Essentials of Adaptive Behavior Assessment of Neurodevelopmental Disorders

Essentials of Psychological Assessment Series

Series Editors, Alan S. Kaufman and Nadeen L. Kaufman

Essentials

of Adaptive Behavior
Assessment of
Neurodevelopmental
Disorders

Celine A. Saulnier
Cheryl Klaiman

WILEY

Registered Office
John Wiley & Sons, Inc., 111 River Street, Hoboken, NJ 07030, USA

Editorial Office
111 River Street, Hoboken, NJ 07030, USA

For details of our global editorial offices, customer services, and more information about Wiley products visit us at www.wiley.com.

Wiley also publishes its books in a variety of electronic formats and by print-on-demand. Some content that appears in standard print versions of this book may not be available in other formats.

Library of Congress Cataloging-in-Publication Data

Names: Saulnier, Celine A., author. | Klaiman, Cheryl, 1972- author.
Title: Essentials of adaptive behavior assessment of neurodevelopmental
    disorders / by Celine A. Saulnier, Cheryl Klaiman.
Description: Hoboken, NJ : John Wiley & Sons, 2018. | Includes
    bibliographical references and index. |
Identifiers: LCCN 2017052028 (print) | LCCN 2017054486 (ebook) | ISBN
    9781119075509 (pdf) | ISBN 9781119075554 (epub) | ISBN 9781119075455 (pbk.)
Subjects: LCSH: Developmental disabilities–Treatment. | Behavioral
    assessment. | Adjustment (Psychology)
Classification: LCC RC570.2 (ebook) | LCC RC570.2 .S28 2018 (print) | DDC
    616.85/88–dc23
LC record available at https://lccn.loc.gov/2017052028

Cover image: © Greg Kuchik/Getty Images
Cover design: Wiley

Set in 10.5/13pt AGaramondProStd by SPi Global, Chennai, India

PB Printing   10 9 8 7 6 5 4 3 2 1

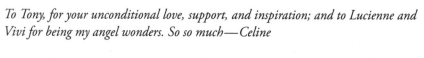

To Tony, for your unconditional love, support, and inspiration; and to Lucienne and Vivi for being my angel wonders. So so much—Celine

To Lee, for your unwavering support, patience, and love—your encouragement and willingness to let me follow my path make anything possible; and to Emma and Madlyn, my hearts and my reason for constantly striving—Cheryl

CONTENTS

SERIES PREFACE

I n the Essentials of Psychological Assessment series, we have attempted to provide the reader with books that will deliver key practical information in the most efficient and accessible style. The series features instruments in a variety of domains, such as cognition, personality, education, and neuropsychology. For the experienced clinician, books in the series will offer a concise yet thorough way to master use of the continually evolving supply of new and revised instruments as well as a convenient method for keeping up-to-date on the tried-and-true measures. The novice will find here a prioritized assembly of all the information and techniques that must be at one's fingertips to begin the complicated process of individual psychological diagnosis.

Whenever feasible, visual shortcuts to highlight key points are used alongside systematic, step-by-step guidelines. Chapters are focused and succinct. Topics are targeted for an easy understanding of the essentials of administration, scoring, interpretation, and clinical application. Theory and research are continually woven into the fabric of each book, but always to enhance clinical inference, never to sidetrack or overwhelm. We have long been advocates of "intelligent" testing—the notion that a profile of test scores is meaningless unless it is brought to life by the clinical observations and astute detective work of knowledgeable examiners. Test profiles must be used to make a difference in the child's or adult's life, or why bother to test? We want this series to help our readers become the best intelligent testers they can be.

In *Essentials of Adaptive Behavior Assessment of Neurodevelopmental Disorders,* the authors underscore the universal role that adaptive behavior plays to functional independence across many neurodevelopmental disorders. The authors review various standardized measures of adaptive behavior and how to best assess for areas of strengths and weaknesses that can be translated into treatment and intervention goals. Case examples are provided to illustrate profiles of adaptive functioning that are often prognostic indicators for specific disorders. The end goal is to provide the reader with an understanding that adaptive behavior is modifiable and strongly predictive of optimal outcome into adulthood.

Dr. Alan Kaufman and Dr. Nadeen Kaufman

ACKNOWLEDGMENTS

The completion of this book would not have been possible without the help and support of many people, from those who have mentored and guided us through the years, to those who have helped in various aspects of this book, and to our families for providing us with their unwavering support for taking on writing a book on top of our crazy lives! We would like to offer special thanks to the following individuals:

First, we provide our heartfelt thanks to and remembrance of Sara Sparrow, PhD, for teaching us the value of adaptive behavior in the lives of individuals with disabilities. We miss her constant wisdom and guidance but know that she would be proud of our efforts to promote the understanding of adaptive behavior through our clinical and scientific endeavors as well as carrying out her legacy in developing the Vineland.

We would also like to thank Ami Klin, PhD, our exceptional leader, for your guidance and support of our careers. You have taught us the art of comprehensive developmental assessments, and we continue to learn from you today. We are so thankful for your mentorship and could not have done this without you!

To Chris Gunter, PhD, our dear friend and colleague, we thank you greatly for your editorial genius and genuine tolerance for our pestering questions. We also thank you for helping us find laughter, even in the valley of despair.

To Chloe Beacham and Hannah Grosman, we can't thank you enough for your thoughtful edits, comments, and suggestions, even amid hard deadlines and long nights. We could never have met our deadline without you. We will miss you when you leave us for graduate school to spread your wings, but we look forward to when we can collaborate again.

A very special thankyou to our editors, Dominic Bibby and Patricia Rossi—without your guidance, patience, and flexibility (and much needed deadline nudges) throughout this process, we would still be working on this book! We are also extremely grateful to Wiley and Drs. Alan and Nadeen Kaufman for their recognition of the importance of better understanding and incorporating measures of adaptive behavior into the assessment of individuals with neuro-developmental disorders.

Finally, we would like to thank the children and families who inspire and teach us every day. Thank you for contributing to our clinical and scientific knowledge of neurodevelopmental disorders.

One

INTRODUCTION AND HISTORY OF ADAPTIVE BEHAVIOR

INTRODUCTION

The construct of adaptive behavior is defined as the independent performance of daily activities that are required for personal and social sufficiency (Sparrow, Cicchetti, & Saulnier, 2016). This is qualitatively different from intelligence, which is conceptualized more as a repertoire of skills that is innate or acquired over time. This book provides a comprehensive overview of profiles of adaptive behavior seen across neurodevelopmental disorders. Though there are many distinct or complex and multiplex causes for neurodevelopmental complications that result in extremely heterogeneous presentations, the delays or deficits in practical, "real-life" skills are the common thread throughout these disorders. Moreover, positive outcome is often associated with adaptive functioning and, as such, interventions to target adaptive behavior can be successful in an individual's ability to attain levels of independence in life.

DON'T FORGET

If cognition or IQ is an individual's repertoire of skills or capacity to perform a given behavior, adaptive behavior is an individual's independent performance of the behavior when life demands it.

THE BIRTH OF ADAPTIVE BEHAVIOR

When measures of cognitive ability were introduced in the early 1900s, the classification of intellectual disability (ID) relied solely on the assessment of intelligence quotient (IQ). Henry Herbert Goddard was one of the first to bring comprehensive intelligence tests to the United States when he translated and modified the Binet Intelligence Scale that was developed in France by Alfred Binet (Zenderland, 2001). Goddard's version, the Binet and Simon Tests of Intellectual Capacity, was published in 1908. At the time, Goddard was working as the research director at the Training School for Feeble-Minded Girls and Boys in Vineland, New Jersey, seeking ways to accurately assess children with IDs. The Vineland Training School was dedicated to the study of ID and, thus, defining and measuring intelligence became a strong focus.

Goddard defined feeble-mindedness as mental deficits originating at birth or early in development that resulted in an individual's incapacity for functioning independently in society (Goddard, 1914). The following labels were designated based on levels of cognitive impairment:

- *Idiot* designated a person with a mental age up to 2 years
- *Imbecile* designated a 3–7 years mental age
- *Morons* designated a 7–12 years mental age (though still designating cognitive delay, these individuals were not regarded as "defective" or "incapable of learning")

Goddard, similar to many of his time, believed in the heritable nature of feeble-mindedness, publishing a book about a family with mental retardation that crossed generations (Goddard, 1912). The notion that cognitive impairment was inherited reinforced the eugenics movement—one of selective breeding and sterilization in an attempt to eliminate undesired traits and maximize desired ones. This resulted in the institutionalization, sterilization, and limited immigration of many individuals with ID in the United States so as to increase the average IQ. These practices would not be fully eradicated until the 1960s and, thus, intelligence tests remained at the forefront of identifying the cognitively inferior, including children (Reilly, 1987). Despite the controversy surrounding his early involvement in the eugenics movement, Goddard is considered one of the founders of intelligence testing in our country and, in some regards, of the field of clinical psychology (Gelb, 1999).

During Goddard's tenure at the Vineland Training School, he had an assistant named Edgar Doll. Doll had recently received his bachelor's degree from Cornell University and began working with Goddard as a clinical psychologist. Doll believed that level of impairment was dependent on one's limited ability to meet designated social expectations, highlighting the necessity of social competence for functional independence (Doll, 1936). He therefore advocated that social criteria be established against which to measure intelligence. In 1917, Doll published *Clinical Studies in Feeble-Mindedness* calling for clarification of the definition of intellectual disability.

After spending several years training with Goddard, Doll left the Vineland Training School to obtain his doctorate in psychology at Princeton University. He took a break from graduate school to join the Army during World War I, where he conducted cognitive assessments on army recruits. After leaving the Army and completing his doctorate at Princeton in 1920, Doll directed the Division of Classification and Education in the New Jersey State Department of Institutions and Agencies, where he assessed prisoners up for parole. Doll's experiences working with army recruits and prisoners revealed similar IQ levels between the groups. This was against the thinking at the time that criminality was caused by mental retardation (Doll, 1941). Doll's research debunking the theory that prisoners were "mentally deficient" was seminal to the field. However, this work would become overshadowed by Doll's subsequent focus on adaptive behavior.

In 1925, Doll returned to the Vineland Training School as the director of research where he remained through 1949. The practice of defining cognitive impairment on a single measure had become highly controversial, as had the theories of what caused ID (Brockley, 1999). Although some professionals such as Doll believed ID to be a genetically based and constitutional condition that resulted in social deficiencies, others argued that it was more developmental in nature arising from impaired social competence (Reschly, Myers, Hartel, & National Research Council, 2002). Evidence arose that not all individuals with ID had parents with cognitive impairment and it was discovered that ID could actually result from a host of non-genetically related factors, such as disease, physical trauma, poverty, and so on, placing into question the heritability of ID. These discoveries helped contribute to the demise of the eugenics theory and encouraged more sympathetic views toward the intellectually disabled.

Doll was a pioneer in developing the construct of adaptive behavior and emphasizing the need for assessing adaptive functioning in addition to IQ when diagnosing ID. Doll's definition for what was then called *mental deficiency* evolved over time. In his earlier work, Doll described a threefold criterion for diagnosing mental deficiency: "social incompetence, due to low intelligence, which has been developmentally arrested" (Doll, 1936, p. 429). Yet, he would later expand on this definition to include the following six criteria: (1) social incompetence, (2) mental subnormality, (3) developmental arrest, (4) obtains at maturity, (5) constitutional origin, and (6) essentially incurable (Doll, 1941, 1953).

≝ *Rapid Reference 1.1*

Doll's Criteria for Mental Deficiency

- Social incompetence
- Mental subnormality
- Developmental arrest
- Obtains at maturity
- Constitutional origin
- Essentially incurable

Although some of Doll's proposed criteria for mental deficiency were contro-versial for his time (e.g., that mental deficiency was constitutional and incurable), several of his principles have sustained generations and still hold true in our con-temporary definitions of ID. In fact, it was in one of his earliest works, *Clinical Studies in Feeble-Mindedness,* that Doll wrote about the criteria for intellectual disability: "social inefficiency is at present prerequisite, and is the most important practical manifestation of the condition" (Doll, 1917, p. 23). He stipulated that although all people with cognitive impairment were socially incompetent to some degree, not all people who were socially incompetent were "feeble-minded."

CAUTION

Despite early theories that intellectual deficiencies were innate and incurable, cur-rent views of cognition are more forgiving in that intelligence levels can improve with intervention.

Doll was instrumental in highlighting the role of social competence in intelli-gence. He believed that social competence was a universal human attribute, but one that was challenging to measure. He struggled with the barriers that pre-vented a universal definition of social competence and took strides to identify the behaviors that defined personal responsibility and independence across all individuals who were not influenced by factors such as race, geographic location, culture, or sex. These behaviors were, however, age-based in that one's repertoire of adaptive skills expanded with age. He ultimately defined social competence as the ability to demonstrate personal independence and social responsibility in everyday contexts, stating that "in short, social competence may be defined as a functional composite of human traits which subserves social usefulness as reflected in self-sufficiency and in service to others" (Doll, 1953, p. 2).

With an increased focus on self-sufficiency and social competence for functional independence, Doll developed the first standardized assessment of adaptive behavior. The Vineland Social Maturity Scale (Vineland SMS) was named for the location of the training school and was published by American Guidance Services (AGS) in 1935 (the comprehensive manual to accompany the scale was not published until 1953) (Doll, 1953). The Vineland SMS was a 117-item instrument that assessed social competence in addition to a broad range of practical skills via a third-party interview with, for example, a parent, caregiver, or teacher. It would be the most widely used measure of adaptive behavior for decades to follow (see Chapter 2 for a more detailed description of the Vineland SMS).

ADAPTIVE BEHAVIOR IN THE DEFINITION OF INTELLECTUAL DISABILITY

With the publication of the American Association on Mental Deficiency (AAMD) *Manual on Terminology and Classification* (5th ed.) in 1959, adaptive behavior was formally included in the definition of *mental retardation* (Heber, 1959). Definitions in all prior AAMD publications dating back to 1921 focused solely on cognitive impairment. Heber's definition in the sixth edition of the AAMD manual (Heber, 1961), however, included the stipulation that in addition to adaptive deficits, the "subaverage general intellectual functioning" (which specified an IQ cutoff of one or more standard deviations below the mean) had to originate in the developmental period, prior to age 16. Heber was the first to introduce a three-factor structure of adaptive behavior skills. These included *practical* skills (activities of daily living), *conceptual* skills (concepts of learning, e.g., reading, writing, language, arithmetic skills), and *social* skills (interpersonal and play skills, social problem-solving, rule-following). Yet, this specific factor structure would not be operationalized into the definition of intellectual disability until 2002. Concurrent to the AAMD fifth edition, the first edition of the *Diagnostic and Statistical Manual of Mental Disorders (DSM-I)* would be published in 1952 by the American Psychiatric Association (APA, 1952). However, it would not be until the second edition (*DSM-II*) was published in 1968 that the criteria for mental retardation included adaptive impairment (APA, 1968).

In the seventh edition definition of AAMD (Grossman, 1973), the IQ cutoff changed to two standard deviations below the mean, and the age limit for the "developmental period" was raised from 16 to 18 years. This significantly decreased the expected prevalence of ID from 16% to the 1% to 2% of the general population that we see today (Richards, Brady, & Taylor, 2015). However, in order to advocate for those individuals with IQs above the cutoff who still had significant adaptive deficits, Grossman later modified the definition to allow for "clinical judgment" to be considered in the eighth edition (Grossman, 1977). For instance, a highly experienced clinician could make a diagnosis of ID in the case of, for example, an individual with a borderline IQ (between 70 and 85) who, based on available data, had adaptive deficits that impeded the individual's ability to function independently in the absence of supports (Grossman, 1977; Richards et al., 2015). In a 1983 publication, Grossman modified the age of onset of ID to be conception rather than birth so as to capture prenatal etiologies (Grossman, 1983).

In 1975, the US Congress enacted the Education for All Handicapped Children Act (which evolved into the Individual with Disabilities Education Act; IDEA, 2004) requiring federally funded public schools to provide free and appropriate education to children with physical and mental disabilities (P.L. 94-142). This law reaffirmed the need to conduct standardized tests of adaptive behavior in addition to cognition, especially as states across the United States began to mandate both assessments. Adaptive behavior assessments also became instrumental for intervention planning and placing individuals in the most appropriate or "least-restrictive" environment for educational, residential, and community programming. This movement led AGS to update the Vineland SMS, which resulted in the publication of the original Vineland Adaptive Behavior Scales in 1984 (Vineland ABS; Sparrow, Balla, & Cicchetti, 1984). By the 1970s and 1980s, numerous adaptive behavior instruments were developed, with the most prominent measures being the Vineland ABS, AAMD's Adaptive Behavior Scale (Nihira, Foster, Shellhaas, & Leland, 1974), the Woodcock-Johnson Scales of Independent Behavior (Bruininks, Woodcock, Weatherman, & Hill, 1985) and eventually the Adaptive Behavior Assessment System (Harrison & Oakland, 2000). See Chapter 3 for more detailed descriptions of the most commonly used measures of adaptive behavior.

DON'T FORGET

With the introduction of P.L. 94-142, standardized measures of cognition and adaptive behavior became standard for eligibility assessments for students with disabilities.

The ninth edition of the American Association of Mental Retardation manual (AAMR, 1992) included substantial changes to the definition of ID. First, it listed specified areas of adaptive deficit that were required for a diagnosis (Luckasson et al., 1992). Though Heber wrote about the three-factor structure of adaptive behavior skills in 1959 (i.e., practical, conceptual, and social areas of adaptive delay), subsequent definitions retained the broader (and thus more abstract) construct. This made it very challenging to research and identify what specific adaptive behaviors to prioritize and target in educational, treatment, and vocational programs to optimize outcome. It would take more than 30 years for the definition of ID to include specific adaptive skills that needed to be delayed or deficient to merit a diagnosis. The ninth edition did just this, specifying the following 10 areas of adaptive deficit: *Communication, Self-Care, Home Living, Social Skills, Community Use, Self-Direction, Health and Safety, Functional Academics, Leisure,* and *Work* (AAMR, 1992). By this point in time, standardized measures had been developed to formally assess adaptive behavior and many broke down the construct into specific domain areas. However, the Adaptive Behavior Assessment System, Second Edition (Harrison & Oakland, 2003) would be the first to include these 10 specific areas that were introduced in the AAMR ninth edition definition.

≡ *Rapid Reference 1.2*

Areas of Adaptive Deficit in the AAMR (Ninth Edition)

- Communication
- Self-Care
- Home Living
- Social Skills
- Community Use
- Self-direction
- Health and Safety
- Functional Academics
- Leisure
- Work

The second major change to the definition of ID in the AAMR ninth edition was the elimination of the levels of cognitive impairment in place of levels of support needed for intervention (Richards et al., 2015). The *mild, moderate, severe,* and *profound* levels that specified respective ranges of IQ would be replaced with *intermittent, limited, extensive,* and *pervasive* supports. The focus became less on how intelligence levels affected functioning and more on the intensity of supports needed for an individual to be functional. This change would not be incorporated into the *DSM* criteria (and truly set into clinical practice) until the publication of the fifth edition (APA, 2013).

Finally, the ninth edition of the AAMR manual would be the first time that ID was conceptualized as a transient condition and one that could be the product of an interaction between an individual's current state and his or her environment (AAMR, 1992). This debunked Doll's description that ID was of constitutional origin and expanded the range of possible causes from congenital (e.g., chromosomal disorders) to peri- and postnatal medical complications (e.g., cerebral palsy, hypoxia, trauma) to environmental influences (e.g., malnutrition, infectious disease, toxins). The notion that ID could also be transient was a paradigm shift from the previous theories in which IQ was innate and unchangeable. In fact, given that the majority of individuals with ID have only mild intellectual impairment (Richards et al., 2015), interventions that directly affect individuals, their family, and their environment can certainly result in improved cognitive functioning and, consequently, elimination of the diagnostic label. Thus, IQ was no longer considered as inherently stable as was earlier presumed.

The 10th edition of the AAMR manual (2002) would introduce Heber's three-factor structure for adaptive skills in the areas of practical, conceptual, and social skills, but it would not be until 2013 for these to be included in the *DSM-5* (APA, 2013). Both definitions specified that adaptive deficits must fall approximately two standard deviations below the mean. An important addition to the AAMR 10th edition was also the inclusion of assumptions for clinicians to consider when making a diagnosis of ID. These included considering the individual's community, culture, individual profile of strengths and weaknesses, supports needed for intervention, and potential for improvement when provided with these necessary supports (AAMR, 2002). These assumptions were in line with the protections in evaluative procedures that were included in law P.L. 94–142 outlining safeguards for evaluating children within the school system.

With the 11th edition of the manual, the organization had changed its name to the American Association on Intellectual and Developmental Disabilities, with this change eliminating the term *mental retardation* in favor of *intellectual disability* from the diagnostic category (Schalock et al., 2010). Also in 2010, the federal government enacted P.L. 111–256 (Rosa's Law), which changed terminology throughout all laws from *mental retardation* to *intellectual disability.*

The subsequent publications of the *DSM-III* in 1980 (APA, 1980), the *DSM-III-R* in 1987 (APA, 1987), the *DSM-IV* in 1994 (APA, 1994), the *DSM-IV-TR* in 2000 (APA, 2000), and the *DSM-5* in 2013 (APA, 2013) would similarly revise the nomenclature and diagnostic criteria for ID on the level of cognitive impairment (i.e., one or two standard deviations below the mean or a specified IQ cutoff of, e.g., 70–80), on the areas of adaptive deficits, and on the specification of the developmental period (i.e., below the age of 16 or 18 or without a specified age). Nevertheless, this three-part structure defining ID based on cognitive and adaptive impairment originating during early development has endured the test of time and remains the structure of our current diagnostic criteria. Table 1.1 provides an overview of the history of definitions of ID.

PRINCIPLES OF ADAPTIVE BEHAVIOR

Modern principles of adaptive functioning that reflect Doll's original narratives are outlined as follows (Sparrow et al., 2016): (1) Adaptive behavior is age-related, (2) adaptive behavior is defined by the expectations of others within a social context, (3) adaptive behavior is modifiable, and (4) adaptive behavior is defined by typical performance not ability.

≡ *Rapid Reference 1.3*

Principles of Adaptive Behavior

- Adaptive behavior is age-related.
- Adaptive behavior is defined by the expectations of others within a social context.
- Adaptive behavior is modifiable.
- Adaptive behavior is defined by typical performance not ability.

First, adaptive behavior is *age-related* because expectations change over time (i.e., what is important for a preschooler is not the same for an adult) and individuals can accumulate a larger and more complex repertoire of skills as they age. Second, adaptive behavior is evaluated within a *social context* because the world in which we live is inherently a social one. This is why it is so important that a parent, caregiver, and teacher assess for the behaviors in naturalistic contexts rather than

Table 1.1 Time Line of Definitions of Intellectual Disability That Include Adaptive Behavior

Year	Author	Definition
1941	Doll	**Mental Deficiency:** "Social incompetence, due to mental subnormality, which has been developmentally arrested, which obtains at maturity, is of constitutional origin, and is essentially incurable"
1952	APA (*DSM-I*)	**Mental Deficiency:** • Mild: IQ of approximately 70–85 • Moderate: IQ of about 50–70 • Severe: IQ below 50
1957	AAMD Committee on Nomenclature	
1959	AAMD (*Manual on Terminology and Classification* [5th ed.]) (Heber)	**Mental Retardation:** "Subaverage general intellectual functioning" that originates during the developmental period and is associated with impairment in adaptive behavior
1961	AAMD (*Manual on Terminology and Classification* [6th ed.]) (Heber)	**Mental Retardation:** Specified that "subaverage intellectual functioning" was one or more standard deviations below the mean (IQ of 85 or below)
1968	APA (*DSM-II*)	**Mental Retardation:** "Subnormal general intellectual functioning originating in the developmental period and associated with impairment of either learning and social adjustment or maturation, or both." • Borderline: IQ = 68–85 • Mild: IQ = 52–67 • Moderate: IQ = 36–51 • Severe: IQ = 20–35 • Profound: IQ = < 20
1973	AAMD (*Manual on Terminology and Classification* [7th ed.]) (Grossman)	**Mental Retardation:** "Significantly subaverage general intellectual functioning" (at least two standard deviations below the mean; IQ of 70 or below) with deficits in adaptive behavior and manifested during the developmental period (designated as birth to 18 years)

Table 1.1 (*Continued*)

Year	Author	Definition
1977	AAMD (*Manual on Terminology and Classification* [8th ed.]) (Grossman)	**Mental Retardation:** This update included individuals with borderline intelligence (IQ 70–80) to be classified as having MR and potentially eligible for services.
1980	APA (*DSM-III*)	**Mental Retardation:** "Significantly subnormal intellectual ability (IQ 70 or below) that leads to deficits in functioning. Levels of mild, moderate, severe, and profound are intended to correspond to an individual's capability for adaptive functioning to the degree to which training will result in independent functioning."
1987	APA (*DSM-III-Revision*)	**Mental Retardation:** The diagnosis of MR was moved from Axis I to Axis II (Personality Disorders and Developmental Disorders—including Mental Retardation and Borderline Intellectual Functioning)
1992	AAMR (*Manual on Terminology and Classification* [9th ed.])	**Mental Retardation:** This update included specifications of deficits in at least two areas of adaptive behavior, including communication, self-care, home living, social skills, self-direction, health and safety, functional academics, leisure, and work.
1994 and 2000	APA (*DSM-IV* and *DSM-IV-Text Revision*)	**Mental Retardation:** Axis II changed its name to Personality Disorders and Mental Retardation. Adaptive behavior deficits in at least two of the following areas: communication, self-care, home living, social-interpersonal skills, use of community resources, self-direction, functional academic skills, work, leisure, health, and safety. Overall IQ falling below two standard deviations from the mean (with a stipulation about confidence intervals on standardized assessments ranging from, e.g., 65–75 and, thus, allowing for variability). Onset prior to the age of 18.

(continued)

Table 1.1 *(Continued)*

Year	Author	Definition
		Levels of MR: Borderline: IQ range 71–84 Mild: IQ range 50/55–approximately 70 Moderate: IQ range 35/40–50/55 Severe: IQ range 20/25–35/40 Profound: IQ range below 20/25 Option for Severity Unspecified
2002	AAMR (*Manual on Terminology and Classification* [10th ed.])	**Mental Retardation:** Specification of adaptive deficits falling two or more standard deviations below the mean in conceptual, social, or practical adaptive skills, or overall level of adaptive behavior falling two or more standard deviations below the mean
2010	American Association on Intellectual and Developmental Disabilities (AAIDD) (*Intellectual Disability: Definition, Classification, and Systems of Supports* [11th ed.]) (Schalock et al.)	**Intellectual Disability:** "A disability characterized by significant limitations both in intellectual functioning and in adaptive behavior as expressed in conceptual, social, and practical adaptive skills. This disability originates before age 18."
2013	APA (*DSM-5*)	**Intellectual Disability (Intellectual Developmental Disorder):** "A disorder with onset during the developmental period that includes both intellectual and adaptive functioning deficits in conceptual, social, and practical domains." Removal of a specified IQ score. Deficits in intellectual functioning need to be confirmed by "both clinical assessment and individualized, standardized intelligence testing." Severity levels matched specifically to adaptive behavior domains rather than IQ score ranges. Removal of specified age of onset; back to "during the developmental period."

try to probe for the behaviors within a contrived, less-naturalistic (i.e., clinical) setting. Third, adaptive behavior is *modifiable* in that levels of functioning can deteriorate or improve over time for a variety of reasons. For instance, changes in the environment can affect adaptive functioning (e.g., moving to a different culture-geographical location, adoption or foster care, hospitalization, imprisonment, etc.), as can traumatic life events (e.g., physical or emotional abuse and neglect). Moreover, treatment and intervention (or lack thereof) can certainly result in changes in adaptive behavior. This is in contrast to intelligence, which is considered more stable over time and less influenced by the effects of intervention. Finally, adaptive behavior is defined by *typical performance,* not ability. If cognition is viewed as an individual's ability or repertoire of skills (what the person "can do"), adaptive behavior is the independent functional application of those skills to daily contexts and routines (what the individual "does do"). Thus, adaptive skills are those that an individual does when expected on a daily basis without prompts, supports, or reminders and *not* merely what an individual can do or is capable of doing. This last tenant is a critical issue in autism spectrum disorder in which there is often a discrepancy between an individual's cognition or capacity and his or her adaptive functioning by nature of the social disability.

CAUTION

Adaptive skills are defined by what an individual does do with independence and not what an individual is capable of doing but doesn't.

SUMMARY

The history of intellectual disability is fraught with controversies over the taxonomy and theories of causality. However, the nomenclature of adaptive behavior has remained surprisingly consistent in comparison. The current *DSM-5* and AAIDD definitions carry forth Doll's original descriptions of functional social, conceptual, and daily living skills. Moreover, the *DSM-5* severity levels for the diagnosis of ID are tied directly to levels of functional, adaptive independence. This exemplifies the importance of measuring adaptive behavior not merely for diagnostic purposes but also for determining appropriate treatment and intervention strategies for educational, community, daily living, and occupational purposes.

With this book, we hope to provide a comprehensive account of adaptive behavior profiles in neurodevelopmental disorders across the life span. Similar to

Doll's view of social competence, we believe that adaptive behavior is the universal thread that ties together functional outcome for individuals with all neurodevelopmental disorders. As such, the goal of the book is to provide the reader with knowledge about the current state of adaptive behavior assessments, profiles of functioning, and optimizing outcome into adulthood. In Chapter 1, we provided the framework for how we define adaptive behavior as well as the fascinating history behind its inception. Chapter 2 provides the reader with information on important constructs in understanding and selecting the best measure of adaptive behavior to meet the needs of the person being assessed. Chapter 3 describes a variety of adaptive behavior measures that are used to assess adaptive behavior. Chapters 4, 5, and 6 then discuss profiles of adaptive behavior across a wide range of disabilities and disorders—from intellectual disabilities and autism spectrum disorder, which offer the largest body of literature on adaptive behavior profiles, to less common genetic syndromes as well as other developmental disorders. Chapter 7 discusses adaptive behavior profiles in adults and the complicating factors when assessing adults. In Chapter 8, the current status of treatments and interventions are discussed. Finally, Chapter 9 ties assessments and treatments together by providing some case studies with sample reports. Our hope is that this book will be useful for clinicians in training and those just starting in the field, as well as seasoned professionals who are interested in adding a measure of adaptive behavior to their battery or are seeking more information on children with various developmental disabilities and the impact this has on the development of their day-to-day living skills.

TEST YOURSELF

1. **What are the four principles of adaptive behavior?**
2. **Of the following, who is considered to be one of the founders of intelligence testing in the United States?**
   a. Alfred Benet
   b. Henry Herbert Goddard
   c. Edgar Doll
   d. Ivan Pavlov
3. **True or false? Intellectual deficiencies cannot be improved, despite intervention.**
4. **Heber's three factor structure included the following *except*:**
   a. Practical skills
   b. Conceptual skills

    c. Motor skills
    d. Social skills

5. **True or false? The AAMR ninth edition was updated to reflect level of support needed versus level of cognitive impairment.**

6. **The law that changed terminology from *mental retardation* to *intellectual disability* throughout all laws was called:**
    a. Rosa's Law
    b. Ava's Law
    c. Maddie's Law
    d. Emma's Law

7. **True or false? Adaptive skills are defined by what an individual can do but doesn't do rather than what he or she does independently.**

8. **Which of the following does not measure adaptive behavior skills?**
    a. Vineland ABS
    b. Adaptive Behavior Assessment System
    c. Woodcock-Johnson Scales of Independent Behavior
    d. Mullen Scales of Early Learning

9. **Factors that a clinician should consider about an individual when making a diagnosis of ID include:**
    a. Community
    b. Culture
    c. Strength and weaknesses
    d. All of the above

10. **True or false? According to the *DSM-5*, the most recent version of this manual, ID must originate before age 18.**

Answers: (1) Age-related, defined by the expectations of others within a social context, modifiable, and defined by typical performance not ability; (2) b; (3) False. Intellectual deficiencies can be improved with intervention; (4) c; (5) True; (6) a; (7) False. Adaptive skills are defined by what an individual does independently; (8) d; (9) d; (10) False. The *DSM-5* was updated to remove specified age of onset.

Two

METHODS OF ASSESSING ADAPTIVE BEHAVIOR

This chapter will discuss the various methods of assessing adaptive behavior. The goal is to provide the reader with information about the various methodologies that can be used as well as things to look for when evaluating a particular assessment tool. In this way, it is hoped that the reader will be able to make an informed choice when deciding what measures would best be administered to a particular client.

In the mid-20th century, when universal definitions of intellectual disability (ID) began to include criteria for deficits in adaptive functioning in addition to cognitive delays, numerous standardized measures began to be developed. In fact, at various times in the United States, there have been more than 200 adaptive behavior measures in use (Doucette & Freedman, 1980)—only some have been long-standing and continue to be used in various forms today. Many measures were created to serve various purposes, including for eligibility and diagnostic confirmation, clinical use and treatment monitoring, or more targeted purposes such as for a specific skill area or age range. There has been some controversy about whether actually having the depth and breadth of one scale is feasible to meet clinical and diagnostic purposes (Spreat, 1999). Spreat argues that it is "unrealistic" to have one measure accomplish the various purposes of diagnosis, classification, individual programming, and program evaluation. Further, the majority of the measures do not have adequate norms and reliability needed to diagnose ID in individuals with mild ID or those with cognitive functioning between standard scores of 60 and 80.

CAUTION

Beware of choosing a measure that purports to assess and serve every purpose.

17

With these caveats, it is important to choose a measure that helps to better understand the phenomenon an examiner is trying to assess. One needs to consider the following when deciding which measure to use:

- The age of the individual one is assessing
- Available norms
- Who the respondent is
- The context in which the individual is known
- The training of the rater

≡ Rapid Reference 2.1

Choose a measure of adaptive behavior based on the following:
- Age of the individual one is assessing
- Available norms
- Who the respondent is
- The context in which the individual is known
- The training of the rater

Despite the importance of adaptive behavior in better understanding an individual's diagnosis and strengths and weaknesses, and given all of the available measures, assessment of adaptive behavior is not frequently incorporated into an assessment battery conducted by clinical psychologists (Watkins, Campbell, Nieberding, & Hallmark, 1995). In the Watkins et al. (1995) study, only 13% of clinical psychologists included an assessment of adaptive behavior as part of their clinical practice. However, assessment of cognitive functioning was conducted 66% of the time. By contrast, surveys of school psychologists indicate that measures of adaptive behavior are some of the most frequent measures used and their use has increased over time (Hutton, Dubes, & Muir, 1992; Ochoa, Powell, & Robles-Pina, 1996; Stinnett, Havey, & Oehler-Stinnett, 1994). School districts rely on measures of adaptive functioning to help guide their education plans, involve parents in the evaluation process, and monitor treatment progress. Clinical psychologists could also better understand their client's presentation and help to better inform school and home recommendations if measures of adaptive behavior were used more frequently.

TYPES OF MEASURES

The primary use of adaptive behavior scales has been to classify whether an individual meets criteria for ID (i.e., to confirm that a low IQ is associated with delayed acquisition or manifestation of everyday personal and social competencies). However, assessing adaptive behavior can be complicated. One must consider not only general competencies across relevant domains but also the level, quality, and fluency of those behaviors (National Research Council, 2002). There also needs to be consideration of the difference between the ability to perform the particular behavior (i.e., can do) versus the actual performance of the various skills (i.e., does do).

DON'T FORGET
....

The primary use of adaptive behavior scales has been to classify whether an individual meets criteria for ID.

How scales are scored and behaviors are determined also varies across measures. Some tools classify behaviors along a frequency dimension (e.g., "never" to "usually or always"), whereas others may use a dichotomy rating (e.g., "yes-no" as to whether the behavior is present). Different measures have distinct numbers of behavioral anchors, for example, a three-point rating scale versus five-point rating scale. Scales may also attempt to address quality or appropriateness of a given level of adaptive behavior skill.

There are a number of ways to ascertain adaptive behavior competencies, each with their own pros and cons.

Interviews
- Unstructured
- Semi-structured
- Structured
- Direct observation

Checklists
- Self-administered
- Other-administered

> ## ≡ Rapid Reference 2.2
> ....
>
> ### Ways to Measure Adaptive Behavior
>
> *Interviews*
> * Unstructured
> * Semi-structured
> * Structured
> * Direct observation
>
> *Checklists*
> * Self-administered
> * Other-administered

INTERVIEWS

Interviews are a direct style of gathering clinical information between an examiner and a respondent. In the case of adaptive behavior, a respondent is interviewed to obtain the necessary information about an individual in question's level of functioning. There are several different types of interviews—from unstructured to structured—and also a range of possible respondents that know the individual well. The following section will review the different types of interviews to measure adaptive behavior.

Unstructured Interviews

In an unstructured interview, clinicians or examiners (hereon referred to as *examiners*) use their own judgment to decide what questions to ask on what topics and when to ask them. There are no preset or prearranged questions and no anchors set for scoring. Examiners, thus, need to be well trained in the theoretical construct behind adaptive behavior as well as on open-ended clinical interviewing techniques. Examiners would then apply personal, experience-based clinical norms to determine an individual's adaptive behavior competency. A benefit of unstructured interviews is that they truly can be tailored to the unique needs of an individual and the functioning level of the respondent. The downside of unstructured interviews is that examiners may impose their own subjective criteria on the assessment, which would threaten the reliability and the validity of the assessment.

CAUTION

Be careful in using unstructured interviews because they can be affected by training of the examiner as well as inherent biases.

Semi-Structured and Structured Interviews

Semi-structured and structured interviews, when performed by well-trained and experienced examiners, are the best safeguard against threats to the reliability and validity of adaptive behavior assessment. The tool, however, is extremely important. If the measure is not reliable or valid, then there will be no accuracy of the interview, even with the most skilled examiners. Semi-structured interviews require the highest level of professional expertise, because the questioning and interpretation of answers requires a high level of training.

CAUTION

Tools used to measure adaptive behavior need to have adequate reliability, validity, and norms or even the most skilled examiners will not get valid data.

Direct Observation

As pointed out by Doll (1953), direct observation of adaptive behavior skills is typically not very practical given that adaptive behaviors are generally displayed in the context of a broad range of everyday living skill situations across a wide variety of settings. It would be difficult, for example, to set up situations in which individuals can demonstrate their ability to perform a wide variety of social, communicative, and daily living behaviors. Though an increasing number of special education programs, schools, and residential placements are creating domestic and community-based environments where adaptive skills can be taught and practiced, they are typically well-controlled settings and, consequently, the assessment of the broad range of independent skills would still be challenging.

CHECKLISTS AND RATING SCALES

Whereas interviews and direct observations require an examiner to conduct the assessment, checklists and rating scales can be completed by a third-party respondent in the absence of an examiner. Self-administered measures are completed by the individual being assessed. Other administered measures are typically completed by a parent, caregiver, teacher, or respondent who is very knowledgeable about the individual being assessed. Although the interview format is generally considered best practice in assessing for adaptive behavior, there are instances when a face-to-face interview is not possible or not ideal. For instance, families from extremely rural areas or disadvantaged communities might not be capable of traveling to a clinic, or there is no examiner who can speak Spanish to conduct an interview with a Spanish-speaking caregiver. In this regard, checklists and rating scales can provide a reliable and valid alternative for measuring adaptive behavior.

Self-Administered

When developing the Vineland Social Maturity Scale (SMS), Doll cautioned against self-assessment of adaptive behavior given that many individuals with cognitive impairment and developmental disorders such as autism might lack the insight and awareness into their own behavioral strengths and weaknesses (Doll, 1953). For this reason, the Vineland SMS did not have an option for self-assessment. Later measures, however, have been developed specifically for this purpose given that the defining features of some neurodevelopmental disorders, in particular those with autism spectrum disorder, have broadened significantly over the years to include individuals who do indeed have the insight and awareness to be able to respond to questions about themselves. Caution needs to be rendered, however, particularly pertaining to the validity of an individual's ability to engage in self-assessment.

Other-Administered

Checklists and rating scales completed by teachers, parents, interventionists, or other practitioners or caregivers who have intimate knowledge of an individual's level of functioning across domains are often used to rate adaptive behaviors. Similar to semi-structured and structured interviews, checklists can range from rating behavior on frequency scales or by the presence or absence of specified behaviors. However, just as an examiner would want to ensure the validity and reliability of an interview or self-assessment, it is critical that examiners who are providing these rating scales to a respondent ensure that the respondent understands the nature of the assessment. As emphasized in Chapter 1, adaptive behavior differs from cognition in that it is the independent application of skills to daily contexts and routines when life demands that the behavior be displayed. It is not the capacity or ability of an individual to perform the skill. This differentiation can be extremely subtle to some respondents, resulting in an overinflation of adaptive behavior. This is evident by comparing normative sample means between, for example, Vineland-II and Vineland-3 Survey/Interview scores and Parent/Caregiver Form scores for which the interview scores are often lower (and presumed more accurate) than Parent/Caregiver Form ratings (Sparrow, Cicchetti, & Balla, 2005; Sparrow, Cicchetti, & Saulnier, 2016).

Examiners also need to be cognizant of rater biases that can influence the validity of checklists and rating scales when the informant does not have a trained person present to ensure accuracy of results. For instance, respondents can intentionally, or even unintentionally, over- or underreport adaptive behavior based on a desire to, for example, not qualify or qualify for services, respectively. In addition, a respondent's limited memory could affect results in the absence of an examiner assisting in cueing memory.

CAUTION

Be cautious of potential rating biases when using checklists or rating scales, as shown in the following examples:

- A respondent's intentional or unintentional overreporting of adaptive behavior so as to present the individual as higher functioning
- A respondent's intentional or unintentional underreporting of adaptive behavior so as to present the individual as more impaired
- A respondent's limited memory
- A respondent's inability to differentiate what the individual can do compared to what the individual does do

Despite these limitations, checklists and rating scales can add valuable information and insights to an individual's adaptive behavior in the following ways. First, when respondents are appropriately instructed on the construct of adaptive behavior and how to rate the items, and when examiners can recontact the respondents as needed to obtain additional information (especially if basals and ceilings are not obtained), then results can be reliable and valid. Second, rating scales are extremely useful when time to complete an evaluation is limited, when there is not direct access to a parent or caregiver, or when an examiner is not trained to conduct an interview. Moreover, when there are language barriers between an examiner and a respondent, rating scales in the native language (e.g., Spanish) can provide accurate assessment of adaptive behavior that otherwise could not be ascertained.

≡ *Rapid Reference 2.3*
....

Advantages of Using Rating Scales Over Semi-Structured Interviews for Assessing Adaptive Behavior

· When there is limited time to conduct an in-person interview
· When there is limited access to a parent or caregiver
· When there is limited access to a trained examiner
· When English is not the primary language and there is a rating scale in the respondent's native language (e.g., Spanish)

PURPOSE OF MEASURE

Measures of adaptive behavior can be used solely to help identify whether an individual meets diagnostic criteria for ID, but they are also useful for intervention planning and treatment progress regardless of diagnosis and can be more broad, aiding in intervention planning and tracking progress.

Depending on the purpose, there may be different items and different content domains. For example, measures that are used in schools may not include vocational or domestic domains, whereas a measure used to assess adaptive behavior in adults would not need items on school-related behaviors (Kamphaus, 1987). Thus, age, culture, and context always need to be considered when measuring adaptive behavior (Thompson, McGrew, & Bruininks, 1999).

Many adaptive behavior scales also contain assessments of problem or maladaptive behavior. Maladaptive behaviors are behaviors that interfere with a person's ability to engage in daily activities. These behaviors can often impede an individual's ability to perform skills that they are capable of doing. Differentiating whether there is a deficit in the adaptive skill versus a maladaptive behavior getting in the way of applying the skill is important for diagnosis and intervention. Correlations between adaptive and maladaptive behavior domains are generally low, with correlations tending to be around .25 or lower. Division 33 of the American Psychological Association makes it clear that significant maladaptive behaviors *do not* meet the criterion for limitations in adaptive function (Jacobson & Mulick, 1996) but, rather, information on maladaptive behavior is still extremely informative in understanding the context of some deficits in adaptive behaviors.

DON'T FORGET

Maladaptive behaviors are not the opposite of adaptive behaviors; rather, they can impede an individual's ability to display adaptive behavior. As such, assessing for maladaptive behaviors can help provide context to an individual's adaptive behavior profile.

PSYCHOMETRIC PROPERTIES

The psychometric properties of various tests can have an influence on the accuracy of the measurement of adaptive behaviors.

Floor and Ceiling Effects

As previously stated, the primary reason adaptive behavior scales were developed was to assess the adaptive behavior development of children thought to have ID. Thus, most measures designated their norming sample, item development, and scale selection at groups ages 3 to 18 or 21 years. This facilitated the early identification of preschool children at risk of ID and allowed for confirmation of persisting developmental delays. Many measures also include adult norming samples, but most of the norming samples include only people with already identified disabilities, and the adult normative samples are quite small. Therefore, depending on the age range of adult participants without disabilities sampled during norming studies, the ceiling (i.e., the highest level of behavioral performance assessed) may differ across scales and may affect the characterization of the degree of delay. Though several measures assess adaptive behavior of children younger than 36 months, these younger ages between birth and 3 years are also weaknesses of adaptive behavior measures. It is therefore important to ensure that the measure you have chosen to use has an appropriate norming sample so that you do not run into floor or ceiling effects.

The other issue that comes into play is wording of the specific items. Because adaptive behavior scales are designed with applicability for a wide age range, some items may not be age-relevant for all individuals. For example, an item may tap skills associated only with childhood (e.g., riding a tricycle) or with adulthood (e.g., menstrual care for an adult or adolescent woman). Some scales contain modifications for alternative items or alternative performance of items.

However, depending on the nature of these modifications, they may reduce the comparability of measures of the related skills from different adaptive behavior scales.

In other instances, scales may be constructed so that they are relevant to only certain age groups such as the Motor Scale of the Vineland Adaptive Behavior Scales (Sparrow, Balla, & Cicchetti, 1984; Sparrow et al., 2005, 2016), or different versions of the same scale may be used in different settings (e.g., school versus residential and community settings). For example, the Adaptive Behavior Assessment System (ABAS) (Harrison & Oakland, 2003) is available in four forms: Parent, Teacher, Adult Self-Report, and Adult Reported by Others. The two versions of the AAMR ABS differ with respect to the age groups emphasized and the settings about which items are structured and weighted in item selection.

Item Density

Item density refers to the number of items that target a specific domain. There can be a single item or many items, and measures of adaptive behavior attempt to balance the number of items given to each behavioral construct. Adaptive behavior scales are structured to be comprehensive without being overly burdensome (Adams, 2000). As such, a number of factors and descriptive categories of behavioral development must be adequately represented in order to ensure comprehensiveness and documentation of strengths and limitations for clinical and diagnostic purposes. A number of considerations go into this. First, the number of items associated with each descriptive category must be sufficient to be applicable across a relatively wide age range. In order to balance comprehensiveness without being too cumbersome, there also has to be relative uniformity of items across the range of ages. This means, for example, that on a given subscale, there may be only one or two items typical of performance for any given age. When scores are then combined to create summary scores, there becomes a meaningful number of age-related items, despite the limited number of items in each subdomain. Nonetheless, it is important to remember that the items that are retained in a measure of adaptive behavior are a sampling of items that have passed reliability and validity checks, rather than a complete characterization of adaptive behavior.

Reliability

Adaptive behavior scales are typically completed through interviews or checklists and, as such, the reliability of informant responses may be of concern.

These concerns are increased when informants have a stake in the outcome of the assessment (e.g., when responses may affect eligibility for services). Test developers have addressed this issue by (1) assessing the interrater and test-retest reliabilities, (2) providing instructions to raters for specific coding of items (e.g., Sparrow et al., 1984), and (3) specifying training for clinicians and preparation of raters (e.g., Bruininks, Woodcock, Weatherman, & Hill, 1996).

In addition to evaluating the reliability of informant responses, there is a need to evaluate the reliability of the measure. Internal consistency refers to how strong items from one-half of the measure compare to items from the other half. Reliability coefficients range from 0 to 1.0, with reliability scores above .80 considered strong.

≡ Rapid Reference 2.4

Types of Reliability

Inter-rater reliability. The strength of the correlation of scores between two different informants on the same measure

Test-retest reliability. The strength of the correlation of scores between time points when the same measure is given repeatedly

Internal consistency. How items from one-half of a measure compare to items from the other half

Validity

Validity refers to the accuracy of an assessment measure; there are many types of validity. Manuals present analyses of data gathered in the process of test development that address the various forms of validity. Content validity refers to the representativeness of the measure and what inferences can be made from the age norms. For example, if there is a domain that purports to assess adaptive communication skills, then items should be representative of adaptive communication behaviors. Construct validity refers to the extent that a test measures a psychological construct or trait, that is, adaptive behavior in this case. Two types of construct validity include convergent validity, or how well two measures of a similar construct have similar results, and discriminant or divergent validity, or how two measures of unrelated constructs have differing results. External validity refers to whether the measure's results can be generalized across contexts, people, and time.

≡ Rapid Reference 2.5

Types of Validity

Content validity. Whether the items on the scale are representative of the domain that the test is supposed to be measuring

Construct validity. The extent to which a test measures a psychological construct or trait; examines whether the measure has a solid theoretical rationale (e.g., adaptive behavior)

   a. **Convergent validity.** Whether the results on one measure are similar to results found on similar measures of adaptive behavior, for instance, evaluating how well the Vineland correlates with the ABAS

   b. **Discriminant-divergent validity.** Whether the results of one measure are different from results found on a measure of an unrelated construct (e.g., adaptive behavior results differ from reading abilities)

Criterion validity:

   c. **Concurrent validity.** Whether the test scores can distinguish between groups, for example, do adaptive behavior scores distinguish between the normative sample and clinical groups?

   d. **Predictive validity.** How well the measure predicts abilities over time

External validity. Whether the measure is generalizable across contexts, for example, does the measure generalize to the population being assessed as well as across populations?

As a result of the high potential for informant bias, the major adaptive behavior scales encourage the use of multiple informants, for example, parents *and* teachers. In addition to ensuring whether an individual truly has an adaptive behavior deficit and is not just underperforming in a certain area, these scales enable the rater to obtain a more complete picture of the adaptive functioning of the person being assessed. They also allow for reconciliation of ratings among these informants. Legislative action and judicial decisions at the federal level have focused on the fact that parents may underreport their children's skills in order to obtain benefits such as Supplemental Security Income.

Adequacy of Normative Samples

Another property to consider is whether the norming samples are adequate. To ensure this, the psychometric properties need to include an adequate representation of people with and without ID as well as have enough of a sample across the various age groups the measure is purporting to assess.

Sociocultural Biases

This bias refers to a consistent distortion of scores that is attributed to demographic factors, mostly ones that cannot be changed, such as age, gender, race, and ethnic or cultural membership. In the United States there have been significant concerns about the relationship between ethnicity or racial origin and performance on intelligence tests (see Chapter 1; Neisser et al., 1996). Similar concerns have generalized to adaptive behavior measures. As documentation of adaptive behavior deficits has become a necessary part of the diagnostic criteria for ID, this concern has been raised because a disproportionate number of minority children have been identified as having ID (Boyle et al., 1996). To some extent, inclusion of participants representative of the general population, including racial and ethnic minorities, in norming samples, should mitigate against biases in scoring of adaptive behavior scales.

Comparable performance on adaptive behavior scales in majority and minority ethnic groups was found in research conducted in the 1970s and 1980s (Bryant, Bryant, & Chamberlain, 1999; Craig & Tasse, 1999). However, despite this comparability, linguistic factors remain a concern in administering measures of adaptive behavior. Concerns center on the ability to interview informants in their primary language and dialect and the comparability of translations of items in adaptive behavior scales. With regard to translation, rarely has a measure had the highest standard of translation, which involves confirming comparability through back-translation from the translated content to the initial language or through confirmatory analysis through further retranslation (Craig & Tasse, 1999). Incomparability of items may alter norms due to the way an item is worded in the translated language. Also, norms may be different in different cultures; for example, English language norms may be lower or higher than the typical performance of a same-age child in another culture. As such, one must use caution when using a measure of adaptive behavior on individuals who are from different cultures than the test was normed on or who speak different languages from which a translation is available. In addition, it is important to know, in choosing a measure, what the quality of the translation was. More research is needed across different cultural groups and cross-cultural comparisons.

Overall, culturally competent assessment practices require an examiner to consider the possible impact of differences in culture or language between the examiner and the client and his or her family or other informants. This impact could affect the clinical validity of the information you are obtaining and how it is interpreted. Obviously, it is ideal to administer an assessment in one's primary language and that that language and dialect matches that of the informant. However, at times an interpreter or a translator is necessary, and the training and experience of that person should also be considered.

Choosing a Measure

The decision as to which standardized measure of adaptive behavior to use must be informed by knowledge of the following:

- The instrument must be appropriate to the individual's age and approximate level of functioning.
- An appropriate respondent, knowledgeable about the individual being tested, is required for most adaptive behavior instruments. If an appropriate respondent is not available, use of the instrument in some other, non-standardized way (e.g., as self-report when there is no self-report version) violates basic standardization procedures, rendering normative comparisons invalid. However, there are some modifications that are able to be done that allow for some flexibility in respondents. For example, some instruments permit more than one respondent to answer different items, depending on which respondent is most knowledgeable about the behavior (Adams, 2000). Another instrument permits adult client self-report (Harrison & Oakland, 2003). Other measures allow guessing on items involving behaviors that have not been observed. However, as modifications are made or guessing is allowed, the instrument becomes less valid. So, if a respondent indicates that he or she has guessed a lot, the results become increasingly unreliable as the number of those guesses increase.
- Scores from the instrument that are useful in diagnostic decisions must be provided and, in turn, interpretations need to be guided by the structure and organization of the adaptive behavior inventory. Diagnostic decisions about ID nearly always involve normative comparisons using various derived scores. Scales with standardized norms are preferred for those comparisons. Useful score scales and appropriate norms are vital features of adaptive behavior instruments used in diagnostic decisions.

SUMMARY

Standardized adaptive behavior instruments have been used historically alongside assessments of cognition in order to determine eligibility for a diagnosis of ID. Over time, with the development of a variety of measures, these instruments have also been used in the diagnostic evaluations of other neurodevelopmental disorders, such as autism, as well as in treatment and intervention planning. It has therefore become important to consider a range of factors when deciding what type of measure to choose, including the format and age range of the measure, the culture, disability, and environment of the individual being assessed. The reliability and validity of the measure used and the results obtained are also of great importance in order to ensure that results are meaningful, especially when used for scientific research.

🖋 TEST YOURSELF 🖋

1. **List the five considerations that must be made when choosing a measure of adaptive behavior.**
2. **What is the primary use of an adaptive behavior scale?**
   a. To assess how well an individual was raised
   b. To classify whether an individual meets criteria for ID
   c. To indicate all potential disorders an individual might be affected by
   d. To quantify the rater's personal opinion on the individual being assessed
3. **List the four interview styles of adaptive behavior measures.**
4. **True or false? Tools measuring adaptive behavior need only two of the following in order to get valid data: adequate reliability, validity, and norms.**
5. **Which of the following is *not* a potential rating bias?**
   a. A respondent's limited memory
   b. A respondent's inability to differentiate what an individual can do compared to what the individual did do
   c. A respondent taking a long time to respond to the rater's question
   d. A respondent's intentional or unintentional overreporting of adaptive behavior to present the individual as higher functioning
6. **Define *maladaptive behaviors*.**
7. **What is item density?**
   a. The number of items in the measure
   b. The ratio of items in the maladaptive scale to items in the adaptive behavior domains
   c. The number of additional items that can be substituted to increase the applicability of questions
   d. The number of items that target a specific domain
8. **Define reliability and list the three types of reliability.**
9. **What is a category of concerning factors that influence sociocultural bias on adaptive behavior measures?**

10. True or false? An adaptive behavior measure is best used on its own in order to inform the clinician about further testing decisions.

Answers: (1) The age of the individual being assessed, available norms, the respondent, the context that the respondent knows the individual being assessed, the level of training of the rater; (2) b; (3) Unstructured, semi-structured, structured, direct observation; (4) False. Adaptive behavior measures must have all three: adequate reliability, validity, and norms; (5) c; (6) Maladaptive behaviors are behaviors that impede an individual's ability to display adaptive behaviors, and, as such, they can provide context to an individual's adaptive behavior profile; (7) d; (8) Reliability is degree to which a measure is consistent across situations and raters, and the three types of reliability are inter-rater reliability, test-retest reliability, and internal consistency; (9) Linguistic factors; (10) False. An adaptive behavior measure is best understood in the context of a full diagnostic assessment.

Three

STANDARDIZED MEASURES OF ADAPTIVE BEHAVIOR

With the inclusion of adaptive behavior deficits in the definitions of intellectual disability (ID) came the need for the development of standardized measures of adaptive behavior. This chapter outlines in detail the most commonly used measures of adaptive behavior as well as provides information on less common measures that can be useful for specific purposes. As outlined in Chapter 2, considerations when choosing a measure of adaptive behavior include reliability, validity, standardization sampling and norms, age range of domains assessed, training of the examiner, and type of respondent.

VINELAND SOCIAL MATURITY SCALE

In Chapter 1, we outlined the history that led to the development of the Vineland Social Maturity Scale (Vineland SMS), developed by Edgar Doll and published by American Guidance Services (AGS) in 1935. The Vineland SMS was the first standardized measure of adaptive functioning developed in an era that was focused on standardized intelligence testing. Doll was a staunch advocate for measuring what he referred to as "accustomed performance in mastered attainment" in addition to intelligence when diagnosing ID (Doll, 1953). Thus, the Vineland SMS was developed to assess the meaningful application of skills to daily contexts. As mentioned in Chapter 1, Doll was seeking to create a measure that was universal in nature and was applicable across factors such as race, geography, culture, or sex, but he understood the limitations this posed. As such, the Vineland SMS was designed with the following parameters (Doll, 1953):

- For use within "ordinary" urban and rural US contexts
- Within the limits of general US socioeconomic status
- Over the entire range of literacy
- For the range of large population samples of varying nationalities within the United States

The measure was created as a 117-item scale administered to individuals with disabilities from birth through maturity, which, at the time, defined the parameters of when ID could be diagnosed. Items were arranged in order of average developmental acquisition based on age-group norms obtained for the entire scale. Scoring was based on the same year-scale and point-scale principles used by Binet for intelligence tests at the time, and the scale yielded one single score. Items were scored as follows:

- Plus (+): When the behavior was performed without assistance or with minimal assistance or incentive
- Formerly (+F): If successful performance of the behavior has been outgrown but could be easily reestablished
- Plus-Minus (+/−): When the behavior is occasionally performed
- Minus (−): When the behavior has not yet been performed when expected or only with a great deal of assistance or incentive

Additional qualifiers were as follows:

- No Opportunity (+NO): If the behavior has never been performed due to lack of opportunity or environmental constraints (can also be scored No Occasion)
- No Information (NI): If the informant does not have adequate information or is unwilling to inform
- Basal: At least two plus scores established at the beginning of each category
- Ceiling: At least two minus scores established at the end of each category

Though Doll used total score norms, items were grouped by the following categories: (1) self-help general, (2) self-help dressing, (3) self-help eating, (4) communication, (5) self-direction, (6) socialization, (7) locomotion, and (8) occupation. As illustrated across these categories, the Vineland SMS was a multidimensional measure even though social competency was at the forefront of Doll's theory of adaptive behavior. Doll believed that the most accurate way to obtain information about an individual's social competence was through an examination of the person's behavior with a third-party respondent, such as a parent, caregiver, or teacher. In the manual, Doll explained that a rating scale could invite personal biases of an observer that could be minimized with a semi-structured interview. Alternatively, he felt that direct assessment would be challenging due to the difficulty in providing opportunities for practical application of skills within a confined or contrived clinical environment. Moreover, any observations would be limited to what the individual *can do* at the time of testing rather than what the individual *does do* routinely, resulting in a skewed estimate of independence (Doll, 1953). Doll's early differentiation of *can do* (innate ability) and *does do* (overt behavior) elucidates the very distinction between intelligence and adaptive functioning, respectively, while highlighting the importance of both for defining ID.

≡ *Rapid Reference 3.1*

···

Vineland Social Maturity Scale Categories

- Self-help general
- Self-help dressing
- Self-help eating
- Communication
- Self-direction
- Socialization
- Locomotion
- Occupation

At the time, the Vineland SMS had a variety of uses, including assessing level of social competence along with cognition when determining the following: (1) if a person with ID was competent to stand trial, (2) institutional placement, (3) identifying areas for program planning, and (4) guardianship. The clinical samples for which the assessments were most useful included individuals of varying levels of cognitive impairment, individuals with visual and hearing impairments, and those with seizure and movement or motor disorders. Many of the qualities of the Vineland SMS, as well as the uses and function of the original measure, still hold strong today.

CAUTION

··

Functional independence is defined more by competencies in adaptive behavior than cognition.

AAMD/AAMR/AAIDD ADAPTIVE BEHAVIOR SCALES

What is currently named the American Association on Intellectual and Developmental Disabilities (AAIDD) is the oldest professional nonprofit association that has focused on individuals with developmental disabilities. Dating back to 1876 when it was originally named the Association of Medical Officers of American Institutions for Idiotic and Feeblemindedness, AAIDD has changed names five times. Yet, it has maintained its own manual for the diagnostic criteria of ID, updating these criteria over decades. Adaptive behavior was first included in the organization's definition of ID when it was called the American Association on Mental Deficiency (AAMD). The next section outlines the measures of adaptive behavior published by this organization since 1969.

Adaptive Behavior Scale (ABS)

When the formalized definitions of ID consistently included adaptive deficits for classification, there became a need to develop more standardized measures of adaptive behavior. As such, the American Association on Mental Deficiency (AAMD) developed the Adaptive Behavior Scale (ABS) in 1969, with Nihira Kazuo, Ray Foster, Max Shellhaas, and Henry Leland. The original ABS measured an individual's personal independence and social skills from ages 3 through adulthood. It was standardized on a diverse sample of 6,523 individuals in the states of California and Florida, ages 3 to 17 years.

Adaptive Behavior Scale, Public School Version (ABS-PSV)

The introduction of P.L. 94-142 in the 1970s called for enhanced standardized assessments of adaptive behavior along with IQ. Given the psychometric shortcomings of the ABS, AAMD updated the scale with the Adaptive Behavior Scale, Public School Version (ABS-PSV; Lambert, Windmiller, Cole, & Figueroa, 1975). The newer ABS-PSV allowed for the assessment of individuals within the school system, not just those who were institutionalized. Given the focus on the school environment, certain areas of daily living from the previous version were excluded, and the measure was used on children ages 7 years, 3 months to 13 years, 2 months. It consisted of two parts: Part 1 assessed daily living and personal responsibility skills and Part 2 assessed maladaptive social functioning. Items in Part 1 were organized in developmental progression. Item responses yielded domain, factor, and comparison scores. It could be administered to a parent or teacher via an interview or through an examiner's knowledge of the individual being assessed. The ABS-PSV had norms that would place individuals with mental retardation by class: either "educable mentally retarded" (EMR) or "trainable mentally retarded" (TMR). Though the psychometrics for Part 1 were stronger than Part 2, the ABS was criticized for lacking reliability analyses, most specifically test-retest and interrater reliabilities (Givens & Ward, 1982).

DON'T FORGET

It was the introduction of P.L. 94-142 (now known as the Individual with Disabilities Education Act) that called for the enhancement of standardized assessments of adaptive behavior along with IQ when evaluating students with disabilities for ID.

Adaptive Behavior Scale, School Edition, and AAMR Adaptive Behavior Scale–School:2 (ABS-S:2)

The ABS-PSV was updated in 1981 to the ABS, School Edition (Lambert, 1981), after AAMD was renamed the American Association on Mental Retardation (AAMR). A second edition of this revision would be published in 1993: AAMR Adaptive Behavior Scale–School:2 (ABS-S:2; Lambert, Nihira, & Leland, 1993). There were two versions of the ABS-S:2: a school version (ABS-2:2; Lambert et al., 1993) and a residential and community version (ABS-Residential and Community, ABS-RC:2; Nihira, Leland, & Lambert, 1993). The measure assessed individuals with ID, autism, or behavioral disorders who were between 3 and 18 years. The scales were used to identify students who were significantly below their peers in adaptive functioning for diagnostic purposes. They also determined strengths and weaknesses, documented progress, and assessed the effects of intervention programs.

Similar to the ABS-PSV, Part 1 of the ABS-S:2 focused on the following nine behavior domains for personal independence:

- Independent Functioning
- Physical Development
- Economic Activity
- Language Development
- Numbers and Time
- Prevocational or Vocational Activity
- Self-Direction
- Responsibility
- Socialization

Part 2 of the ABS-S:2 focused more on maladaptive behaviors or those associated with personality or behavior disorders in the following seven domains:

- Social Behavior
- Conformity

- Trustworthiness
- Stereotyped and Hyperactive Behavior
- Self-Abusive Behavior
- Social Engagement
- Disturbing Interpersonal Behavior

Collectively, the ABS-S:2 yielded five factor scores: (1) Personal Self-Sufficiency, (2) Community Self-Sufficiency, (3) Personal-Social Responsibility, (4) Social Adjustment, and (5) Personal Adjustment.

The standardization sample for the ABS-School:2 included 2,074 students (ages 3–21) with ID living in 40 states and a sample of 1,254 students (ages 3–18) without ID from 44 states. Standard scores, age-equivalent scores, and percentile ranks were converted from raw scores on the adaptive behavior subscales and three factor scores for ages 3–21 on the school form. The standardization samples had been judged to be excellent, although the sample of individuals with ID did not include people with IQs between 71 and 75 and, thus, likely overestimated adaptive behavior when using the norms for individuals with IDs (Stinnett, 1997). The Residential and Community form was developed to be used with individuals through 79 years of age. Norms, however, were not available for adults with typical functioning, and the norm-referenced scores were generally available only to compare to adults with developmental disabilities. Although it was linked to AAMR by name, the ABS did not provide subscale scores in the 10 adaptive skill areas listed in the 1992 AAMR definition of ID. In fact, research suggested that the ABS-School:2 was best considered as a two-factor model assessing personal independence and social functioning, rather than the five-factor model proposed in the measure (Stinnet, Fuqua, & Coombs, 1999). The measure went out of print in 2016.

DIAGNOSTIC ADAPTIVE BEHAVIOR SCALE (DABS)

The AAIDD is currently developing a new adaptive assessment measure called the Diagnostic Adaptive Behavior Scale (DABS; Tassé et al., 2018; Tassé, Schalock, Balboni, Spreast, & Navas, 2016). The DABS assists clinicians in making a diagnosis of ID by allowing one to determine if individuals present with significant limitations in their adaptive behaviors. The DABS is exclusively used for establishing a diagnosis of ID in individuals 4 through 21 years of age. There are three versions: one for individuals 4 through 8 years of age, another for individuals 9 through 15 years of age, and the third for individuals 16 through 21 years of age.

Diagnostic
Adaptive
Behavior Scale
User's Manual

Marc J. Tassé
Robert L. Schalock
Giulia Balboni
Henry (Hank) Bersani, Jr.
Sharon A. Borthwick-Duffy
Scott Spreat
David Thissen
Keith F. Widaman
Dalun Zhang

Source: Tassé et al. (2018). Cover of upcoming *Diagnostic and Adaptive Behavior Scale User's Manual.* Reproduced with permission of the American Association on Intellectual and Developmental Disabilities.

Similar to the Vineland, the DABS is a semi-structured interview that is conducted between an examiner and a respondent who has direct knowledge of the individual being assessed. Respondents can be anyone who knows the individual well (i.e., someone who has interacted with him or her on a daily basis over several months), including family members, friends, teachers, coworkers, support staff members, employers, or other adults meeting these criteria. Similar to the ABAS, the DABS is based on the Conceptual, Social, and Practical domains of adaptive behavior. The DABS was developed as a brief measure, taking approximately 30 minutes to complete. There is a total of 75 items on the scale, including items assessing higher-order social adaptive skills such as gullibility, naiveté, and the ability to avoid victimization. The DABS is normed on the general population and has a mean of 100 and a standard deviation of 15. The DABS does not have a Maladaptive subscale, and there is no self-report form.

The scale ranges from 0 to 3, with 0 being used when an individual rarely or never does a particular task and 3 indicating that an individual always or almost always does a task independently. Scores of 1 and 2 indicate that an individual does a task with reminders or assistance or sometimes independently. A score of NS can also be given if the respondent does not have direct knowledge of the individual's typical performance or if there is lack of opportunity due to cultural, gender, geographic factors, or environmental constraints.

The scale was developed using item response theory, allowing examiners the flexibility of tailoring the assessment to meet the needs of the individual being evaluated. Sensitivity and specificity of the DABS are .88 and .90, respectively, with regard to including and excluding individuals who meet criteria for an ID. The DABS standard scores compare favorably with the Vineland-II, with convergent validity coefficients ranging from .70 to .84.

VINELAND ADAPTIVE BEHAVIOR SCALES

The Vineland Adaptive Behavior Scales is one of the original standardized measures of adaptive functioning, having been the revision of the Vineland Social Maturity Scales (SMS). Similar to the Vineland SMS, it was developed as a semi-structured clinical interview between an examiner and a parent or caregiver to obtain the broadest and most accurate information regarding an individual's level of practical skills.

Vineland Adaptive Behavior Scale (Vineland ABS)

About the same time that AAMD was developing the ABS-PSV in the 1970s, AGS set out to update the Vineland SMS. Sara Sparrow, an esteemed psychologist with expertise in intellectual disabilities at the Yale Child Study Center within Yale University School of Medicine, was recruited as the author. Sparrow, along with her colleagues David Balla, an associate professor of psychology also at the Yale Child Study Center, and Domenic Cicchetti, a biostatistician at Yale University School of Medicine, would develop the revision of the Vineland SMS. Sparrow, Balla, and Cicchetti significantly expanded on the content and psychometrics of the Vineland SMS with the publication of the Vineland Adaptive Behavior Scales (Vineland ABS) in 1984.

The Vineland ABS would have three versions: (1) A Survey Interview edition that, true to Doll's view of a third-party informant, was a semi-structured interview conducted with a parent or caregiver of individuals from birth through 18 years, 11 months; (2) An Expanded Interview edition that included more

Table 3.1 Vineland ABS Adaptive Behavior Domains and Subdomains

Communication	Daily Living Skills	Socialization Skills	Motor Skills
Receptive (language a person understands)	Personal (eating, dressing, bathing, toileting, etc.)	Interpersonal (engaging and interacting with others, conversation)	Fine (manipulation of small objects with hands and fingers, such as writing, cutting, opening doors, fasteners)
Expressive (language a person uses)	Domestic (cleaning, organizing, cooking, etc.)	Play and leisure (make-believe play, independent play, leisure activities)	Gross (large body movements and balance, such as running, jumping, coordination, kicking)
Written (reading and writing skills)	Community (understanding use of money and time concepts, use of the telephone, vocational abilities)	Coping (emotional regulation, manners, following community rules and norms, responsibility toward others)	

items across a more comprehensive range of behaviors than the Survey Interview; and (3) a Classroom edition to be completed by teachers that was published a year later in 1985 for use with children ages 3 years to 12 years, 11 months (Sparrow, Balla, & Cicchetti, 1985). The Vineland ABS expanded on the content areas of the Vineland SMS, assessing adaptive behavior in four domains and 11 subdomains (see Table 3.1).

Similar to the Vineland SMS, items in the Vineland ABS were listed in developmental order and were scored based on frequency of performance, with a score of 2 denoting "frequently," a score of 1 denoting "sometimes" or "emergent performance of the skill," and a score of 0 denoting "seldom" or "never." Also similar were the options to score "no opportunity" and "don't know." In order to avoid having to administer all items on the Survey Form, basal and ceiling rules were developed, with a basal consisting of seven consecutive scores of 2 and a ceiling consisting of seven consecutive scores of 0 within a subdomain. Standard scores were available for the overall Adaptive Behavior Composite as well as each broad domain, with a mean of 100 and standard deviation of 15. Subdomain scores were reported in age-equivalents.

The Vineland ABS Survey Form also included a Maladaptive Behavior domain that measured more negative behaviors that get in the way of adaptive functioning. The Maladaptive Behavior Domain was composed of externalizing and internalizing behaviors, as well as "critical" behaviors (e.g., suicidality, setting fires, etc.). Administration of this domain was optional for children over the age of 3 (i.e., the Maladaptive Behavior domain is not completed on children under the age of 2).

The Vineland ABS was standardized on 3,000 individuals across 15 age groups matching US Census data from 1980. The final Survey Form consisted of 265 items within the four domains and an additional 36 items in the Maladaptive Behavior domain, for a total of 301 items. The Expanded Form was not standardized and included twice as many items as the Survey Form, and items were arranged by topic content area, or "cluster," rather than in developmental order. For the Survey Form, internal consistency reliability coefficients across domains ranged from .70 to .95. Test-retest reliability coefficients were above .80. Concurrent validity between the Vineland ABS Adaptive Behavior Composite with the Vineland SMS Social Quotient was moderate at .55, though the major revisions would account for this. Correlations with the AAMD ABS ranged between .40 and .70. The strong standardization of the Vineland ABS set the stage for the scale becoming one of the leading measures of adaptive behavior worldwide.

Vineland Adaptive Behavior Scales, Second Edition (Vineland-II)

In 2005, the second edition of the Vineland ABS was published by the same authors (Sparrow, Cicchetti, & Balla, 2005b). Originally published by AGS but subsequently acquired by Pearson Clinical, the Vineland-II retained the organizational structure of the Vineland ABS, including all domains, subdomains, and maladaptive domains, but extended the age range through 90+ years and added a Parent Rating Form. Items were revised and updated to be more current, and content was expanded to include behaviors associated with autism spectrum disorder, including items assessing social communication, interpersonal reciprocity, and play. Basal and ceiling rules for the Survey Interview Form were modified to four consecutive scores of 2 for a basal and four consecutive scores of 0 for a ceiling. A Spanish translation of the Survey Interview Form was added, for use with the English norms.

Though the Survey Interview Form retained the open-ended interview format, the newly added Parent Rating Form offered the same content to be administered in a questionnaire format that was given to the third-party respondent to complete on his or her own. Because the items were identical across the Survey and Parent

Rating Forms, the two were standardized together on the same sample of 3,695 individuals matched to US population data from 2001 in regard to race-ethnicity, community size, geographic region, and socioeconomic status (as measured by maternal education). Internal consistency reliability coefficients for the Survey Interview Form domain scores ranged from .77 to .93. Test-retest reliability coefficients ranged from .53 to .80. The correlations between the Vineland-II and original Vineland ABS domains ranged from .69 to .96. The correlation between the Vineland-II Adaptive Behavior Composite and the Adaptive Behavior Assessment System, Second Edition's General Adaptive Composite was .70.

The Vineland-II Teacher Rating Form that replaced the Classroom Edition of the Vineland ABS was also published in 2005, with norms extending from age 3 to 21 years (Sparrow, Cicchetti, & Balla, 2005a). The standardization sample consisted of 2,500 students ages 3–18, with the 18-year-old norms used for students 19–21 (given that typically developing students of this age range would not be readily accessible within the school systems). Though the four domains remain consistent with the Survey Interview and Parent Rating Forms, the Domestic subdomain was renamed *Academic* and the Community subdomain was renamed *School Community*, with respective associated items to match behaviors observable within the school environment.

The Vineland-II Expanded Interview Form was published in 2008 by Pearson Clinical (Sparrow, Cicchetti, & Balla, 2008). This version offered a more comprehensive set of items that were useful primarily for developing treatment and intervention plans, whether for educational, vocational, or living purposes. Similar to the Vineland ABS, items in the expanded form were arranged by content cluster areas rather than developmental level and, as such, basal and ceiling rules differed. Please refer to the Vineland-II Expanded Interview Form manual for a detailed description of these rules (Sparrow et al., 2008). Though the Expanded Interview Form was often used in clinical trials research (i.e., primarily drug studies conducted by pharmaceutical companies) and occasionally used in autism research, commercial interest in this version of the Vineland-II was limited. As such, it would not be included as a separate measure in the third revision.

Vineland Adaptive Behavior Scales, Third Edition (Vineland-3)

The third edition of the Vineland was published by Pearson Clinical in June 2016 by Sparrow, Cicchetti, and Saulnier. Saulnier trained at the Yale Child Study Center with Sparrow, conducting research on profiles of adaptive behavior in autism spectrum disorder. On Sparrow's passing in 2010, she (along with Cicchetti) bequeathed coauthorship to Saulnier to carry on her legacy with the Vineland-3.

Source: Sparrow, Cicchetti, and Saulnier (2016). The cover page image of the *Vineland Adaptive Behavior Scales, Third Edition (Vineland-3)*. Copyright © 2016 NCS Pearson, Inc. Reproduced with permission. All rights reserved.

Given the vast changes in technology, many contemporary assessment instruments were being developed with options for online administration and use. The Vineland-3 would be no exception, and it was developed with an option for online administration through Pearson Clinical's Q-Global platform (a secure online testing platform that provides automated scoring and reporting). The structure of the Vineland-3 remains consistent with the Vineland-II in that there are three administration forms: the Interview Form (formerly Survey Form), Parent Form (formerly Parent Rating Form), and Teacher Form (formerly Teacher Rating Form). The four domains of Communication, Daily Living Skills, Socialization, and Motor Skills remain (including the 11 respective subdomains), with the modification of making the Motor domain (Fine- and Gross-Motor subdomains) optional and, therefore, not included in the overall

Adaptive Behavior Composite score. The Motor domain age norms were also extended to age 9. This change in making the Motor domain optional was to be consistent with concurrent diagnostic criteria for ID in the *Diagnostic and Statistical Manual of Mental Disorders,* Fifth Edition (American Psychiatric Association [APA], 2013), which does not include motor impairments in the definition of ID. The Vineland-3 continues to offer the option of administering the Maladaptive domain, which is now also included in the Parent and Teacher Forms.

The items in the Vineland-3 consist of updated items from the Vineland-II as well as the addition of new content items, particularly in the following areas: pre-reading and pre-writing skills, advanced reading and writing, awareness and use of healthy eating and exercise behaviors, social gullibility, and perspective taking. For the Interview Form, items from the Survey Form and Expanded Form of the Vineland-II were considered and, thus, the total number of 502 items in the Vineland-3 Interview Form actually exceeds that of the Vineland-II Survey Form. The Parent Form items, though identical in content to the Interview Form, are written at a fifth-grade reading level. For this reason, the Parent Form was standardized separately from the Interview Form and, thus, they each have separate norms. The Parent Form is also now available with the option of a Spanish translation. Basal and ceiling items remain the same for the Interview Form, with four consecutive scores of 2 and 0, respectively. Given the ease in automation with the online platform, basal and ceiling scores were also added to the Parent and Teacher Forms, with five consecutive scores of 2 and 0, respectively. Original paper administration options remain for use with all forms.

A new addition to the Vineland-3 includes the development of domain-level versions of all three forms. These are brief administration options that consist of items sampled across all subdomains within a domain, but only offer domain-level scores and an overall Adaptive Behavior Composite. The domain-level forms allow for a much quicker administration option when the primary need for the assessment is to determine eligibility for ID. The standard scores meet American Association on Intellectual and Developmental Disabilities (AAIDD) and *DSM-5* criteria for ID. Administration times range from 10–20 minutes. Domain-level forms can be administered online or in paper form.

All forms of the Vineland-3 can be scored manually or through Q-Global's online scoring system. Computer-generated reports are available that can include multi-rater comparisons, progress monitoring comparisons over time, and intervention guidance to inform treatment programs.

⟰ Rapid Reference 3.2

Overview of the Vineland-3

	Interview Form		Parent/Caregiver Form		Teacher Form	
	Compre-hensive	Domain Level	Compre-hensive	Domain Level	Compre-hensive	Domain Level
Core Adaptive Scores	Three domains Nine sub-domains Overall ABC	Three domains Overall ABC	Three domains Nine sub-domains Overall ABC	Three domains Overall ABC	Three domains Nine sub-domains Overall ABC	Three domains Overall ABC
Optional Domains	Motor skills Maladaptive behavior	Motor skills Maladaptive behavior	Motor skills Maladaptive behavior	Motor skills Maladaptive behavior	Motor skills Maladaptive behavior	Motor skills Maladaptive behavior
Age Range	Birth–90+	3–90+	Birth–90+	3–90+	3–21	3–21
Total Item Count	502	195	502	180	133	149
Completion Time	35–40 minutes	23–27 minutes	20–25 minutes	10–15 minutes	15–20 minutes	8–10 minutes

Primary clinical uses for the Vineland continue to be for determining eligibility for ID, diagnosing autism spectrum disorder, identifying areas for intervention and treatment planning, and measuring and monitoring progress over time. Moreover, the Vineland is the most widely used measure of adaptive behavior for scientific research. To date, it has been informally translated into more than a dozen languages, including Italian, German, Dutch, Vietnamese, and Hindi, among others, for use across the world. Formal translations with standardizations have been published in Japan (Tsujii et al., 2015). It is also modeled in the National Institutes of Health's National Database for Autism Research as a required measure for phenotypic characterization of research participants with autism spectrum disorder.

ADAPTIVE BEHAVIOR ASSESSMENT SYSTEM

The Adaptive Behavior Assessment System is a comprehensive, norm-referenced measure to assess adaptive behavior. It was among the first measures to align areas of adaptive skills with those specified within the *Diagnostic and Statistical Manual of Mental Disorders* for a diagnosis of intellectual disability.

Adaptive Behavior Assessment System (ABAS)

Though Heber described a three-factor structure of adaptive behavior deficits in the areas of practical, conceptual, and social skills in 1959, it would not be until the 10th edition of the AAMR manual in 2002 that this trifecta of deficits was included in the definition of mental retardation. Two years prior, in 2000, the Adaptive Behavior Assessment System (ABAS) was developed by Patti Harrison and Thomas Oakland and published by the Psychological Corporation. The major difference between the ABAS and the Vineland ABS was that the ABAS was a rating form that parents, caregivers, teachers, or adults actually completed themselves (i.e., rather than a clinical interview conducted with an examiner). Whereas the original Vineland ABS only measured adaptive behavior through age 18 years, the ABAS could be administered to individuals from birth through 89 years. Items were measured on a four-point rating scale from 0 (not able) to 3 (always) and three forms were provided: (1) a Parent Form, (2) a Teacher Form, and (3) an Adult Form. However, the original ABAS was just a one-factor measure providing only an overall composite score. This would become one of the major criticisms of the measure, which led to its early revision (Sattler, 2002).

Adaptive Behavior Assessment System, Second Edition (ABAS-II)

Shortly after its publication in 2000, the ABAS was revised by Psych Corp to be consistent with AAMR guidelines (i.e., with the trifecta of deficits in practical, conceptual, and social skills) and the diagnostic criteria for mental retardation set forth by the *Diagnostic and Statistical Manual of Mental Disorders,* Fourth Edition, Text Revision (American Psychiatric Association [APA], 2000). In fact, the ABAS, Second Edition (ABAS-II; Harrison & Oakland, 2003) would include all 10 adaptive skill areas listed in the *DSM-IV-TR* criteria. The 10 adaptive skill areas within the three broad domains were as follows: The Conceptual domain included Communication, Functional Academics, and Self-Direction; the Social domain included Leisure and Social Skills; and the Practical domain included Community Use, Home-School Living, Self-Care, Health and Safety, and Work. Motor skill scores were available for children under the age of 5 years. Given that the ABAS-II was a rating form, it could be completed in as few as 20 minutes. Examiners also had the option of reading items aloud to respondents who might have difficulty reading.

☰ *Rapid Reference 3.3*

Adaptive Domains and Skill Areas of the ABAS

Conceptual Skills
- **Communication.** Skills needed to communicate with others (e.g., conversational skills, nonverbal communication skills)
- **Functional Academics.** Foundational skills for learning (e.g., reading, writing, mathematics)
- **Self-Direction.** Skills needed for independence (e.g., making choices, task initiation and completion, following instructions and routines)

Social Skills
- **Leisure.** Engaging in play and leisure activities (e.g., interactive play, playing with games and toys, following rules in games)
- **Social.** Social interaction skills (e.g., emotional expression, friendships, manners)

Practical Skills
- **Community Use.** Skills necessary for navigating the community (e.g., getting around through transportation, engaging in activities outside the home)
- **Home-School Living.** Basic living skills in the home or school environment (e.g., cleaning, organizing, chores)
- **Health and Safety.** Taking care of health needs (e.g., medications, following safety rules, avoiding danger)
- **Work.** Holding a job, part-time or full-time (e.g., completing work tasks, following schedules)
- **Motor** (replaces the Work domain on the Infant-Preschool Forms): Basic fine- and gross-motor skills (standing, walking, jumping, kicking)

The ABAS-II also included new Infant-Preschool Forms. As such, it separated out the Parent/Primary Caregiver Rating Forms for ages 0 to 5 years and the Parent Form for 5 to 21 years, and the Teacher–Daycare Provider Rating Forms for children ages 2 to 5 years and the Teacher Form for 5 to 21 years. The Adult Form was from 16 to 89 years and could be completed by a parent or caregiver or as a self-rating. The Parent and Teacher Forms were available in Spanish. Collectively across all forms, the standardization sample across groups was more than 7,000 individuals throughout the United States. Composite scores were available for all broad domain scores and a General Adaptive Composite (GAC) with a mean score of 100 and standard deviation of 15. Skill area scores had a mean of 10 and standard deviation of 3. The ABAS-II had strong reliability, with internal consistency scores above .90, and test-retest reliability scores averaging between .80 and .90. Correlations between the ABAS-II GAC for the Teacher Form and the Vineland ABS Adaptive Behavior Composite for the Classroom Edition was .76.

Adaptive Behavior Assessment System, Third Edition (ABAS-3)

In 2015, the third edition of the ABAS was published by Western Psychological Services (ABAS-3; Harrison & Oakland, 2015). Although the overall composition and structure of the ABAS-3 remains consistent with the ABAS-II, item content was updated and made more comprehensive at the very early and later developmental stages and to better represent behaviors associated with ID, autism spectrum disorder, and attention deficit/hyperactivity disorder. The three broad domains and 11 adaptive skill areas (including motor) remain intact, again consistent with the former AAMR and now AAIDD (Schalock et al., 2010) and *DSM-5* (American Psychiatric Association [APA], 2013) definitions of adaptive behavior domains. The five forms remain intact, including the Parent/Primary Caregiver Form, the Parent Form, the Teacher/Daycare Provider Form, the Teacher Form, and the Adult Form (the last of which can be a self-rating). All forms are available in Spanish. Items are scored on a four-point scale from 0 reflecting "not able to" perform the behavior to 4 reflecting "always" performing the behavior when needed. Completion time is 15–20 minutes.

The ABAS-3 has an online administration option that was developed using the Western Psychological Services Online Evaluation System. Another addition to the third edition was the inclusion of rater comparisons between, for example, a parent and teacher. The Intervention Planner is also available for the paper and online administrations to inform treatment and intervention based on item content.

Updated norms for the ABAS-3 were obtained from a national sample of 4,500 individuals from birth through 89 years. Internal consistency reliability coefficients continue to be strong, with GCA scores for all forms ranging from .85 to .99. Average test-retest correlations for all forms range between .70 and .89. Corrected correlations between the ABAS-3 Parent/Primary Caregiver Form and the Vineland-II Parent/Caregiver Rating Form averaged .66 across skill areas, and the ABAS-3 GAC correlated with the Vineland-II ABC at .77.

SCALES OF INDEPENDENT BEHAVIOR–REVISED (SIB-R)

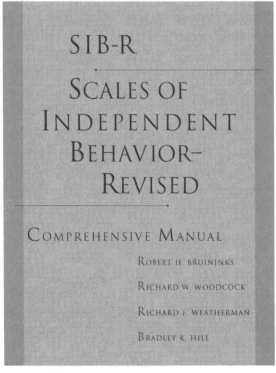

SIB-R

•

SCALES OF
INDEPENDENT
BEHAVIOR–
REVISED

•

COMPREHENSIVE MANUAL

ROBERT H. BRUININKS

RICHARD W. WOODCOCK

RICHARD F. WEATHERMAN

BRADLEY K. HILL

Source: Bruininks, Woodcock, Weatherman, and Hill (1996). Cover of the Scales of Independent Behavior–Revised. Reproduced with permission from Houghton Mifflin Harcourt.

The Scales of Independent Behavior–Revised (SIB-R) was developed by Robert Bruininks, Richard Woodcock, Richard Weatherman, and Bradley Hill and published by Houghton Mifflin Harcourt in 1996. It is a component of the Woodcock-Johnson Psycho-Educational Battery and is a comprehensive, norm-referenced assessment of adaptive behavior across 14 different areas including eight areas of maladaptive behavior. The assessment can be used for individuals from birth through 80+ years of age and assesses functional independence and adaptive functioning in school, employment, and community settings. It also assesses people with mild to profound disabilities and people without disabilities, and it is one of the only instruments that has a form specifically for blind individuals.

There are two forms of the SIB-R; the Full Scale, which takes 45 to 60 minutes to administer, and the Short Form or Early Development Form, which takes 15 to 20 minutes to administer. The SIB-R can be administered as a structured interview or given in a checklist format. The SIB-R enables examiners to obtain standard scores, percentile ranks, and age equivalents. A support score is also obtained which provides a weighted measure of maladaptive and adaptive behaviors to evaluate the levels of support, supervision, and resources that an individual needs. The support score is categorized into six broad levels: Pervasive, Extensive, Frequent, Limited, Intermittent, and Infrequent or No Support, with lower scores indicating greater adaptive impairment and need for services. The primary uses of the SIB-R are to identify areas for training, for planning programs and services, for systematic monitoring of individualized training programs, for program evaluation, for clinical assessment and diagnosis, for research and psychometric training, and to determine eligibility for developmental disability services.

The norming sample for the SIB-R (Bruininks et al., 1996) included 2,182 individuals ages 3 years 11 months to 90 years, with a sampling frame based on the general population of the United States stratified for gender, race, Hispanic origin, occupational level, geographic region, and community size.

ADAPTIVE BEHAVIOR EVALUATION SCALE, THIRD EDITION (ABES-3)

Source: McCarney and House (2017). Cover of *Adaptive Behavior Evaluation Scale, Third Edition, School Version Technical Manual.* Reproduced with permission from Hawthorne Educational Services, Inc.

Unlike the other measures of adaptive behavior described previously, the Adaptive Behavior Evaluation Scale, Third Edition (ABES-3; McCarney & House, 2017) is a direct observation rating scale of an individual's adaptive behavior published by Hawthorne Educational Services. The prior revised second edition (ABES-2R) was developed by Stephen B. McCarney and Tamara Arthaud in 2006. Similar to the ABAS-3, the ABES-3 is keyed into the *DSM-5* criteria for ID with 10 areas of adaptive skills under the three domains of Conceptual, Social, and Practical Skills. It assesses individuals from 4 through 18 years of age and is divided into two age groups: one for children 4 through 12 years of age and another for adolescents 13 through 18 years of age. Each age group also has a home and a school version. Each version takes approximately 20 minutes for an individual to complete. Parents or guardians or educators can complete the scale based on observations of the individual in an educational or residential setting.

The ABES-3 can be used to measure adaptive skills in individuals with ID, behavioral disorders, learning disabilities, and those with visual, hearing, or physical impairments. In addition, there is an Adaptive Behavior Intervention manual for each version that provides goals, objectives, and interventions for each of the items from the school version that can be directly included in a child's individualized education program (IEP). The ABES-3 is available in English and Spanish. With regard to psychometrics, for all versions, internal consistency was above 0.80 and test-retest reliability ranged from 0.60 to 0.85. Interrater reliability ranged from 0.61 to 0.73.

DON'T FORGET

The ABES-2R is a direct observation measure of adaptive behavior skills.

DEVELOPMENTAL ASSESSMENTS WITH ADAPTIVE BEHAVIOR SECTIONS

In addition to standardized assessments that were developed specifically to measure adaptive behavior, there are sections of broader assessment batteries that also measure adaptive functioning. Two commonly used developmental measures that include sections on adaptive behavior are the Battelle Developmental Inventory,

Second Edition, and the Bayley Scales of Infant and Toddler Development, Third Edition.

Battelle Developmental Inventory, Second Edition, Normative Update (BDI-2)

The Battelle Developmental Inventory, Second Edition, Normative Update (BDI-2; Newborg, 2016) is a test of early developmental abilities that includes an Adaptive domain consisting of two subdomains: Self-Care and Personal Responsibility. The BDI-2 is appropriate for children from birth through 7 years, 11 months of age with norms based on a nationally representative sample of children using US Census projections for 2015.

Bayley Scales of Infant and Toddler Development, Third Edition (Bayley-III)

The Bayley Scales of Infant and Toddler Development, Third Edition (Bayley-III; Bayley, 2006) is one of the leading measures for assessing early development between the ages of 1 and 42 months. With the third edition came the addition of the Adaptive Behavior Subtest that was developed by Patti Harrison and Thomas Oakland (see ABAS). This domain assesses for the following adaptive areas: Communication, Community Use, Functional Pre-Academics, Home Living, Health and Safety, Leisure, Self-Care, Self-Direction, Social, and Motor Skills.

SUMMARY

Though this chapter highlights the most commonly used and historical measures of adaptive behavior, many more exist and are under development. Please refer to Chapter 2 for variables to consider when choosing the most appropriate measure to fit the needs of the individual being evaluated. These include the age of the individual being assessed, the type of respondent available, the context in which the individual is known, the training of the rater or examiner, and the reliability and validity of the measure. Table 3.2 summarizes the measures described in this chapter in the order in which they were published.

Table 3.2 Measures of Adaptive Behavior

Measure	Year Published	Authors	Publisher	Age Range
Vineland Social Maturity Scale	1935	Doll	American Guidance Services	Birth through maturity
AAMD Adaptive Behavior Scale	1969	Kazuo, Foster, Shellhaas, and Leland	AAMD	3 to 17 years
AAMD Adaptive Behavior Scale, Public School Version	1975	Lambert, Windmiller, Cole, and Figueroa	AAMD	7 years, 3 months to 13 years, 2 months
AAMR Adaptive Behavior Scale, School Edition	1981	Lambert et al.	AAMR	3 to 18 years
Vineland Adaptive Behavior Scales	1984	Sparrow, Balla, and Cicchetti	American Guidance Services	Birth to 18 years, 11 months
Vineland Adaptive Behavior Scales, Classroom Edition	1985	Sparrow, Balla, and Cicchetti	American Guidance Service	3 years to 12 years, 11 months
AAMR Adaptive Behavior Scale, School:2	1993	Lambert et al.	AAMR	3 to 18 years
Scales of Independent Behavior, Revised	1996	Bruininks, Woodcock, Weatherman, and Hill	Houghton Mifflin Harcourt	Birth to 80+ years
Adaptive Behavior Assessment System	2000	Harrison and Oakland	Psychological Corporation	Birth to 89 years
Adaptive Behavior Assessment System, Second Edition	2002	Harrison and Oakland	Psychological Corporation	Birth to 89 years
Vineland Adaptive Behavior Scales, Second Edition	2004, 2006, and 2008	Sparrow, Cicchetti, and Balla	Pearson Assessments	Birth to 90+ years
Adaptive Behavior Evaluation Scale, Revised, Second Edition	2006	McCarney and Arthaud	Hawthorne Educational Services	4 to 18 years

Table 3.2 (Continued)

Measure	Year Published	Authors	Publisher	Age Range
Adaptive Behavior Assessment System, Third Edition	2015	Harrison and Oakland	Western Psychological Services	Birth to 89 years
Vineland Adaptive Behavior Scales, Third Edition	2016	Sparrow, Cicchetti, and Saulnier	Pearson Assessments	Birth to 90+ years
Adaptive Behavior Evaluation Scale, Third Edition	2017	McCarney and House	Hawthorne Educational Services	4 to 18 years
Diagnostic Adaptive Behavior Scale	In development	Tassé, Schalock, Balboni, et al.	AAIDD	4 to 21 years

TEST YOURSELF

1. True or false? In the Vineland SMS, a score of Plus-Minus is a behavior that is performed without assistance or with minimal assistance or incentive.
2. True or false? Functional independence is defined more by cognition than competencies in adaptive behavior.
3. Name the five factor scores that the Adaptive Behavior Scale–School:2 (ABS-S:2) yields.
4. Name the four domains of the Vineland ABS.
5. Which of the following is *not* a subdomain of the Socialization Skills domain of the Vineland ABS?
   a. Interpersonal
   b. Play-Leisure
   c. Coping
   d. Domestic
6. Which of the following is *not* one of the three administration options for the Vineland-3?
   a. The Interview Form
   b. Parent Form
   c. Self-Administered Form
   d. Teacher Form

7. **What are the three domains of the Adaptive Behavior Assessment System, Second Edition (ABAS-II) that followed Heber's three-factor structure of adaptive behavior deficits?**

8. **In what format is the Vineland-II administered?**
   a. Unstructured interview
   b. Semi-structured interview
   c. Direct observation
   d. Self-administered

9. **In what format is the Diagnostic Adaptive Behavior Scale (DABS) administered?**
   a. Unstructured interview
   b. Semi-structured interview
   c. Direct observation
   d. Self-administered

10. **In what format is the Adaptive Behavior Evaluation Scale, Third Edition (ABES-3) administered?**
    a. Unstructured interview
    b. Semi-structured interview
    c. Direct observation
    d. Self-administered

11. **Which two of the following are adaptive behavior sections that the Battelle Developmental Inventory, Second Edition, Normative Update (BDI-2) uses?**
    a. Communication
    b. Self-care
    c. Self-direction
    d. Personal responsibility

12. **True or false? The Individual with Disabilities Education Act (formerly known as P.L. 94-142) called for standardized assessments of adaptive behaviors along with IQ when evaluating student with disabilities for ID.**

Answers: (1) False. A score of a Plus-Minus indicates the behavior is occasionally performed; (2) False. Functional independence is defined more by competencies in adaptive behavior than cognition. (3) Personal Self-Sufficiency, Community Self-Sufficiency, Personal-Social Responsibility, Social Adjustment, and Personal Adjustment; (4) Communications, Daily Living Skills, Socialization Skills, and Motor Skills; (5) d; (6) c; (7) Conceptual, Social, and Practical Skills; (8) b; (9) b; (10) c; (11) b and d; (12) True.

Four

ADAPTIVE BEHAVIOR PROFILES IN INTELLECTUAL DISABILITY AND GENETIC DISORDERS

B y definition, there are adaptive delays observed in every individual with intellectual disability (ID). Yet, the levels of adaptive functioning certainly vary based on the level of cognitive impairment, and these profiles can also be specific to causes of ID (i.e., syndromes). Because the sheer number of etiologies for ID are far too enumerable to review in detail given the nature of this book, this chapter will focus on profiles of adaptive functioning observed in individuals with the most common forms of ID, whether the causes be pre-, peri-, or postnatal, or even unknown.

To recap from Chapter 1, the most recent *Diagnostic and Statistical Manual of Mental Disorders, Fifth Edition* (*DSM-5;* American Psychiatric Association, 2013) defines ID according to the following criteria:

- Deficits in intellectual functioning (confirmed by clinical assessment and standardized testing) in which standard scores fall approximately two or more standard deviations below the population mean
- Deficits in adaptive functioning in one or more areas of daily life, including conceptual, social, and practical areas, that pervade across multiple contexts (i.e., home, work, school, community) and require ongoing support
- Onset of deficits in intelligence and adaptive functioning occurring during the developmental period

The *DSM-5* defines adaptive skills in the following manner: Conceptual skills are defined as those that are more academically based (e.g., language, reading, writing, memory, numerical reasoning, and problem-solving, etc.). Social skills are defined as interpersonal, play, leisure, and conversational abilities, as well as friendships, empathy, caring, and social awareness. Practical skills are defined as self-management, personal care, recreational and vocational aptitude, money management, and task completion.

≡ *Rapid Reference 4.1*

Adaptive deficits in the *DSM-5* are defined by the following three areas:

- **Conceptual skills.** Those that are more academically based, including language, reading, writing, memory, numerical reasoning, and problem-solving
- **Social skills.** Interpersonal, play, leisure, and conversational abilities as well as friendship, empathy, caring, and social awareness
- **Practical skills.** Self-management, personal care, recreational and vocational aptitude, money management, and ability to complete tasks

In contrast to prior definitions in the *DSM-IV* and *DSM-IV-TR,* the *DSM-5* severity levels for ID (i.e., Mild, Moderate, Severe, and Profound) are keyed more to the degree of adaptive impairments across Conceptual, Social, and Practical domains rather than to level of IQ. This better aligns with evaluating levels of support needed for an individual to apply functional skills to daily life. However, as previously noted, there historically has been some resistance to transitioning away from classifying individuals based on level of IQ (Richards, Brady, & Taylor, 2015).

ELIGIBILITY VERSUS DIAGNOSIS

What is often unclear to patients and families, as well as to some professionals, is the differentiation between a diagnosis of ID (or any neurodevelopmental disorder for that matter) and eligibility for services under the same or similar label. To clarify, just because a community-based clinician or physician provides a diagnostic label to an individual, this does not automatically make that individual eligible for educational or state services.

DON'T FORGET

A diagnostic label from a community-based assessment does not necessarily translate into eligibility for local, state, or federal services.

Though the diagnostic criteria for ID are now relatively stable across systems and include cognitive and adaptive deficits and onset within the developmental period, eligibility criteria can vary across states and laws. For instance, many states will require that the cognitive and adaptive deficits negatively affect educational or academic performance in order to meet eligibility requirements. The Individual with Disabilities Education Act (IDEA, 2004) is a public law that ensures all children with disabilities receive a free and appropriate education that will prepare them for future education, employment, and independent living. IDEA was amended in 2015 under the Every Student Succeeds Act (ESSA). Under IDEA, a "child with a disability" must be deemed in need of special education and related services by a team that includes parents and qualified professionals (e.g., the child's teacher and a person trained in conducting diagnostic assessments) to be eligible for special education services. Autism spectrum disorder (ASD), ID (or developmental delays between the ages of 3 and 9, depending on the state or local agency), hearing and visual impairments, traumatic brain injury, learning disabilities, severe emotional disturbance, physical disabilities, multiple disabilities, and "other health impairment" all fall under IDEA's definition of "disability." Typically, evaluations are conducted by the school system's qualified professionals and then an individualized education program (IEP) is developed that includes the recommended educational placement along with treatment and intervention goals and objectives.

Eligibility for state and federal funding also comes with distinct criteria. The Social Security Administration (SSA) offers individuals with ID financial, medical, and rehabilitation benefits (National Research Council, 2002). These benefits can come through Social Security Income (SSI) or disability income (DI). DI is a benefit solely for adults. SSI is a benefit for adults, children, and their families and is based on financial and medical need. For SSI, the cause of ID is not of importance; rather, the individual needs to meet criteria and demonstrate need for support because the disability negatively affects the individual's level of functioning. For example, adults with ID would need to show that their disability results in severe restrictions on vocational skills.

The SSA's criteria for ID differs from the *DSM* and American Association on Intellectual and Developmental Disabilities (AAIDD) criteria in that IQ can be broken down, if needed. That is, nonverbal or verbal IQ can be used in place of an overall or Full Scale IQ score—and only one of these has to fall at least two standard deviations below the mean to meet eligibility requirements. Moreover, a SSA diagnosis of ID is not contingent on educational or clinical diagnoses (National Research Council, 2002).

DON'T FORGET

Nonverbal or verbal IQ scores as well as specific areas of adaptive deficit can be used in place of overall standard scores to determine eligibility for SSA services.

When providing community-based diagnoses, it is important to have discussions with parents and family members about eligibility for local, state, and federal resources. This is especially important in the developing years (i.e., prior to young adulthood), when documenting early development of the disorder is necessary for funding. Oftentimes, families are denied available services for adults with disabilities because they applied for eligibility too late.

ADAPTIVE BEHAVIOR PROFILES BY LEVEL OF COGNITION IN ID

The relationship between adaptive behavior and IQ can vary depending on the level of functioning of the individual. For instance, in individuals with extremely low levels of cognition, adaptive behavior tends to fall on par with cognitive ability or mental age (Meyers, Nihira, & Zetlin, 1979). That is, if cognition is substantially impaired, so are adaptive skills—but they tend to be equally impaired. Several factors could account for this high correlation, the most likely being limitations in the floor levels of assessment measures for IQ and adaptive behavior. However, this could also be due to an overlap in behaviors being assessed at these low levels. For instance, conceptual skills at very low mental age levels are often part of a repertoire of skills (e.g., number of words expressed or understood), as are adaptive skills at similar developmental levels.

Correlations between IQ and adaptive behavior are much more variable for individuals with higher cognitive levels, such as those with borderline or mild to moderate ID (Fernell & Ek, 2010; National Research Council, 2002). Mild ID can be challenging to accurately diagnose when overall levels of either IQ or adaptive functioning fall just above cut-off requirements, leaving the diagnosis to rely heavily on clinical judgment. For instance, individuals with borderline ID (i.e., IQ falling between 71 and 85) could certainly have cognitive deficits in some skill areas, but if their overall IQ is above 70, they might not meet criteria for diagnosis even if adaptive delays are also present. Nevertheless, they could still benefit from specialized services or intervention. This phenomenon has been exemplified in a Swedish study examining profiles of students in a specialized school for mild ID where only about half of the students met diagnostic criteria after testing (Fernell & Ek, 2010). Yet, many of the individuals who failed to meet criteria still benefited from the educational placement. This makes it extremely important for clinicians who are conducting evaluations for eligibility to use comprehensive measures (i.e., rather than brief IQ tests, for example) in order to effectively advocate for the needs of these individuals.

CAUTION

Though adaptive behavior levels can be on par with mental age in individuals with lower levels of cognition, there is much more variability in individuals with mild, moderate, or borderline ID.

It is also quite challenging to accurately ascertain all individuals with mild ID. Many individuals may be functioning just well enough to blend into society and not be identified as having a disability. Their vulnerabilities might be overlooked because they are considered less severe. Also of concern, individuals with milder ID who come from disadvantaged communities where access to and resources for care are more limited can also fail to obtain the appropriate diagnosis and subsequent care. Increased awareness about milder forms of ID is needed so that these individuals can be accurately identified and appropriately treated.

DON'T FORGET

The true prevalence of mild ID could be underestimated given that many individuals with milder cognitive and adaptive delays may not be flagged for evaluations to determine eligibility for services despite their need for them.

COMORBIDITIES WITH ID

The prevalence of multiple disabilities on cognition also affects an individual's level of adaptive behavior skills and, subsequently, the possible increased needs for service development and resource allocation. Common comorbidities with ID include physical, neurological, sensory, and psychiatric disabilities (Harries, Guscia, Nettelbeck, & Kirby, 2009). In a study examining the Australian Institute of Health and Welfare report (2007), 52% of individuals with ID who were receiving state government–funded services also reported the presence of an additional disability (Australian Institute of Health and Welfare, 2007). For those with funded accommodation support services, 73% of them reported the presence of an additional disability. Estimates of comorbid disabilities with ID from other sources range from 22% (Murphy, Yeargin-Allsopp, Decoufle, & Drews, 1995) to 58% (van Isterdael, Stilma, Bezemer, & Tijmes, 2006).

Children with IQ levels between 55 and 70 tend to have comorbid challenges with abstract thinking, problem-solving, attention, and working memory, but profiles of cognitive strengths and weaknesses can vary (Soenen, Van Berckelaer-Onnes, & Scholte, 2009). The mental age of a person with this level of ID tends to fall to about 6 to 11 years. Thus, even with adaptive delays in the required two or more areas compared to chronological age, these individuals can possess a large repertoire of adaptive skills that should be fostered. Learning disabilities and attention deficit/hyperactivity disorder (ADHD) can also be comorbid with ID, oftentimes in children with milder forms of ID. These relationships are covered in more detail in Chapter 6.

Estimates of comorbid psychopathology found in individuals with ID are as much as four times as in the general population (Rush, Bowman, Eidman, Toole, & Mortenson, 2004). Yet, psychopathology is a greater risk to those with milder ID, whereas the more severely cognitively impaired individuals (especially with medical complications such as epilepsy) tend to be spared (Cowley et al., 2004). Depression is one of the most common comorbid psychiatric conditions in individuals with mild to borderline IQ, with the cognitive error of "under-estimation of the ability to cope" being most predictive of depressive symptoms (Weeland, Nijhof, Otten, Vermaes, & Buitelaar, 2017). Deficits in intellectual and adaptive behavior skills have been found to increase the risk of psychopathological disorders, including depression (Harries et al., 2009; Tremblay, Richer, Lachance, & Côté, 2010). Additional information on adult outcomes of individuals with ID with comorbid psychopathology is provided in Chapter 7. Given the increased risk, it is extremely important to determine these diagnostic differentials as early as possible in development so as to ensure that individuals receive appropriate treatment and intervention for their respective needs.

CAUTION

Individuals with mild to borderline ID are at heightened risk for psychopathology, especially depression.

INCIDENCE AND PREVALENCE OF ID

Determining incidence and prevalence rates for ID is challenging given how much cultural, geographic, and socioeconomic (SES) factors have an impact on these rates (e.g., higher rates of ID are often found in lower SES areas). Additionally, changes in diagnostic criteria have played a significant role in varying rates. Prevalence estimates have historically ranged from < 1% to 3%, but a meta-analysis conducted between 1980 and 2009 concluded that the best estimate of ID worldwide is 1% (Maulik, Mascarenhas, Mathers, Dua, & Saxena, 2011). Primary and secondary prevention methods, such as immunizations and peri- and postnatal screenings, have also contributed to a decrease in prevalence of ID over time, but primarily in the Western world (Leonard & Wen, 2002).

DON'T FORGET

The worldwide prevalence of ID is estimated to be about 1% of the population.

The incidence rate for ID is assumed to be higher than the prevalence given high infant mortality rates (Grossman, 1983). However, modern medical and health care advances have resulted in increased survival rates of infants at risk for ID (e.g., extremely premature infants), which in turn can increase prevalence rates (Leonard & Wen, 2002; McKenzie, Milton, Smith, & Ouellette-Kuntz, 2016). Males have been found to have a 1.5-fold increase in prevalence for ID than females, but this difference appears in children more than adults (Leonard & Wen, 2002).

Mild ID makes up the vast majority of individuals with ID, with about 85% affected. Moderate ID rates are about 10%, severe ID about 4%, and profound ID about 2% (King, Toth, Hodapp, & Dykens, 2009). However, many factors can contribute to fluctuations in prevalence, especially in mild ID, due to the Flynn effect (the population's increase in IQ over time, requiring the re-norming of instruments to calibrate), changes in diagnostic criteria for ID, and also common comorbid disorders, and diagnostic substitution (McKenzie et al., 2016). Diagnostic substitution has especially affected prevalence rates of autism in which the ASD diagnosis is now more commonly the primary educational or clinical label, with ID being secondary for those individuals with both disorders (McKenzie et al., 2016). These rates, however, vary state by state.

More attention needs to be given to disparities observed in ID. Minorities, especially African American individuals, tend to score lower on traditional standardized intelligence tests than Caucasian individuals (Reschly, Grimes, & Ross-Reynolds, 1981; Taylor & Partenio, 1983), and this would certainly also apply to individuals with ID. Research has found this bias to be reduced when controlling for SES (Valencia & Suzuki, 2001), but the fact that being from a disadvantaged community negatively affects cognition merits much more concern and attention than is currently given.

CAUTION

Be cognizant of the impact of race, geographical location, and socioeconomic status on the prevalence of ID and disparities in cognitive levels.

ETIOLOGIES OF ID

For about 30% to 75% of ID cases, there is no known etiology (Leonard & Wen, 2002). Of the known biological causes for ID, the vast majority occur prenatally (Grossman, 1983). These include infectious disease in the mother, congenital (rarer) or acquired; genetic disorders in the fetus; prematurity and low birthweight (more correlational rather than causal); and other biomedical causes such as toxins, malnutrition, traumatic birth, and so on. Postnatal factors contributing to ID during infancy or early childhood include infectious diseases, trauma, toxins, nutritional disorders, and in some cases, accidents. It is important to note, however, that some cases of ID that are actually prenatal in origin might not present with symptoms until later in life. Moreover, some biological causes may not be detected until after educational or psychological testing identifies delays in development that result in, for example, genetic or medical testing. The combination of biological vulnerabilities with environmental factors can also result in ID, when in the absence of an environmental trigger, the individual might not otherwise be affected.

⇒ Rapid Reference 4.2

Known Causes of ID

- Infectious disease in the mother (congenital or acquired)
- Infectious disease in the child
- Genetic disorders
- Low birthweight
- Biomedical causes (e.g., toxins, malnutrition, traumatic birth)
- Nutritional disorders (e.g., PKU)
- Accidents

Genetic Causes of ID

Many of the various genetic syndromes are associated with comorbid intellectual disability and, as such, impairments in adaptive behavior (though adaptive deficits can still be present in those without ID). Research often characterizes syndromes by various profiles—of cognitive strengths and weaknesses, neuropsychological, as well as physical and medical features. Adaptive behavior is another area that can characterize different genetic disorders and, taken collectively, these profiles are often referred to as a *behavioral phenotype*. A behavioral phenotype is the characteristic patterns of behavior that describe a specific disorder (Flint & Yule, 1994). As described by Dykens (1995), having a particular phenotype helps predict that a person affected by a specific syndrome would show a constellation of certain features and behaviors. Hodapp (1997) and Dykens and Hodapp (2001) summarized the various possible patterns:

- **No-specificity.** Syndromes that do not have individualized cognitive and adaptive profiles and, as such, the cognitive deficits are the common outcome; in this way, within-syndrome differences are higher than across-syndrome differences
- **Total specificity.** Syndromes that have unique cognitive and adaptive outcomes and, therefore, differences between syndromes are specific
- **Partial specificity.** Overlaps in profiles between some syndromes but not others

Understanding these behavioral phenotypes is relevant for treatment and intervention as well as helpful for understanding what behaviors can be expected. However, the research on adaptive behavior profiles in various genetic syndromes has not been straightforward. First, between 4,000 and 6,000 syndromes have been identified, with about 1,000 of these associated with ID (Abbeduto & McDuffie, 2010). There is also marked within-profile variability (Dykens, 1999).

The syndromes with the most research on adaptive profiles are Down syndrome, Williams syndrome, fragile X syndrome, and Prader-Willi syndrome—each of which is discussed in detail in this chapter. However, it is important to recognize that knowledge in this area is continuing to grow. New studies continue to emerge and collaborations across research sites have enabled increased sample sizes as well as better statistical techniques for analyzing longitudinal data. As such, more specific information is being gathered and profiles are sometimes changing.

DON'T FORGET

Our knowledge of genetic disorders and behavioral profiles continues to grow as more research is being conducted.

Down Syndrome

Down syndrome, also known as Trisomy 21, is the most prevalent chromosomal cause of ID. It was first described in 1866 by H. Langdon Down, a physician working in a psychiatric institution in England. Down syndrome is caused by the presence of all or part of an extra copy of chromosome 21. Most occurrences of Down syndrome are not familial and thus, parents have a relatively low chance of a second child being born with the syndrome. The risk of having a child with Down syndrome, however, increases as a woman gets older. Down syndrome was the first developmental disorder to become publicly identified and recognized (Dykens, Hodapp, & Finucane, 2000).

The prevalence of Down syndrome is about 1 in 700 to 1,000 births, affecting males and females of all ethnic and socioeconomic backgrounds (Dykens et al., 2000). Characteristic features include a small head with a flat-looking face, small ears and mouth, protruding tongue, broad neck, and an upward slant to the eyes, with epicanthal folds at the inner corners. Significant motor deficits are also found (Vicari, 2006). In individuals with Down syndrome, motor deficits are more pronounced than would be predicted given their cognitive disability (Piek, Dawson, Smith, & Gasson, 2008; Volman, Visser, & Lensvelt-Mulders, 2007) and are marked by hypotonia and poor control of muscle stiffness (Fidler, Most, & Philofsky, 2009; Lauteslager, Vermeer, Helders, & Mazer, 1998).

Individuals with Down syndrome have distinctive cognitive, linguistic, and behavioral profiles. Intelligence is variable, though most individuals function within the moderate range of ID, with mean IQ scores in the 50s (Connolly, 1978; Gibson, 1978). In addition, language skills tend to be delayed, particularly expressive language, syntax, and verbal (Davis, 2008; Grieco, Pulsifer, Seligsohn, Skotko, & Schwartz, 2015; Silverman, 2007).

Adaptive behavior in individuals with Down syndrome is marked by varied trajectories over time. Children with Down syndrome tend to show greatest strengths in adaptive socialization skills and greatest weaknesses in communication skills (Coe et al., 1999; Dykens, Hodapp, & Evans, 2006; Fidler, Hepburn, & Rogers, 2006; Griffith, Hastings, Nash, & Hill, 2010; Van Duijn, Dijkxhoorn, Scholte, & Van Berckelaer-Onnes, 2010). Despite documented weaknesses, adaptive behavior tends to be better than expected given cognitive and academic abilities (Hodapp, 2006; Rondal, Perera, & Nadel, 1999). Loveland and Kelley (1991) hypothesized that adaptive behavior in individuals with Down syndrome shows a similar trajectory to those with typical development, though development occurs at a slower pace.

Longitudinally, adaptive behavior profiles also vary with the age of the child, and different profiles may emerge dependent on the degree of ID (Buckley, Broadley, MacDonald, & Laws, 1995; Chapman & Hesketh, 2001; Dykens et al., 2006; Grieco et al., 2015; Jobling, 1998; Patterson, Rapsey, & Glue, 2013; Silverman, 2007; Tsao & Kindelberger, 2009; Vicari, 2006). One study examined developmental outcomes in children between 2 and 10 years of age and, similar to past work, socialization skills were found to be a relative strength (Marchal et al., 2016). Yet, by contrast, daily living skills were found to be the greatest weakness. Differences in profiles were found when groups were split between those with below-average skills and those with above-average skills. In the below-average group, as per past studies, socialization skills were the relative strength and communication skills were the relative weakness. In the above-average group, however, socialization remained the overall strength but daily living skills were a strong weakness, being markedly weaker than the other domains. In examination of the data using multiple linear regression, it was found that more years in mainstream education related to better communication and socialization skills whereas daily living skills were predicted only by overall cognitive abilities. This argues that mainstream education specifically promotes communication and socialization skills but not daily living skills. Overall, adaptive skills in Down syndrome appear to increase with age and, compared to individuals with other IDs, individuals with Down syndrome have fewer maladaptive behavior deficits (Chapman & Hesketh, 2001; Dykens & Kasari, 1997; Myers & Pueschel, 1991).

It should be emphasized that comorbid medical and psychiatric conditions that co-occur with Down syndrome can significantly affect outcome. These include, most specifically, depression, cardiac issues, and dementia. Chapter 7 provides more details on these co-occuring conditions and the impact into adulthood. However, comorbidities in Down syndrome can certainly negatively affect level of functioning in children as well. In a retrospective study on individuals with Down syndrome who regressed in functioning, loss of independent daily living skills, language, and academic functioning was found in a subsample of individuals who experienced some form of emotional distress—and regression was not associated with level of cognitive disability (Mircher et al., 2017). This calls into question the need for assessing individuals with Down syndrome for comorbidities so that appropriate monitoring, diagnosis, and intervention can take place.

Fragile X Syndrome

Fragile X syndrome was first identified in the 1970s and is the most common known *inherited* cause of ID. It is caused by a mutation in the fragile X mental retardation 1 gene (FMR1). As is similar to many genetic discoveries, the story of how the FMR1 gene was discovered is an interesting one. In 1943, Martin and Bell described a large family in which multiple males were affected by intellectual disability. No females in the large pedigree were affected. All the males had a phenotypic pattern of large, protruding ears, a long and narrow face, and enlarged testicles, known as macroorchidism. The disorder was thus initially known as Martin-Bell syndrome, after those who discovered it. In 1969, Herbert Lubs described the presence of an abnormal "marker X" chromosome in a family of males. In 1977, that "marker X" was shown by Grant Sutherland as having a thread-like appearance on the X chromosome, which then become known as the "fragile X."

In 1991, the gene responsible for fragile X syndrome, FMR1, was discovered (Verkerk et al., 1991). The gene in its normal state produces a protein thought to play a key role in pre- and postnatal brain development. The FMR1 gene contains a repetitive sequence of the trinucleotide CGG. In individuals without fragile X syndrome, that sequence is repeated between 6 and 50 times. A carrier for fragile X syndrome would have 50 to 200 repeats and an individual with fragile X syndrome has more than 200 repeats. Premutation carriers do not show any phenotypic characteristics of fragile X syndrome; however, they can pass the mutation on to their children (Mazzocco & Holden, 1996; Reiss, Freund, Abrams, Boehm, & Kazazian, 1993). Individuals with the full mutation do not make the protein, and this results in the symptoms of fragile X syndrome. The prevalence of fragile X syndrome is approximately 1 in 4,000 males and 1 in 2,000 females (Turner, Webb, Wake, & Robinson, 1996), secondary to the fact that it is an X-linked disorder (Warren, Brady, Fleming, & Hahn, 2017). It is found in all racial and ethnic groups.

Behaviorally, individuals with fragile X syndrome tend to have cognitive and language difficulties, social anxiety, avoidance of eye contact, and hand stereotypies (Wadell, Hagerman, & Hessl, 2013). In addition, there appears to be a high overlap with autism, with 30% to 45% of individuals with fragile X syndrome also meeting criteria for ASD (Bailey et al., 1998; Denmark, Feldman, & Holden, 2003; Feinstein & Reiss, 1998; Hagerman & Jackson, 1985; Kaufmann et al., 2004; Philofsky, Hepburn, Hayes, Hagerman, & Rogers, 2004; Warren et al., 2017). The combination of ID, comorbid ASD, and increased rates of psychopathology may lead to difficulties in adaptive behavior.

Although there is certainly some behavioral overlap between individuals with ASD and those with fragile X syndrome, there is controversy about whether the "autism" is the same in those with and without fragile X syndrome. For example, males with fragile X syndrome have been shown to perform similar to IQ-matched controls on tasks of facial and emotional expressions (Simon & Finucane, 1996; Turk & Cornish, 1998), and females with fragile X syndrome have performed similarly to IQ-matched controls on theory of mind tasks (i.e., perspective taking and emotional perception in others), which are the very skill areas that are commonly observed as weaknesses in individuals with ASD. Other studies examined gaze avoidance in children with fragile X syndrome and children with ASD (Cohen, Vietze, Sudhalter, Jenkins, & Brown, 1989). Findings revealed that children with fragile X syndrome were sensitive to parental gaze and were avoidant of direct eye contact, whereas children with ASD were not sensitive to the gaze of others and did not appear to avoid it. It has thus been suggested that social anxiety leads to the reduction in eye gaze in individuals with fragile X syndrome, whereas a more primary social deficit leads to the eye-gaze reductions seen in individuals with ASD.

Though there are conflicting findings regarding exact profiles of adaptive behavior in individuals with fragile X syndrome, generally, when compared to individuals with other developmental disabilities matched for mental age, socialization and communication skills tend to be a weakness (Carpentieri & Morgan, 1996; Freund, Peebles, Aylward, & Reiss, 1995; Vig & Jedrysek, 1995). Differential findings may be influenced by the ages of the participants, sex, number of assessment time points, and types of scores used—that is, standard scores, raw scores, or age-equivalent scores. Most studies have used either standard scores that represent how discrepant performance is from the average performance in the normative sample or age-equivalent scores that represent the average chronological age of the given raw score. In individuals with ID, age-equivalent scores may increase over time denoting progress, whereas standard scores can be observed to decline over time despite a true increase in skills (Kover, Pierpont, Kim, Brown, & Abbeduto, 2013; Mervis & Klein-Tasman, 2004). Analyzing age-equivalent scores, however, can have methodological issues, including having an ordinal scale of measurement, which limits the types of appropriate analysis methods available for use (Maloney & Larrivee, 2007).

Raw scores can help determine if there is a true decline in adaptive behavior. For example, Fisch, Simensen, and Schroer (2002) and Fisch and colleagues (2012) reported declines in adaptive behavior based on two time-point analyses of males with fragile X between the ages of 2 and 24 years. The first was completed with 18 males with fragile X (Fisch et al., 2002) and the second included 28 males with fragile X (Fisch et al., 2012). In a contrasting study, Hatton and colleagues (2003) used a longitudinal analysis with an average of 4.4 assessment points of 60 males and 10 females with fragile X from 12 months through 12 years. They reported increases in adaptive behavior overall and across domains for males and females, with females showing higher trajectories (Hatton et al., 2003). Klaiman and colleagues (2014) also observed higher adaptive behavior trajectories for females ($n = 89$) than for males ($n = 186$) between 2 and 18 years of age, but both groups showed declines over time.

Overall, there is evidence that many children with fragile X syndrome show gains in their communication, daily living, and socialization skills during early and middle childhood (Dykens, Hodapp, Ort, & Leckman, 1993; Dykens et al., 1996; Fisch et al., 1999; Hahn, Brady, Warren, & Fleming, 2015; Hatton et al., 2003). However, studies are finding that many individuals with fragile X begin experiencing declines in their adaptive skills starting in middle childhood and extending into adolescence (Fisch et al., 2012; Freund, Peebles, Aylward, & Reiss, 1995; Hahn et al., 2015; Klaiman et al., 2014). In the study by Hahn and colleagues (2015), whereas 44% of children with fragile X syndrome showed improvements in adaptive behavior from toddlerhood through middle childhood, the remaining 56% showed declines in adaptive behavior at or before 10 years of age (in their study, the average age for the start of decline was 7 years of age). This study used raw scores suggesting that this decline was truly a regression in functioning, indicating that children were no longer performing the skills that they were performing approximately 18 months earlier. These studies suggest that childhood may be a pivotal time period for adaptive behavior in children with fragile X syndrome (Hahn et al., 2015).

Williams Syndrome

Williams syndrome was first identified in the 1960s by two independent teams of physicians—Williams, Barrett-Boyes, and Lowe (1961) and Beuren, Apitz, and Harmjanz (1962). As such, it is sometimes referred to as Williams-Beuren syndrome. Williams syndrome is a result of a microdeletion on the long arm of chromosome 7, at 7q11.23 (Bellugi, Lichtenberger, Mills, Galaburda, & Korenberg, 1999; Ewart et al., 1993). The deletion involves up to 28 genes, including the gene for elastin, a connective tissue protein that provides strength and elasticity to the skin, blood vessels, and walls of organs and arteries. Prominent features include mild to moderate ID, distinctive facial features, and a cardiac anomaly called *supravalvular aortic stenosis,* which is a narrowing of the arteries that reduces blood flow. In addition, individuals have also been found to have connective tissue abnormalities and growth deficiency (Morris,

2006). Behavioral features have been found to include difficulties with attention, increased prevalence of anxiety and other phobias, visual-spatial deficits, hypersociability, and mild to moderate adaptive behavior deficits. Children with Williams syndrome also have difficulties with eating and sleeping (Annaz, Hill, Ashworth, Holley, & Karmiloff-Smith, 2011; Davies, Udwin, & Howlin, 1998). Axelsson, Hill, Sadeh, and Dimitrou (2013) found that infants and toddlers with Williams syndrome had significantly reduced and disrupted sleep, which likely is a contributing cause to the increased emotionality and attention problems that are observed. Failure to thrive and other feeding difficulties, as well as reflux and constipation, have also been reported in Williams syndrome (Morris, 2010).

The prevalence of Williams syndrome occurs between 1 in 7,500 to 1 in 20,000 live births, with equal rates in males in females and in all races and cultures. The deletion can be transmitted through the mother or the father but the risk of recurrence in subsequent children is low because Williams syndrome occurs sporadically in the general population. There is, however, about a 50% chance that a male or female with Williams syndrome could transmit the disorder to his or her offspring.

Williams syndrome is associated with distinctive profiles of cognitive functioning. Approximately 75% of young children have cognitive and adaptive scores consistent with developmental delay (Mervis & Klein-Tasman, 2000), with one study showing an average overall IQ score to be 64.56 (Mervis & John, 2010). Relative strengths are typically found in verbal short-term memory, nonverbal reasoning skills, and receptive vocabulary (Mervis & John, 2010), whereas weaknesses are found in spatial skills, psychomotor skills, and processing speed (Mervis & Klein-Tasman, 2000). Using the Bayley Scales of Infant Development (Bayley, 1969), Mervis and Bertrand (1997) found that infants and toddlers with Williams syndrome showed better verbal than nonverbal abilities and extreme difficulties on tasks that assessed visuospatial skills.

Adaptive behavior profiles have also been found. Using the Vineland Adaptive Behavior Scales (Sparrow, Balla, & Cicchetti, 1984), children with Williams syndrome showed overall deficits in adaptive behavior (Greer, Brown, Pai, Choudry, & Klein, 1997). In this study, 40% of children and adolescents with Williams syndrome fell within the Moderately Deficient range on the Vineland (i.e., scores between 40 and 50), 33% scored within the Mildly Deficient range (i.e., scores between 55 and 70), and 27% scored in the Moderately Low range (i.e., scores between 70 and 85). Relative strengths have been found in adaptive socialization and communication skills as compared with daily living and motor skills (Fisch et al., 2012; Greer et al., 1997; Mervis, Klein-Tasman, & Mastin, 2001; Mervis & Pitts, 2015). However, within Vineland Adaptive Behavior domains, no one area has been found to be a significant strength or weakness (Brawn & Porter, 2014).

In a study by Hahn and colleagues (2015), children with Williams syndrome under the age of 5 years showed stronger adaptive communication than daily living skills (as measured by the Vineland), and socialization skills were found to be better developed than daily living and motor skills (Hahn et al., 2015). In a group of infants and toddlers, assessed with the Adaptive Behavior Assessment System, Second Edition (ABAS-2; Harrison & Oakland, 2003), overall adaptive behavior scores fell within the Mildly Delayed range (mean = 64.0; standard deviation = 10.6), with no specific area representing a strength or weakness.

Although IQ has been found to remain stable with age in Williams syndrome, adaptive behavior outcome has been more variable. Several studies have shown adaptive behavior to significantly decline with age (Davies et al., 1998; Fisher, Lense, & Dykens, 2016; Greer et al., 1997; Mervis et al., 2001). Some studies have found that chronological age is associated with lower communication skills (Dimitropoulos, Ho, Klaiman, Koenig, & Schultz, 2009), lower community living (Mervis & John, 2010), and lower social interaction skills (Fu, Lincoln, Bellugi, & Searcy, 2015). However, other studies have demonstrated a plateau in skills with age (Di Nuovo & Buono, 2011; Elison, Stinton, & Howlin, 2010; Fu et al., 2015), and even others have shown improvements in adaptive socialization and daily living skills but a plateau in communication skills (Howlin, Elison, Udwin, & Stinton, 2010). Variability in results may be due to methodological differences, with some studies using cross-sectional rather than longitudinal designs and others having large age spreads. A recent study addressed these limitations and found that contrary to the stability of cognitive functioning, adaptive behavior in adolescents through adulthood decreased significantly across all domains except Socialization, which showed a decreasing trend (Fisher et al., 2016).

Prader-Willi Syndrome

Prader-Willi syndrome (PWS) is a genetic disorder first identified in the mid-1950s by Prader, Labhart, and Willi (1956). They identified individuals who tended to be obese, have short stature, hypotonia, and failure to thrive during infancy. The syndrome is caused by either a paternal deletion or maternal uniparental disomy on the long arm of chromosome 15 (15q11–q13). Seventy percent of the time, the deletion is due to the absence of typically active, paternally inherited genes on the long arm of chromosome 15 (Type 1), but the missing paternal genes can also be due to two copies of chromosome 15 from the mother (Mascari et al., 1992; Nicholls, Knoll, Butler, Karam, & Lalande, 1989;

Robinson et al., 1991). In a small percentage of cases, PWS can be the result of a translocation or a microdeletion within the 15q11–q13 area—the part that controls the imprinting process (Buiting et al., 1995; Saitoh et al., 1997). The prevalence of PWS ranges from 1 in 10,000 to 1 in 15,000.

Individuals with PWS typically have mild to moderate ID as well as behavioral profiles consisting of compulsive behavior, irritability, aggression, and hyperphagia. Hyperphagia is a failure to recognize being full and, consequently, a constant seeking out of food. This food seeking can lead to life-threatening obesity (Dykens, Roof, & Hunt-Hawkins, 2017). Individuals with PWS also tend to have perseverative speech, temper tantrums, and social withdrawal (Dykens, Hodapp, Walsh, & Nash, 1992; Dykens & Kasari, 1997). The severity and prevalence of the behavioral phenotype varies across genetic subtypes, with those with Type I deletions showing lower cognitive behavior skills, and those with maternal uniparental disomy having better developed verbal than spatial skills and are more apt to have ASD, autistic features, and psychosis (Boer et al., 2002; Dykens, Lee, & Roof, 2011; Dykens & Roof, 2008; Key, Jones, & Dykens, 2013; Whittington et al., 2004).

In a study by Di Nuovo and Buono (2011), adaptive behavioral profiles were compared across individuals with Down syndrome, Williams syndrome, Angelman syndrome, PWS, and fragile X syndrome. Individuals with PWS were found to have the highest adaptive behavior profiles, with a specific weakness in motor abilities. Adaptive communication skills, as measured by the Vineland Adaptive Behavior Scales, were significantly correlated with IQ.

Other Genetic Syndromes

Smith-Magenis syndrome (SMS) is characterized primarily by a 3.7 megabyte interstitial deletion of 17p11.2. The prevalence is estimated at 1 in 25,000 (Colley, Leversha, Voullaire, & Rogers, 1990; Greenberg et al., 1991). Phenotypically, individuals have craniofacial anomalies including brachycephaly, broad face, midface hypoplasia, prognathism, and an everted upper lip. They also have short hands, short stature, and scoliosis. Vision and hearing loss are also prominent, and 20% of individuals will have a seizure disorder. Behaviorally, individuals with SMS have significant difficulties including hyperactivity, distractibility, temper tantrums, self-injurious and aggressive behaviors such as biting, headbanging, skin picking, and slapping. Sleep disturbances are also common. A behavior unique to SMS is referred to as self-hugging or the "spasmodic upper body squeeze," which is assumed to be an expression of happiness (Dykens et al., 2000)

In a study by Madduri and colleagues (2006), using the Vineland Adaptive Behavior Scales, children with SMS were found to function in the Low range of adaptive behavior, with a relative weakness in daily living skills. In children under 6 years of age, a significant weakness was also found in adaptive motor skills. Size of deletion was also related to level of intellectual and adaptive functioning, with individuals with greater deletion sizes being significantly more likely to have lower cognitive and adaptive behavior skills (Madduri et al., 2006).

Angelman syndrome is a rare neurogenetic disorder with a prevalence of about 1 in 15,000 live births (Clayton-Smith & Pembrey, 1992). It is a result of several genetic mechanisms. The most common is a deletion on chromosome 15 at the 15q12 region of the maternal chromosome. Paternal uniparental disomy is the result of having two copies from the paternal side of chromosome 15. Because the maternal chromosome is absent, this results in Angelman syndrome. Angelman syndrome can also arrive as a result of an imprinting defect whereby a small stretch on the q12 region of chromosome 15 is turned off. Angelman syndrome is associated with very low verbal abilities (Clayton-Smith & Pembrey, 1992). Individuals with Angelman syndrome also tend to have hyperactivity, stereotyped and repetitive behaviors (including what have been described as puppet-like movements), frequent and inappropriate laughing, and sleep difficulties (Smith, 2001; Summers & Feldman, 1999). In comparison with Williams syndrome, PWS, fragile X syndrome, and Down syndrome, individuals with Angelman syndrome have shown the lowest overall adaptive behavior skills, with greatest relative weaknesses found in the socialization and motor domains (Dykens et al., 2000).

Duplication of chromosome 15q11.2–q13.1, otherwise known as Dup15q syndrome, is one of the most common chromosomal abnormalities associated with ASD and ID. The region that is duplicated includes the imprinted Prader-Willi–Angelman syndrome critical region as well as other genes that are responsible for several critical brain functions (Finucane et al., 1993). Individuals with Dup15q tend to exhibit mild to profound ID, motor delays secondary to hypotonia, mild to profound language impairment, and impairments in social communication. Epilepsy often develops early in infancy with rates ranging between 16% and 63% depending on the type of duplication. With regard to adaptive behavior profiles, individuals with Dup15q, show relatively impaired adaptive behavior skills across all domains. Compared with individuals with ASD, scores on the Daily Living Skills and Motor domains were significantly lower. Overall, individuals with Dup15q have a relatively flat profile of adaptive behavior skills more similar to children with idiopathic ID (Miny et al., 1986).

Idiopathic and Biomedical Causes of ID

In addition to identifiable genetic mutations that account for ID, there are cases for which the cause of ID is unknown or idiopathic or for which there is an associated biomedical but nongenetic cause. The most common of these are prenatal alcohol exposure, prematurity, and low birth weight.

Fetal Alcohol Spectrum Disorder

In the Western world, prenatal alcohol exposure tends to be the leading biomedical cause of ID, more prevalent than Down syndrome or cerebral palsy (CP) (Fagerlund et al., 2012). One study compared adaptive profiles of children and adolescents with fetal alcohol spectrum disorders (FASDs) to children with specific learning disabilities (SLDs) matched on IQ and found that the children with FASDs exhibited significantly poorer adaptive skills in all domains despite the same level of cognitive impairment (Fagerlund et al., 2012). In addition, there was a decline in adaptive socialization skills with age in the FASD sample in contrast to an increase in functional social skills in the SLD sample. A study by Crocker, Vaurio, Riley, and Mattson (2009) similarly found adaptive socialization skills to be lower in older versus younger children with prenatal exposure to alcohol. There also appears to be a continuum in that children who have the full syndrome have more significant adaptive delays than those children with prenatal exposure but not FASD, with fine-motor delays being prominent in children under the age of 5 (Kalberg et al., 2006).

As outlined in Chapter 6, adaptive deficits are commonly found in individuals with ADHD. Prenatal alcohol exposure also significantly increases risk for ADHD. Adaptive deficits are observed in all adaptive areas within each of these clinical samples, but children who have prenatal exposure and ADHD have the most impairments in adaptive communication skills (Ware et al., 2014).

Extreme Prematurity and Low Birth Weight

Children born preterm are at risk for a host of neurodevelopmental difficulties, with the greater degree of prematurity increasing risk for various developmental delays. Extreme prematurity, which is when an infant is born before 27 weeks' gestation, happens in about 1.42% of all births registered in the United States (Glass et al., 2015). Adaptive deficits in socialization have been found in extremely premature children when compared to those born at term (Hack et al., 2005). However, a great deal of stressors—developmental, medical, and environmental—may have a deleterious effect on brain development and the social-emotional experiences of children born extremely premature. For instance, medical complications, such as periventricular hemorrhagic infarctions and CP, both of which can also be associated with ID, could affect adaptive functioning. Studies, therefore, need to take into consideration myriad complications that come with extreme prematurity in order to parse out the true predictors of poor outcome.

Over the past couple of decades, researchers and clinicians have started following infants born extremely preterm longitudinally, trying to better understand the impact of prematurity on a host of factors, including adaptive behavior. In an early study by Rosenbaum, Saigal, Szatmari, and Hoult (1995) using the Vineland Adaptive Behavior Scale, the communication subscale correlated as highly or higher than overall adaptive behavior scores in comparison to the variety of other standardized tests (i.e., cognitive, neuropsychological, academic achievement) that were conducted. A longitudinal study examining preterm children with very low birth weight until age 5 found that maternal education, medical complications at birth, early motor assessments, and early cognitive assessments explained 30% of the variance for adaptive behavior deficits (Howe, Sheu, Hsu, Wang, & Wang, 2016). Motor impairments and low cognition accounted for adaptive deficits in preterm children with very low birth weight and CP, and even in preterm children without CP, the presence of abnormal motor behaviors including fidgety movements has been found to associate with poor adaptive functioning (Fjørtoft et al., 2015).

There is a great deal to learn from studies of preterm infants with extremely low birth weight given that many are followed longitudinally from birth. It is important to be aware of the developmental and medical complications that are commonly associated with prematurity so as to be monitoring for each from early on in development.

SUMMARY

Collectively, the literature on adaptive deficits in ID and genetic disorders highlight the need for comprehensive, multidisciplinary evaluations when assessing these individuals. Clinicians need to be aware of the developmental, medical, psychosocial, and behavioral manifestations that accompany individuals with ID and genetic disorders throughout their lifetime. A person's outcome is not always dictated by his or her disability but rather by the level of independence and functional skills. Using appropriate measures to assess adaptive behavior early on and then following these individuals longitudinally can help to ensure the acquisition of functional, practical skills—especially those that are found to be weaker based on associations with comorbid conditions.

🐟 TEST YOURSELF 🐟

1. **List three disorders, impairments, or disabilities that fall under IDEA's definition of "disability."**

2. **What is the most common comorbid psychiatric condition with ID?**
   a. Anxiety
   b. Depression
   c. PTSD
   d. Borderline personality disorder

3. **What is the estimated prevalence of ID in the worldwide population?**
   a. 5%
   b. 2%
   c. 1%
   d. 9%

4. **Which of the following are *all* prenatal causes of ID?**
   a. Infectious disease in the mother; genetic disorders the in fetus; prematurity; infectious diseases in fetus
   b. Prematurity; infectious disease in the mother; accidents; low birth weight
   c. Genetic disorders the in fetus; infectious disease in the mother; prematurity; low birth weight
   d. Infectious disease in the mother; genetic disorders in the fetus; trauma post-birth; low birth weight

5. **Define *behavioral phenotype*.**

6. **How many genetic syndromes are associated with ID?**
   a. 2,500
   b. 4,000
   c. 6,000
   d. 1,000

7. **True or false? Maladaptive behavior scores are a relative strength of those diagnosed with Down syndrome.**

8. **What is the predominant domain of weakness for individuals diagnosed with Prader-Willi syndrome?**
   a. Expressive language
   b. Socialization
   c. Motor skills
   d. Community skills

9. **True or false? Cerebral palsy is the leading biomedical cause of ID in the western world.**

10. **What is the consideration that must be made when examining preterm infants and adaptive behavior?**

Answers: (1) Possible answers include ASD, ID, hearing and visual impairments, traumatic brain injury, learning disabilities, severe emotional disturbance, physical disabilities, multiple disabilities, and "other health impairment"; (2) b; (3) c; (4) c; (5) Characteristic patterns of behavior that describe a specific disorder; (6) d; (7) True; (8) c; (9) False. Fetal alcohol spectrum disorders are the leading biomedical cause of ID; (10) That a host of medical complications are associated with prematurity, such as periventricular hemorrhagic infarctions and CP, leading to difficulties in parsing the cause of adaptive behavior deficits.

Five

ADAPTIVE BEHAVIOR PROFILES IN AUTISM SPECTRUM DISORDER

The most extensive research on adaptive behavior profiles in neurodevelopmental disorders has been conducted in the field of autism. The vast majority of this research, conducted worldwide, has used the Vineland Adaptive Behavior Scales, either the original version or the second edition. The Adaptive Behavior Assessment System (ABAS, ABAS-II, and now ABAS-3) is the next most commonly used measure in autism spectrum disorder (ASD) research. Regardless of the measure used, deficits in adaptive behavior in individuals with ASD are so widely identified that assessment of adaptive behavior is now standard practice in ASD diagnostic evaluations. In fact, one study found that when adaptive behavior assessments were included in ASD evaluations along with the gold-standard diagnostic measures (Autism Diagnostic Observation Schedule [ADOS] and Autism Diagnostic Interview—Revised [ADI-R]), a clinician's diagnostic accuracy improved by 95% (Tomanik, Pearson, Loveland, Lane, & Bryant Shaw, 2007).

This chapter will outline the various relationships between adaptive behavior and cognition, age, autism symptomatology, and adult outcome. When considering these profiles, there is a need to revisit the principles of adaptive behavior that were outlined in Chapter 1; that is, adaptive behavior is (1) age-related, (2) defined by the expectations of others, (3) modifiable, and (4) defined by typical performance and not ability. Thus, profiles are expected to change across development as a result of life experiences. Moreover, profiles will be affected by myriad factors, particularly in ASD when navigating the social world is at the crux of the disability.

DON'T FORGET
....
Adaptive behavior is age-related and modifiable, meaning it is amenable to change, whereas cognition is more stable over time.

RELATIONSHIP BETWEEN ADAPTIVE BEHAVIOR AND LEVELS OF COGNITION

Early studies in ASD highlighted the substantial deficits in adaptive socialization skills that fell not just below age expectations but also below cognitive levels (e.g., Volkmar et al., 1987; Volkmar, Carter, Sparrow, & Cicchetti, 1993). These discrepancies between mental age and social skills in ASD could be more than two standard deviations in size. In fact, patterns emerged such that an "autism profile" was established wherein the greatest deficits in classic autism were identified in adaptive socialization skills in comparison to intermediate communication deficits and relative strengths in daily living skills (Carter et al., 1998; Loveland & Kelley, 1991; Volkmar et al., 1987).

≡ Rapid Reference 5.1

The "autism profile" of adaptive behavior—strongest to weakest skills:
- Daily living skills
- Communication skills
- Socialization skills

The incredible variability between these profiles in individuals with ASD compared to typically developing and intellectually disabled peers led to the development of supplemental norms for adaptive behavior in autism so that these individuals could be compared to their own peer group rather than to the normative sample (Carter et al., 1998). The rationale for developing these specialized norms was to identify attainable goals for intervention planning (Carter et al., 1998).

Given that adaptive and cognitive delays make up the diagnostic criteria for intellectual disability (ID), it is not surprising that these two constructs would be historically associated in autism, particularly in individuals with ASD with cognitive impairment. Though IQ, in general, may be a strong predictor of adaptive behavior, studies differ on whether the associations are in relation to verbal IQ, nonverbal IQ, or both, and if the relationship differs based on cognitive level (e.g., Liss et al., 2001; Schatz & Hamdan-Allen, 1995). For instance, in the study by Liss and colleagues (2001), IQ predicted adaptive behavior for individuals with cognitive impairment with and without autism. Yet, language skills and verbal memory were more predictive of adaptive behavior for individuals with autism without cognitive impairment. In a longitudinal study examining predictors of adaptive behavior in young children with autism and Asperger syndrome, early language and nonverbal skills were indicators of better outcome on the Communication and Socialization domains of the Vineland ABS for children with autism, but less so for those with Asperger syndrome (Szatmari, Bryson, Boyle, Streiner, & Duku, 2003). Taken collectively, these studies highlight that IQ certainly plays a role in adaptive outcome, but that this may be the case more so for individuals with autism who also have cognitive impairment.

Historically, a significant gap has been identified between chronological age and adaptive behavior across levels of cognition. However, more recent research is showing that the gap between mental age and adaptive skills may be dependent on cognitive level. "Higher-functioning" individuals with ASD who have average to above-average cognition tend to exhibit significant and often substantial deficits in their adaptive skills, with standard scores falling two to three standard deviations below IQ despite their cognitive capacity (Kanne et al., 2011; Klin et al., 2007; Perry, Flanagan, Dunn Geier, & Freeman, 2009). Thus, these individuals with ASD have difficulty independently applying their vast repertoire of skills (particularly social communication skills) to daily contexts in the absence of external supports, help, or reminders. This raises the question as to how "high functioning" these individuals truly are when they are constantly struggling to independently apply these behaviors in real life.

Conversely, recent studies have shown that for cognitively impaired individuals with ASD, Vineland standard scores often fall *above IQ scores,* with adaptive behavior being on par with or above mental age in some cases (Fenton et al., 2003; Kanne et al., 2011; Perry et al., 2009). These findings suggest that "lower-functioning" individuals with ASD and ID are potentially better able to apply their repertoire of skills to daily contexts and routines (in relation to their cognitive capacity) than their peers with much higher IQs. This could be a treatment effect, in that teaching daily life skills to very impaired individuals is often a focus in treatment programs. This is the case for individuals with ID with or without ASD. Historically, *cognitively able* individuals with ASD have been less likely to receive the same intensity of interventions (if any) as those individuals with comorbid ID, often because they are faring well academically within school settings.

Although research is suggesting that lower-functioning children with ASD have relatively stronger adaptive skills in comparison to IQ, there is still evidence that adaptive deficits negatively affect functioning. In a large sample of more than 300 minimally verbal school-age children, impairments in social affect were associated with all areas of adaptive functioning, reiterating the need to focus on adaptive skills instruction in addition to other areas of deficit when treating ASD (Frost, Hong, & Lord, 2017).

DON'T FORGET

Adaptive skills tend to fall significantly below age and cognition for individuals with autism without cognitive impairment, whereas individuals with autism and ID tend to have stronger adaptive skills than would be expected given their mental age.

RELATIONSHIP BETWEEN ADAPTIVE BEHAVIOR AND AGE

The relationship between adaptive behavior and age is just as equivocal as that with IQ; for every study showing a positive correlation with age, suggesting that adaptive behaviors improve with age, there are studies showing the opposite.

Several studies examining the relationship between adaptive behavior and age have reported a positive association (Anderson, Oti, Lord, & Welch, 2009; Freeman, Del'Homme, Guthrie, & Zhang, 1999; Schatz & Hamdan-Allen, 1995). Freeman and colleagues (1999) found that adaptive skills in all Vineland ABS domains improved with age. Yet, the rate of progress in communication and daily living skills was related to cognition level at baseline, whereas improvement in socialization skills was not. The study by Anderson and colleagues (2009) showed improvement in adaptive social skills over time as measured by the Vineland ABS, as well as an increase in nonverbal IQ and a decrease in social deficits as measured by the ADOS. A great deal of variability was found across the sample, with some children making gains in adaptive skills that closed the gap in or even exceeded age expectations, even in more cognitively disabled children. A positive association was also found between adaptive skills and maternal education, suggesting that children of more educated mothers made larger gains over time. It should be noted that this cohort of children was identified as having autism at a very young age (i.e., by age 2), and many received subsequent early intervention that could account for these gains.

To the contrary, some studies have identified a negative correlation between adaptive behavior and age (Kanne et al., 2011; Klin et al., 2007). In the study by Klin and colleagues (2007), Vineland ABS scores and age were negatively correlated, whereas ADOS scores did not vary over time. Thus, adaptive skills did not keep pace with chronological age, whereas autism symptomatology remained stable. In the study by Kanne and colleagues (2011), a significant negative correlation was also found using the Vineland-II Adaptive Behavior Composite with age—and this sample included over 1,000 individuals with ASD ages 4 to 18 years. When the sample was split in half by age, the older sub-sample had a wider gap between their IQ and adaptive scores compared to the younger sub-sample, despite having no difference in overall level of IQ.

Despite an individual with ASD's ability to acquire new adaptive skills over time, the gap between IQ and adaptive functioning does appear to widen with age, suggesting that as individuals grow older, they acquire new functional skills at a slower pace than their conceptual development (Kanne et al., 2011; Klin et al., 2007; Szatmari et al., 2003). Longitudinal studies have shed light on whether gains made in adaptive behaviors have actually kept pace with chronological development. There is evidence to suggest that adaptive skill acquisition may plateau by late adolescence or young adulthood (Szatmari et al., 2003). However, factors such as cognition, language functioning, and early treatment need to be controlled for to better understand these trajectories. One very comprehensive longitudinal study followed 192 individuals with ASD from age 2 to 21 years over as many as six time points (Bal, Kim, Cheong, & Lord, 2015). Though adaptive daily living skills were found to fall significantly below age expectations by young adulthood for the entire sample, individuals with ASD who had higher daily living skills at outcome made approximately 12 years of gains in skills over the 19-year study in comparison to the much slower rate of gains in the lower-at-outcome group. The latter group did, however, continue to make 3 to 4 years of gains in late adolescence, highlighting that skill acquisition is possible despite level of functioning. Also of note, nonverbal IQ and intensive parent-implemented intervention prior to the age of 3 were predictors of better outcome.

Another large-scale longitudinal study followed children with autism over 8 to 12 years, some receiving as many as three to four assessments (Gotham, Pickles, & Lord, 2012). Only 15% of the sample changed trajectories over time (i.e., either improved or worsened, overall), whereas the vast majority remained stable in their levels of functioning. Despite autism symptomatology remaining stable over time for all groups, adaptive behavior worsened in the stable group and the declining group, whereas scores remained steady in the group that improved over time—yet, adaptive scores were still impaired in this highest-outcome group.

These findings from longitudinal studies emphasize the need for repeated evaluation of adaptive skills over time to elucidate these trends and to best inform intervention practices. Research also highlights the utility of using standardized measures of adaptive behavior at multiple time points for assessing intervention outcome—especially because adaptive behavior is "modifiable" and, as such, it is so sensitive to change.

CAUTION

The gap between cognition and adaptive skills appears to be greater in older versus younger individuals with autism who do not have cognitive impairment.

RELATIONSHIP BETWEEN ADAPTIVE BEHAVIOR AND AUTISM SYMPTOMATOLOGY

One would intuitively presume that there would be a strong correlation between adaptive behavior and autism symptom severity, assuming that fewer autism symptoms would relate with stronger adaptive skills and vice versa. However, the research in this area is not so clear.

Several studies have found strong inverse relationships between adaptive behavior and autism symptomology. One longitudinal study of children with ASD followed from age 2 to 13 years found strong correlations between the Vineland Socialization score and ADOS social domain scores at all four time points (Anderson et al., 2009). It should be noted, however, that Vineland age-equivalent scores were used instead of standard scores for these analyses, which may account for the variation in findings. Another study using the ABAS-II also found a significant negative relationship (Kenworthy, Case, Harms, Martin, & Wallace, 2010). When high-functioning individuals with ASD age 12 to 21 years were matched on age, IQ, and sex ratio, higher ADOS communication scores (indicating more impairments) were negatively correlated with all ABAS-II composite scores, and higher ADOS social impairments were negatively correlated with ABAS-II Global and Social Composite scores. One study that compared Adaptive Behavior scores from the Vineland ABS Classroom Edition, the Scales of Independent Behavior, Revised, and the Adaptive Behavior Scales, School Edition, found moderate negative correlations with autism severity scores from the Childhood Autism Rating Scale across all three measures (Wells, Condillac, Perry, & Factor, 2009).

To the contrary, several studies using the Vineland ABS and Vineland-II, respectively, have found limited correlations between adaptive behavior and autism symptomatology in school-age children. In a study conducted by Klin and colleagues (2007), minimal associations were found between the Vineland ABS and the ADOS in two independent samples of children with autism without cognitive impairment ranging in age from 8 to 18 years. These findings were replicated in a very large sample of more than 1,000 children with autism of more variable cognitive levels and a wider age range from 4 to 18 years

(Kanne et al., 2011). Results suggested that children with more severe symptomatology did not necessary have worse adaptive skills and vice versa. In fact, symptom severity had very little bearing on adaptive behavior. Even when studies examined samples stratified by subtypes of autism (e.g., autism versus Asperger syndrome versus pervasive developmental disorder, not otherwise specified) or varying levels of autism symptomatology, few differences in adaptive skills between these samples were found (Paul et al., 2004; Saulnier & Klin, 2007). Although these studies were cross-sectional, the longitudinal study conducted by Szatmari and colleagues (2003) also found that autism-related symptoms were a weak predictor of adaptive outcome.

Given the vast variability in findings, it still remains unclear as to whether adaptive skills and autism symptoms affect one another. It does appear that age and level of cognitive functioning may play a role into the strength of these relationships as well as what types of measures are used to assess autism symptom severity and adaptive behavior.

CAUTION

The relationship between adaptive behavior and autism symptomatology in school-age children with ASD remains unclear. Factors that appear to affect this relationship include age, level of cognition, and type of measures used.

RELATIONSHIP BETWEEN ADAPTIVE BEHAVIOR AND SENSORY BEHAVIORS

Sensory sensitivities have long been documented as being prevalent in individuals with ASD. These behaviors can manifest as sensory over-responsivity (e.g., covering ears to mild sounds, aversion to certain fabrics or tags, etc.), under-responsivity (e.g., limited reaction to pain and injury), and sensory-seeking (e.g., seeking out sensory input). Studies that have investigated sensory-processing impairments in ASD have found these behaviors to be associated with adaptive functioning. For instance, a study on school-age children with ASD found that children who were over-reactive to sensory stimuli also tended to have overfocused attention, high-fidelity memory, higher cognitive skills, and high adaptive communication skills. However, this same group of children had the lowest adaptive socialization skills (Liss, Saulnier, Fein, & Kinsbourne, 2006). Lower-functioning children, however, tended to be more under-responsive to sensory stimuli.

In a study on toddlers with ASD and non-ASD developmental disorders, toddlers with ASD were found to have more atypical responses to taste and smell compared to children with fragile X syndrome, children with developmental disorders of mixed etiology, and typically developing children (Rogers, Hepburn, & Wehner, 2003). Moreover, sensory responsivity in ASD affected adaptive behaviors scores more than autism symptomatology. However, developmental level, as assessed by the Mullen Scales of Early Learning, was the best predictor of adaptive functioning in toddlers with ASD.

RELATIONSHIP BETWEEN ADAPTIVE BEHAVIOR AND SEX

Scientific research in the field of autism has been predominantly conducted on males. Comparatively little is actually known about female profiles of ASD and if potential sex differences exist across symptomatology, language, cognitive and adaptive functioning, and behavioral presentation. Using diagnostic criteria (that have been historically developed on male-dominant profiles), girls ascertained as having ASD tend to have lower IQs (Lord & Schopler, 1985; Volkmar, Szatmari, & Sparrow, 1993), and it has been suggested that they require a greater genetic insult to meet diagnostic thresholds (Frazier, Georgiades, Bishop, & Hardan, 2014; Szatmari et al., 2012). The few studies that have examined sex differences in relation to adaptive behavior have been variable in results. For instance, one study found females to have greater deficits in adaptive daily living skills and milder restricted and repetitive behaviors in comparison to males (White et al., 2017), whereas another found higher adaptive daily living skills and no differences in autism symptomatology (Mandic-Maravic et al., 2015). When matching for age and IQ in males and females, one study also found fewer restricted and repetitive behaviors in females but similar levels of social communication impairments (Mandy et al., 2012). Though adaptive behavior, per se, was not directly assessed in this study, the authors did find females to have more emotional problems in comparison to higher levels of externalizing behaviors in males with ASD.

The greatest limitation of the aforementioned studies is small sample size for females. In one of the largest studies conducted to date on 304 females with ASD ascertained as part of the Simons Simplex Collection (a network of 12 university-affiliated sites conducting highly rigorous diagnostic assessments), several sex differences were identified (Frazier et al., 2014). In this rigorously characterized sample using the Vineland-II Survey Form, females with ASD had lower cognition and language abilities, lower adaptive skills, and greater social communication impairments but lower restricted and repetitive behaviors.

Adaptive deficits were lower in females in all areas of adaptive behavior as measured by the Vineland-II, with the greatest impairments in adaptive socialization skills.

CAUTION

More research is needed on adaptive profiles in females with ASD, but the largest study conducted to date identified lower adaptive skills in females versus males in communication, daily living, and socialization skills.

ADAPTIVE BEHAVIOR PROFILES IN TODDLERS AND PRESCHOOL-AGE CHILDREN WITH ASD

With the increase in focus on early detection research in autism, many of the research questions that had been studied in older individuals with ASD are now being explored in toddlers and preschool-age children in order to examine the earliest emerging deficits. Similar to older children, associations have been found between adaptive skills and early cognition in toddlers with ASD. For instance, in a study that included 125 children with ASD ranging in age from 23 to 39 months using the Vineland-II and Bayley-III (to measure adaptive and early cognitive skills, respectively), strong positive correlations were found, indicating that stronger developmental skills related to stronger adaptive skills (Ray-Subramanian, Huai, & Ellis Weismer, 2011). Another study found that toddlers with ASD had more delays on every scale of the Vineland-II when compared to toddlers with non-autism developmental delays (DDs) (Paul, Loomis, & Chawarska, 2014). When these toddlers with and without ASD were matched on age and developmental level, delays in adaptive receptive communication and daily living skills were still evident.

DON'T FORGET

Delays in adaptive functioning are evident as early as toddlerhood in children with ASD, with adaptive socialization and communication skills being vulnerable.

The typical "autism profile," with adaptive socialization skills being the greatest area of deficit, has not been consistently found in toddlers when observing standard scores. For instance, in the study using the Vineland-II and the Bayley-III, adaptive communication skills were found to be the lowest, followed by socialization skills, daily living skills, and then motor skills being the strongest (Ray-Subramanian et al., 2011). Toddlers ranged in age from 24 to 36 months and were of average cognition. However, when examining *age-equivalent* rather than standard scores, one study on young children did observe the traditional "autism profile," with highest scores on the Motor domain of the Vineland-II, followed by Daily Living Skills, Communication, and then Socialization age-equivalent scores (Yang, Paynter, & Gilmore, 2016).

The varying gap between cognition and adaptive functioning has also been observed in young children with ASD. One study found higher adaptive than cognitive scores in young children with ASD who were cognitively impaired but not in those with intact cognition (Yang et al., 2016).

Strong associations between adaptive skills and autism symptomatology have been found in toddlers. In the study by Ray-Subramanian and colleagues (2011), significant negative correlations were found between the Vineland-II Communication and Daily Living Skills domains with the ADOS-calibrated severity scores. However, the effect sizes were small. Yang et al. (2016) also found strong negative associations between autism symptom severity and Vineland-II age-equivalent scores. However, neither study found ADOS-calibrated severity scores to add any significant contribution to Vineland scores after controlling for age and IQ.

CAUTION

A negative association between adaptive behavior and symptom severity is clearer in toddlers with ASD in that more severe symptomatology is related to poorer adaptive functioning.

Few studies have examined specific adaptive behaviors that might contribute to more positive outcomes in young children. A study of 52 Italian preschoolers with ASD and non-ASD DD found that the Play and Leisure subdomain of the Socialization domain of the Vineland-II discriminated between the ASD and non-ASD DD samples (Balboni, Tasso, Muratori, & Cubelli, 2016). When looking further at item-specific clusters, they found that playing and imitating skills were lower than other adaptive socialization skills in the children with ASD. In a larger study comparing 108 children under the age of 3 with ASD and non-ASD, DDs matched on nonverbal ability, 9 out of 20 items from the Interpersonal and Play/Leisure subdomains of the Socialization domain significantly distinguished the groups (Ventola, Saulnier, Steinberg, Chawarska, & Klin, 2014).

These items were early-emerging developmental milestones that would be expected in the first year of life, including responding to another person's voice, showing interest in new people and in children, and anticipation of being picked up by a caregiver.

THE IMPACT OF RACE, ETHNICITY, AND SOCIOECONOMIC STATUS ON ADAPTIVE BEHAVIOR IN ASD

There is an emerging amount of literature exposing significant disparities in race, ethnicity, and socioeconomic status (SES) in ASD. African American and Hispanic children with ASD tend to be diagnosed later than Caucasian, non-Hispanic children; they are more likely to be diagnosed with something other than ASD on initial evaluation; and they have poorer access to health care services and are less likely to have a medical home, or central source providing comprehensive, continuous, and personalized care (Magaña, Lopez, Aguinaga, & Morton, 2013; Mandell et al., 2009; Valicenti-McDermott, Hottinger, Seijo, & Shulman, 2012). African American children with ASD are also more likely to have developmental and cognitive delays than Caucasian children (Cuccaro et al., 2007).

CAUTION

African American and Hispanic children with ASD are more likely to be diagnosed later, misdiagnosed, have poorer access to health care services, and are less likely to have a medical "home" compared to Caucasian children with autism.

Differences observed in adaptive behavior could certainly be affected by IQ, which calls to action the need for stratifying samples by cognitive levels when investigating racial-ethnic differences in adaptive functioning. A study that sampled only African American and Caucasian youth with ASD without ID found the African American sample to have higher scores on measures of executive functioning, adaptive behavior, and social-emotional functioning—and that scores for the African American children were in the nonclinical or impaired range across all measures used (Ratto et al., 2016). These findings remained significant even after controlling for parent education and IQ.

Similar disparities in delays in diagnosis, misdiagnosis, and limited access to health care are also observed in Latino and Hispanic children with ASD (Magaña et al., 2013; Parish, Magaña, Rose, Timberlake, & Swaine, 2012).

A recent study stratified a large sample of children with ASD by Latino with English proficiency, Latino with limited English proficiency, and non-Latino White children to investigate barriers to diagnosis and treatment (Zuckerman et al., 2017). Results indicated that families with limited English proficiency had the most barriers, including high levels of unmet treatment needs and low numbers of treatment hours, with the most frequently endorsed barrier being parent knowledge about ASD—even more common than economical or logistical barriers (e.g., cost or travel, respectively). In addition to lack of autism awareness, other studies have found stigma surrounding the diagnostic label and social isolation from family and community members to be barriers in access to care for parents of Latino and Hispanic children with ASD (Blanche, Diaz, Barretto, & Cermak, 2015; Ijalba, 2016).

The role of SES also complicates matters. Unlike most other disabilities when a negative association is often found between SES and the disability (e.g., language disorders), there is a positive association between SES and ASD (Durkin et al., 2010; Schopler, Andrews, & Strupp, 1979; Wing, 1980). That is, autism is more likely to be diagnosed in families with higher educations, with larger incomes, and that live in more advantaged geographical areas. Therefore, the disparities observed in race and ethnicity could actually be more related to SES—though some studies have found disparities in race-ethnicity to exist even after controlling for SES (e.g., Garland et al., 2005).

DON'T FORGET

Unlike most other developmental disorders, there is a positive correlation between ASD and SES in that children from more advantaged homes and communities are more likely to be diagnosed with ASD.

Given that the field of ASD is still learning about disparities, there will be ongoing questions as to the impact of race, ethnicity, and SES on the phenotypic (i.e., behavioral) and genotypic profiles. For starters, we need to improve on accurate diagnostic ascertainment. Although epidemiological studies have shown a significant increase in the prevalence of African American and Hispanic children (Christensen et al., 2016), there are still many individuals of minority status and from disadvantaged communities that are either misdiagnosed or have yet to be ascertained correctly.

SUMMARY

In summary, the research on adaptive deficits in ASD is staggering, if not sobering. The limited adaptive skills in individuals with ASD—particularly in those without cognitive impairment—stress the need for targeted intervention to enhance functional, real-life skills. In addition, given that adaptive behavior is strongly associated with positive outcomes, researchers need to consider using adaptive behavior assessments more frequently to measure outcome. Dating back to the early 20th century, Doll noted that these very skills are easily identifiable and modifiable, and Chapter 8 will highlight treatments that have been shown to enhance adaptive functioning when specifically addressed. Thus, there should be no limitation on the progress that individuals with ASD can make in acquiring and applying new adaptive skills.

TEST YOURSELF

1. List the skills (strongest to weakest) of the "autism profile" of adaptive behavior.
2. True or false? Cognition is modifiable, whereas adaptive behavior is more stable over time.
3. True or false? Research shows that "higher-functioning" individuals with ASD exhibit substantial deficits in their adaptive skills.
4. The gap between cognition and adaptive skills appears to be _____ in older versus younger individuals with autism with no cognitive impairment.
   a. Smaller
   b. Greater
   c. Almost equal
5. List the three factors that appear to affect the relationship between adaptive behavior and autism symptomatology in school-age children with ASD.
6. Research shows that _____ is the best predictor of adaptive functioning in toddlers with ASD.
   a. Motor skills level
   b. Amount of spoken words
   c. Age
   d. Developmental level
7. True or false? Adaptive behavior profiles in girls with ASD are clear and well defined in comparison to males.

8. **Which two adaptive behavior domains as measured by the Vineland-II and Bayley-III are more vulnerable than other domains for toddlers with ASD?**
   a. Communication skills
   b. Daily Living skills
   c. Socialization skills
   d. Motor skills

9. **True or false? There is a negative correlation between ASD and SES in that children from more-advantaged communities are less likely to be diagnosed with ASD.**

10. **African American and Hispanic children with ASD are _____ likely to be misdiagnosed than Caucasian children with ASD.**
    a. Less
    b. More
    c. Equally

Answers: (1) Daily living skills, communication skills, and socialization skills; (2) False. Adaptive behavior can be modifiable, whereas cognition is more stable over time; (3) True; (4) b; (5) Age, level of cognition, type of measure used; (6) d; (7) False; (8) a and c; (9) False. There is a positive correlation between ASD diagnosis and SES showing that children from more-advantaged communities are more likely to receive and ASD diagnosis; (10) b.

Six

ADAPTIVE BEHAVIOR PROFILES IN OTHER NEURODEVELOPMENTAL DISORDERS

I n addition to intellectual disability (ID) and autism spectrum disorder (ASD), adaptive behavior deficits are also observed in individuals with a variety of neurodevelopmental disorders. Understanding these profiles is important when developing treatment and intervention plans to promote practical skill acquisition and functional independence. This chapter reviews common neurodevelopmental disorders for which adaptive behavior should be considered.

LEARNING DISABILITIES

Learning disabilities are characterized by difficulties in learning and applying academic skills, such as reading, writing, and mathematics. These challenges often affect academic and vocational performance as well as activities of daily living (American Psychiatric Association, 2013).

In learning disabilities, adaptive behavior deficits are often related to the specific area of learning that is vulnerable (Fagerlund et al., 2012; Leigh, 1987). For instance, in a study by Balboni, Incognito, Belacchi, Bonichini, and Cubelli (2017), the overall Communication domain on the Vineland-II was lower than individuals without learning disabilities and this was primarily driven by delays in the written skills as opposed to receptive and expressive skills. In examining specific subsets of items, it was found that reading and writing skills within the Written subdomain and temporal items from the Community subdomain, such as time and date concepts, were the areas of greatest weakness. A direct relationship was not found between symptom severity and corresponding disability (Balboni & Ceccarani, 2003), suggesting that measures of adaptive behavior can be useful to evaluate if and to what extent the learning disability is affecting everyday living skills.

As observed in ASD, the gap between cognitive functioning and adaptive behavior widens with age for individuals with learning disabilities. One study found that secondary-age students showed consistently lower levels of adaptive behavior than elementary-age students (Leigh, 1987). Using the Adaptive Behavior Inventory (ABI), the overall adaptive functioning composite declined from 94.1 to 85.4 as an individual aged, with initial scores within the Average range to scores within the Below Average range (Brown & Leigh, 1986). The areas of greatest decline were within the Self-Care, Communication, and Social Skills domains.

ATTENTION DEFICIT/HYPERACTIVITY DISORDER (ADHD)

Attention deficit/hyperactivity disorder (ADHD) is a common childhood psychiatric disorder characterized by inattention, disorganization, or hyperactivity and impulsive behaviors (Roizen, Blondis, Irwin, & Stein, 1994). According to the CDC, the prevalence of ADHD across the United States in 2011 ranged from 5% to 17%, with a national average of 11%. Despite the commonly understood symptomatology of inattention, distractibility, and impulsivity, children and adolescents with ADHD can also show significant impairment in the areas of conceptual, social, and practical adaptive behavior skills (Clark, Prior, & Kinsella, 2002; Crocker, Vaurio, Riley, & Mattson, 2009; Sukhodolsky et al., 2005). Social deficits are also cited as a central to the challenges with ADHD (Barkley, Fischer, Edelbrock, & Smallish, 1990; Hinshaw, 1992) in that individuals with ADHD are frequently rejected by their peers (Erhardt & Hinshaw, 1994). According to Barkley et al. (1990), 50% to 80% of individuals with ADHD experience problems with peer relationships in adolescence. In addition to social deficits, ADHD can also have an adverse impact on children's academic and family functioning (American Psychiatric Association, 2013; Hinshaw, 2002).

For the most part, assessment of adaptive behavior has not been a standardized component of diagnostic evaluations or treatment plans for individuals with ADHD. However, there are a variety of behaviors consequential of ADHD that are likely to result in adaptive behavior deficits. Examples would include excessive talking, difficulty organizing and communicating information, difficulty modulating communication based on task demands, difficulty with back-and-forth interactions, and responsiveness to questions asked by their peers. Children with ADHD also tend to jump between tasks, have difficulty completing tasks or following through on instructions, and are often messy or sloppy in their performance (for example, losing necessary items needed to complete tasks). Consequently, children with ADHD struggle to meet age-appropriate expectations with regard to following multistep instructions, which can certainly affect social functioning as well as personal and domestic self-care, such as dressing, grooming, and completing household chores.

A subsample of children with ADHD was included as one of the clinical samples for the standardization of the Vineland-II and Vineland-3. In the Vineland-II ADHD sample, the mean Adaptive Behavior Composite score was lower than that of the nonclinical reference group. The Daily Living Skills scores were consistent between groups, but individuals with ADHD had lower scores on the Communication and Socialization domains, including on all three subdomains within each domain. In addition, scores on the Maladaptive Behavior Index were in the clinical range, with higher scores on the Internalizing and Externalizing subscales compared to the normative population. ADHD is highly comorbid with disruptive behavior disorders such as conduct disorder and oppositional defiant disorder (ODD), which can contribute to elevated externalizing symptoms in addition to exacerbated social and emotional dysfunction (Carter et al., 2000).

In a study by Balboni and colleagues (2017), children with ADHD had significantly lower scores on the Adaptive Behavior Composite of the Vineland-II, as well as on the Communication, Daily Living Skills, and Socialization domains. Within the Communication domain, Receptive and Expressive subdomains were weaker than the Written subdomain. Within the Daily Living Skills domain, the Community subdomain was also found to be more impaired than the Personal subdomain. Within the Socialization domain, the Coping Skills subdomain was significantly more impaired than the Interpersonal and Play and Leisure subdomains. This study also broke the Vineland-II into subsets and found that the following subsets were significantly lower in individuals with ADHD than in those without:

- **Receptive:** Understanding, listening and attending, following instructions
- **Expressive:** Interactive speech, speech skills, expressing complex ideas
- **Daily Living Skills:** Money skills and restaurant skills
- **Socialization:** Expressing and recognizing emotions, social communication, friendship, sharing and cooperating, playing games, recognizing social cues, controlling impulses, keeping secrets, responsibility, and appropriate social caution

DON'T FORGET

Individuals with ADHD tend to show lower adaptive receptive, expressive, daily living, and socialization skills than those without ADHD.

In a study examining 104 children between 6 and 16.6 years with ADHD, it was found that, despite overall intelligence within the average range, these individuals had standard scores on the Vineland that were one to two standard deviations (mean of 27.9 points) lower than their cognitive abilities (Roizen et al., 1994; Stein, Szumowski, Blondis, & Roizen, 1995). This split between cognitive and adaptive behavior skills also appears to widen with age, indicating that as individuals with ADHD age, their adaptive skills are increasingly disparate from their peers (Roizen et al., 1994).

Individuals with ADHD often struggle with comorbid conditions, including ID, learning disabilities, obsessive compulsive disorder, Tourette syndrome, and speech and language impairment. Therefore, it can be difficult to discern what symptoms might be affecting adaptive behavior. One study compared adaptive profiles between a sample of children with mild ID, many of whom also had ADHD, and a sample of children with ADHD without ID, many of whom had non-ID comorbid conditions (Lindblad et al., 2013). Although no differences in adaptive behavior were observed between groups on the Adaptive Behavior Assessment System, Second Edition (ABAS-II), when the sample was split by age, older children with ADHD (i.e., above age 11 years) had significantly lower adaptive scores than the children with mild ID, as well as lower adaptive skills than the younger age group. These findings highlight the need to include adaptive skills instruction when programming for individuals without cognitive impairment given that adaptive impairments were greater for this sample despite the children having a cognitive advantage.

In comparison to disorders such as ASD that show similar deficits in adaptive socialization skills as well as significant gaps between cognition and adaptive behavior, attention needs to be given to the nature of social delays and deficits in ADHD. Unlike ASD, social deficits are not hallmark of ADHD, but certainly impulsivity, hyperactivity, and inattention can be strong contributors to challenges in understanding social contexts and, consequently, the development and maintenance of social relationships. Moreover, the presence of aggression and significant disruptive behavior can result in substantial social problems, including being rejected by peers (Ladd & Burgess, 1999). In this regard, intervention strategies to help develop adaptive social skills can be very similar regardless of the diagnostic label (e.g., social skills groups, teaching social rules and norms, enhancing perspective taking and theory of mind, etc.). But because the intervention strategies may be similar does not necessarily merit providing the additional diagnostic label of ASD to a child with ADHD.

OBSESSIVE COMPULSIVE DISORDER (OCD)

Obsessive compulsive disorder (OCD) is a neuropsychiatric condition that results in an individual having distressing and intrusive thoughts, impulses, or obsessions and repetitive overt or covert behaviors, known as compulsions, which are performed to reduce this distress (American Psychiatric Association, 2013). To meet criteria for a diagnosis of OCD, the distress must be marked and interfere with a person's functioning. The prevalence of OCD is estimated at 3% to 4% of adolescents (Flament et al., 1988; Zohar, 1999). However, OCD often co-occurs with other conditions, in particular anxiety, depression, tic disorders, and ADHD. Any of these comorbid conditions can affect adaptive functioning as much as the OCD symptomatology itself, and parsing this out can be quite challenging.

Research on children with OCD has suggested that adaptive impairments in daily living skills as well as diminished participation in daily activities and anxiety are characteristic of OCD (Sukhodolsky et al., 2005). Adaptive deficits are also greater than would be expected given cognitive profiles. Yet, when children with OCD also have ADHD, adaptive socialization skills are more affected in conjunction with emotional adjustment, school performance, and symptoms of depression. The additive ADHD symptomatology, therefore, has an adverse effect on social, emotional, and academic functioning (Geller et al., 2003; Sukhodolsky et al., 2005).

MOVEMENT AND MOTOR DISORDERS

There are several movement and motor disorders that develop during childhood that can affect adaptive functioning. These include developmental coordination disorder, inborn errors of metabolism, cerebral palsy, Tourette's syndrome, and epilepsy.

Developmental Coordination Disorder (DCD)

Developmental coordination disorder (DCD) is a neurodevelopmental disorder marked by significant motor impairments that are not otherwise accounted for by ID, visual impairment, or a known neurological condition, such as cerebral palsy (American Psychiatric Association, 2013). DCD occurs in about 6% of the general population, and symptoms can often be confused for other developmental disorders such as ID or ADHD (Farmer, Echenne, Drouin, & Bentourkia, 2017). The motor impairments (in gross- and fine-motor skills) significantly affect an individual's life in the areas of academic, vocational, home, and community living. Understandably, if an individual suffers from motor impairments, adaptive motor skills are likely to be affected as well as daily living skills that require motor skills to execute the specific behaviors such as eating, dressing, bathing, and so on (Balboni, Pedrabissi, Molteni, & Villa, 2001).

Inborn Errors of Metabolism (IEM)

Inborn errors of metabolism (IEM) are rare inherited disorders that can often result in psychomotor retardation, epilepsy, and (though less often) movement disorders (García-Cazorla et al., 2009). In addition to affecting motor functioning, IEM are also associated with adaptive deficits, particularly in the areas of personal and domestic daily living skills (Eggink et al., 2014). In addition, these adaptive impairments are significantly associated with measures of a child's health-related quality of life.

Cerebral Palsy

Cerebral palsy (CP) is considered a motor disorder in childhood caused by disturbances to a developing fetus or infant brain (e.g., van Schie et al., 2013). The degree of motor impairments in individuals with CP is often measured by a gross motor function classification system (GFMCS) with levels ranging from I (mild impairment) to V (severe impairment). Studies on adaptive deficits in CP vary dependent on the co-occurring conditions that often accompany CP, such as ID, epilepsy, and sensory processing problems. For instance, children with CP and GFMCS level V motor impairments (i.e., nonambulatory) who also have lower cognitive levels and epilepsy tend to show more limited adaptive socialization skills over time. Yet, those with milder motor impairments and no cognitive delays actually show improvement in social functioning over time, often approaching typical levels (e.g., Tan et al., 2014; van Schie et al., 2013). Adaptive communication skills are stronger in children with CP without ID (van Schie et al., 2013), and expressive communication skills, specifically, are stronger in those without ID and with unilateral spastic as opposed to bilateral spastic motor disorders (Vos et al., 2014). Thus, comprehensive assessments of cognition, language level, motor skills, adaptive behavior, and medical comorbidities are needed to fully understand developmental trajectories and outcomes for individuals with CP and to determine the best course of treatment.

Tourette's Syndrome

Tourette's syndrome (TS) is a developmental, neuropsychiatric disorder that is characterized by the presence of motor and verbal tics. The disorder increases and decreases in intensity, location, frequency, and complexity over time (Sukhodolsky et al., 2003). The prevalence of TS in school-age children ranges from 1 to 8 per 1,000 (Hornsey, Banerjee, Zeitlin, & Robertson, 2001; Swain, Scahill, Lombroso, King, & Leckman, 2007). Few studies have investigated adaptive behavior profiles that are specific to TS but those that have reported weaknesses in adaptive socialization skills (Dykens et al., 1990; Meucci, Leonardi, Zibordi, & Nardocci, 2009). However, well-controlled studies are needed to control for potential confounding factors such as comorbidity.

There is high comorbidity with TS and other neurodevelopmental disorders including ADHD, ODD, and conduct disorder (Coffey & Park, 1997; King & Scahill, 2001; Spencer et al., 2001). As with ADHD and OCD, the comorbidity is often what affects adaptive behavior more so than TS, in isolation. For instance, in a study examining adaptive behavior profiles in children with TS only, Vineland Communication and Socialization scores were no different from unaffected controls, and these children participated in age-appropriate extracurricular activities. However, children who suffered from TS and ADHD had lower adaptive scores that negatively affected their social functioning (Sukhodolsky et al., 2003). In fact, children with TS and ADHD were just as impaired as those with only ADHD, suggesting that it is the ADHD symptomatology that is driving the adaptive deficits in children with TS and not the tic disorder, per se.

Epilepsy

Seizures occur when there is abnormal excessive or synchronous neuronal activity in the brain. Epilepsy is a disease defined by enduring seizures and, as such, the neurobiological, cognitive, psychological, and social consequences that result. A commonly used definition of epilepsy has been two or more unprovoked seizures more than 24 hours apart (Dawda & Ezewuzie, 2010). Seizures and epilepsy commonly co-occur in individuals with ID, but seizures can certainly be present in individuals with no cognitive impairment.

Several studies have examined adaptive behavior profiles in individuals with epilepsy, but with varying results. For instance, in children with IQs of 61 to 70, overall adaptive behavior scores fell above their cognitive level and within the average range, with a mean composite score of 87.2 (de Bildt, Kraijer, Sytema, & Minderaa, 2005). In a group of children with IQs over 80, however, overall adaptive behavior scores were significantly delayed and below IQ, with a mean composite of 64.1 (Buelow et al., 2012). A longitudinal study examined adaptive behavior performance for 3 years post-initial diagnosis in a community-based cohort of children with epilepsy (Berg et al., 2004). The Vineland Scales of Adaptive Behavior Screeners were administered at baseline and once a year through the duration of the study. At baseline, adaptive behavior scores were found to be initially slightly below average. Over time, however, significant declines across all four domain scores were found. If a child had a syndrome that was associated with epilepsy, Motor and Socialization scores were lower than those without an epileptic syndrome. In addition, in children who developed intractable epilepsy, or epilepsy that is not managed despite medication, Adaptive Behavior scores were considerably lower at baseline. Age of onset of epilepsy was not associated with overall level of adaptive behavior, but the Vineland Daily Living Skills domain was lower in those with earlier onset epilepsy.

The study by Berg and colleagues (2004) also found differences in adaptive behavior based on the type of epilepsy. In individuals whose seizures were not intractable or when seizures were not associated with a syndrome, adaptive behavior was not found to decrease over time—overall or across domains. However, in children with intractable seizures or those with seizures with a known etiology, adaptive behavior significantly declined over time. This decline was found to be between 3.6 to 12 points per year, or up to almost one standard deviation decline per year. These declines were observed across all domains, with daily living skills and communication skills being the most likely to decline. The Communication domain in particular was found to be the area of greatest weakness.

Adaptive behavior has also been found to correlate with medication use for epilepsy, in that the more medications used (potentially indicating more severe symptomatology), the lower the adaptive scores (Villarreal, Riccio, Cohen, & Park, 2014). This finding is concerning given that medication management for epilepsy is critical for positive outcome (Bautista, 2017). If an individual's adaptive skills are affected by the number of medications, self-management skills are also likely to be negatively affected.

This body of research suggests that adaptive behavior may be independent of cognitive functioning in individuals with epilepsy. Given the concerning findings, children with epilepsy should be screened for adaptive behavior delays, repeatedly assessed and monitored for progress over time, and explicitly taught practical skills and self-management skills, particularly as they pertain to medication management.

HEARING IMPAIRMENTS

More than one-third of children who are deaf or hard of hearing have comorbid disabilities including learning disabilities, ADHD, ASD, motor impairments, developmental or cognitive delays, and visual deficits (e.g., Daneshi & Hassanzadeh, 2007; Van Naarden, Decouflé, & Caldwell, 1999). As with many other clinical conditions, it is these co-occurring conditions that can have the greatest impact on adaptive functioning. An early study by Dunlap and Sands (1990) conducted a cluster analysis on adaptive behaviors in a sample of hearing-impaired children and found that the lowest adaptive scores were not in those children with the most-severe hearing loss but rather in those with multiple disabilities (Dunlap & Sands, 1990).

The Vineland-II normative sample included hearing-impaired individuals as a clinical group. Individuals with hearing impairments showed lower adaptive scores than the nonclinical reference group, with communication and daily living skills falling below socialization skills. However, the hearing-impaired sample had higher adaptive skills in comparison to those with visual impairments (Sparrow, Cicchetti, & Balla, 2005).

With advances in technology, an increasing number of children with hearing impairments are candidates for cochlear implants. The success of these implants and the developmental gains made as a result, often depend on the overall level of disability given co-occurring conditions. Thus, understanding adaptive behavior profiles in hearing-impaired children again takes into consideration the parsing out of comorbidity. Studies examining deaf children who received cochlear implants have shown that children who had additional disabilities still progressed in development but at a slower pace than those without comorbid conditions (Daneshi & Hassanzadeh, 2007; Donaldson, Heavner, & Zwolan, 2004). When specifically studying adaptive behavior profiles, deaf children who have additional disabilities have lower adaptive scores in all areas compared to same-aged peers. However, following cochlear implants, deaf children with and without comorbid conditions made gains in adaptive daily living and socialization skills, even in some children who did not make gains in expressive language (Beer, Harris, Kronenberger, Holt, & Pisoni, 2012).

VISUAL IMPAIRMENTS

Congenital visual impairments are rare and research is complicated by the varying etiologies, particularly when impairments to the central nervous system exist (Greenaway, Pring, Schepers, Isaacs, & Dale, 2017). Prevalence rates of congenital visual impairments are estimated to be around 4 per 10,000 for infants prior to the first birthday, but rising to about 6 per 10,000 by age 16 (Rahi, Cable, & British Childhood Visual Impairment Study Group, 2003).

Research has suggested that theory of mind, or perspective-taking skills, are impaired in younger (but not older) children with congenital visual impairment (Pijnacker, Vervloed, & Steenbergen, 2012). These impairments have been attributed to the lack of ability to observe and, thus, acquire fundamental nonverbal social skills such as joint attention, gestures, mutual gaze, and facial expressions (Green, Pring, & Swettenham, 2004). As such, young children with congenital visual impairments may be at risk for pragmatic language impairments and possibly even for developing ASD (Hobson & Bishop, 2003). Regardless of whether the similarities of autistic features in congenitally blind children are truly characteristic of ASD, the potential for social vulnerabilities—especially in the nonverbal domain—merit attention for intervention.

Individuals with visual impairment ages 6 to 18 years were included as a clinical sample in the standardization of the Vineland-II; however, this sample included individuals with partial sight in addition to those with full blindness. Although the lowest domain score was for Daily Living Skills (with a mean score of 82.6), the lowest subdomain score was for Play and Leisure Time within the Socialization domain, with a v-scaled score of 11.5, more than one standard deviation below the normative mean of 15. Domestic and Personal subdomains were the second and third lowest scores, with means of 11.6 and 11.9, respectively, highlighting the challenges in conducting domestic chores and personal care with independence in this sample. Communication scores were within the average range, demonstrating relatively strong receptive and expressive skills compared to other practical skills (Sparrow et al., 2005).

Individuals with vision and hearing impairments are at risk for deficits in adaptive behavior, particularly with the skills needed for social sufficiency and competence in daily living skills. Careful assessment of adaptive behavior strengths and weaknesses is important in helping parents, caregivers, and educators develop necessary supports and compensatory programs so as to maximize these children's level of independence.

SPEECH, LANGUAGE, AND COMMUNICATION DISORDERS

Childhood apraxia of speech is a disorder affecting motor movements involved in speech. Children with apraxia of speech have problems saying sounds, syllables, and words secondary to motor planning issues. As a result, the brain struggles planning to move the body parts, including lips, jaw, and tongue, which are needed to effectively produce speech sounds (American Speech-Language-Hearing Association [ASHA], 2006). It is estimated that 1 to 2 children per 1,000 have apraxia of speech (Shriberg, Aram, & Kwiatkowski, 1997), and it is likely three to four times more common in boys than in girls (Hall, Jordan, & Robin, 1993). Frequently co-occurring with apraxia are more general motor deficits—from difficulties in timed and complex manual motor tasks (Bradford & Dodd, 1994, 1996; Dewey, Roy, Square-Storer, & Hayden, 1988; Newmeyer et al., 2007; Teverovsky, Bickel, & Feldman, 2009) to more global motor delays such as developmental coordination disorder (Visser, 2003; Zwicker, Missiuna, Harris, & Boyd, 2012).

There have also been reports of delays in adaptive behavior in children with childhood apraxia of speech (Tükel, Björelius, Henningsson, McAllister, & Eliasson, 2015; Winters, Collett, & Myers, 2005). In a study that examined adaptive behavior using the Adaptive Behavior Assessment Scale, Second Edition (ABAS-II), they found that 89% of children with apraxia of speech had some difficulties in at least one of the ABAS-II domains, but the number of behavioral difficulties identified on the ABAS-II did not correspond to the degree of motor difficulties (Tükel et al., 2015). Their overall adaptive profile was found to be at the lower end of the average range.

For children with language impairment, the associated impairments in phonological awareness, level of vocabulary, and understanding of syntactic structure have been associated with challenges in reading (Beitchman, Wilson, Brownlie, Walters, & Lancee, 1996). Identifying early language delays in the preschool years becomes imperative for future academic success. However, parent report measures of language (e.g., rating scales and checklists) can often overrepresent a child's level of language (Hall & Segarra, 2007). But clinical interviews between a clinician and a parent or caregiver are more likely to accurately ascertain language levels. In fact, research has shown that the Communication standard score of the Vineland Adaptive Behavior Scales, Survey (i.e., Interview) Form is most strongly correlated with clinical assessment findings (Aram, Morris, & Hall, 1993). Adaptive communication skills have also been found to be predictive of future reading, writing, and math skills (Hall & Segarra, 2007).

Much of the literature on communication disorders and adaptive behavior is found in the field of autism. Children with autism can struggle with reading, in particular reading comprehension (Arciuli, Stevens, Trembath, & Simpson, 2013; Kjelgaard & Tager-Flusberg, 2001). The often-observed discrepancy between their strong reading decoding skills (usually resultant from memorization of words by sight) and poorer reading comprehension skills places them at risk for hyperlexia. Having stronger adaptive communication skills has been found to correlate with reading ability (Arciuli et al., 2013), similar to findings for children with language disorders (Hall & Segarra, 2007).

SUMMARY

As outlined in this chapter, there are numerous developmental disorders that affect adaptive functioning. Given that many of these disorders overlap with one another, elucidating trends of adaptive strengths and weaknesses can actually help to parse out prognosis, but, more importantly, they inform treatment and intervention planning. In some cases, the unique profiles of adaptive skills can even be predictive of future functioning in other areas, such as academic achievement.

In light of the heterogeneity in profiles across disabilities, the information in this chapter highlights the common thread of adaptive impairments in neurodevelopmental disorders as well as how strongly a good outcome is dependent on these practical skills.

🖋 TEST YOURSELF 🖋

1. **In which area are individuals with learning disabilities appearing *most* vulnerable on the Vineland-II?**
   a. Gross Motor subdomain
   b. Written subdomain
   c. Fine-Motor subdomain
   d. Daily Living Skills domain
2. **What is the prevalence of ADHD across the United States?**
   a. Range of 5% to 17% with an average of 11%
   b. Range of 10% to 20% with an average of 11%
   c. Range of 5% to 10% with an average of 7%
   d. Range of 5% to 17% with an average of 9%
3. **List three of the ADHD symptoms that are likely to result in adaptive behavior deficits.**
4. **List the four adaptive behavior subsets that were significantly lower in individuals with ADHD according to Balboni et al. (2017).**
5. **True or false? Adaptive behavior measures are highly sensitive to comorbid symptomatology, and these measures help to understand what is actually affecting adaptive behaviors.**
6. **Which subset of individuals diagnosed with OCD is most vulnerable to greater adaptive behavior deficits?**
7. **True or false? Adaptive behavior profiles in children with CP vary according to level of impairment and cognitive functioning.**
8. **True or false? There is a positive correlation between dosage of medication and level of adaptive functioning in individuals with epilepsy.**
9. **Which of the following is *not* a characteristic of adaptive behavior profiles in individuals with hearing impairments?**
   a. Understanding these adaptive behavior profiles requires parsing out comorbid conditions.
   b. Deaf children with and without comorbidities improved in daily living and socialization skills after receiving cochlear implants.
   c. Deaf children without comorbidities who received cochlear implants improved at a faster rate than those with comorbidities.
   d. Deaf children with and without comorbidities improved in daily living and communication skills after receiving cochlear implants.

10. True or false? Parents of children with language delays and communication disorders are accurate reporters on parent-completed questionnaires, but they show overreporting bias in clinical adaptive behavior interviews.

Answers: (1) b; (2) a; (3) Possible answers include excessive talking, difficulty organizing and communicating information, difficulty modulating communication based on task demands and difficulty with back-and-forth interactions, responsiveness to questions asked by peers, jumping between tasks, difficulty completing tasks or following through on instructions, and general sloppiness; (4) Receptive Language, Expressive Language, Daily Living Skills, and Socialization; (5) False. Comorbid symptomatology makes it more difficult to discern what is actually affecting adaptive behaviors; (6) Those with comorbid conditions, specifically ADHD; (7) True; (8) False. There is a negative correlation with increased dosage of medicine correlating with more-severe adaptive behavior deficits; (9) d; (10) False. Adaptive behavior measures are more likely to resemble actual language skill level than are parent-report measures in the language delay and communication disorder population.

Seven

ADAPTIVE BEHAVIOR PROFILES IN ADULTS WITH NEURO-DEVELOPMENTAL DISORDERS

C urrently in the United States, about 1.3 million adults have an intellectual disability (ID) (Woodman, Mailick, Anderson, & Esbensen, 2014). With recent medical and technological advances, an increasing number of individuals with ID are living into adulthood with normal life expectancies. As such, there is a substantial increase in the demand for residential and vocational services, with nearly 700,000 residents with ID in the United States living in out-of-home settings in 2015 (American Association on Intellectual and Developmental Disabilities [AAIDD], 2017). Of these individuals, 82% were living in residences with six or fewer people, with the majority living in supported living environments followed by group homes. Nearly 70,000 were living in settings such as nursing homes or state institutions that house 16 or more individuals. In 2011, there were about 500,000 individuals with ID living in residential placements (Larson, Salmi, Smith, Anderson, & Hewitt, 2013). Despite this increase over time, many states actually decreased funding for public institutions between 2013 and 2015 (AAIDD, 2017). Costs of residential settings in 2015 ranged from $27,593 to $210,110 per year, depending on the level of supported care.

CAUTION

Despite the increase in the number of individuals with ID living in residential placements since 2011, funding for public institutions has decreased in many states.

This chapter highlights the role that adaptive behavior plays in adult outcome, not only for successful residential and vocational placements but also for emotional and medical well-being. Regardless of the type of disability and level of cognitive functioning, adults require functional, practical skills to meet the demands of everyday life. Thus, strong adaptive skills become the common thread across disabilities when considering optimal outcome.

ADAPTIVE PROFILES IN ADULTS WITH INTELLECTUAL DISABILITY

By definition, adults with ID will have adaptive deficits. As mentioned in Chapter 4, adaptive skills tend to be on par with cognitive skills for severely cognitively impaired individuals, whereas adaptive profiles vary in comparison to cognition for individuals with mild, moderate, or borderline ID, especially across specific genetic disorders. The majority of research in this regard has sampled individuals in the school-age years, but an increasing amount of longitudinal studies has followed individuals with various disabilities into adulthood. Just as profiles of cohort samples vary, trajectories over time are variable depending on the type of disability.

Few studies have focused on adults with severe or profound ID given the low incidence of this level of severity compared to more mild and moderate levels of ID (Belva & Matson, 2013), not to mention the challenges in researching this population given restrictions on residential placements, consenting or assenting procedures, and access to caregivers or guardians. Yet, for this population, having even a modicum of fundamental adaptive skills—especially daily living skills—is imperative. Belva and Matson (2013) have been among the few to investigate adaptive profiles in individuals with severe ID and found that for items on the Vineland Adaptive Behavior Scales, Daily Living Skills domain, domestic items (e.g., dressing, eating, bathing) were endorsed the most by this group of adults, followed by personal items and then community items. Given that community items were the least endorsed raises concerns as to whether highly restricted inpatient or residential placements provide adults with severe ID access to the community to practice these skills. This study also found younger adults to have stronger personal and domestic skills than older adults with ID (Belva & Matson, 2013).

Adaptive profiles in individuals with mild, moderate, and borderline ID are more variable, likely due to the heterogeneity in causes and comorbid conditions. Though most adults with severe and profound ID were likely identified in their developmental years, those with milder deficits might not have been identified early on in life and either missed out on intervention in their formative years or were denied eligibility for services given their milder delays. Thus, many adults with mild ID might not carry a label and, therefore, are not accessing services under this eligibility despite needing them (Emerson, 2011). This is unfortunate, given that many adults with mild ID have the capacity to make significant contributions to society given their milder cognitive and adaptive impairments and, therefore, optimizing their adaptive skills as early as possible becomes all the more necessary.

It is estimated that more than one-third of adults with ID also suffer from a psychiatric disorder, with depression being the most common and even higher than would be expected in the typical adult population (Bhaumik, Tyrer, McGrother, & Ganghadaran, 2008; van Schrojenstein Lantman-de Valk et al., 1997). Though depressive symptomatology can certainly manifest similarly in ID compared to typical development, adults with ID might also express depression in the form of behavior disruption, aggression, and even a regression in some areas of development (Matson et al., 1999; McBrien, 2003). Also of notable importance, adults with mild ID self-report more affective and cognitive depressive symptoms (e.g., sadness, anhedonia, worry, self-blame, suicidality, helplessness) than would be endorsed by a third-party respondent such as a staff member, whereas staff members are more likely to endorse somatic depressive symptoms, such as feeling fatigued, sick, having loss of appetite, or insomnia (Mileviciute & Hartley, 2015). Therefore, residential and vocational staff members, health care providers, caregivers, and family members need to consider self-report of symptomatology in addition to rating scales that are typically completed by third-party respondents when assessing for depression.

DON'T FORGET

Depression symptoms in adults with ID can manifest as behavior disruption, aggression, or regression of skills in addition to or in lieu of typical depressive symptomatology.

Another risk factor for adults with ID worth noting is obesity. Obesity, in general, has been on the rise worldwide, with more than one-third of adults being obese (Ng et al., 2014). Yet, little research has been conducted on obesity levels in adults with ID. One review that investigated this prevalence found the following risk factors to be associated with ID: being female, having more mild ID, having Down syndrome, being older in age, consuming antipsychotic medications, lacking physical exercise, and living in less-restricted environments such as independently or with family (Ranjan, Nasser, & Fisher, 2017). The prevalence of obesity was estimated to be between 17% and 43%. However, there were several limitations to the studies conducted in this review, leaving many questions still unanswered. Despite the limitations, concern remains regarding adults with IDs and their ability to take care of their personal health needs. Many individuals with mild ID have the capacity to understand these risk factors and, thus, take strides to manage them, even if with guidance and instruction. Newer measures of adaptive functioning, such as the Vineland Adaptive Behavior Scales, Third Edition (Sparrow, Cicchetti, & Saulnier, 2016), have included items to assess for knowledge and execution of healthy eating and exercise habits in addition to the already existing assessment of medication management and self-care that it is hoped will help to identify areas of vulnerability in these important adaptive skills.

≡ Rapid Reference 7.1

....

Risk factors for obesity in adults with ID include the following:

- Being female
- Having milder cognitive deficits
- Having Down syndrome
- Being older in age
- Consuming antipsychotic medications
- Lacking physical exercise
- Living in less-restricted environments

ADAPTIVE PROFILES IN ADULTS WITH GENETIC DISORDERS

As outlined in Chapter 5, distinct adaptive profiles can be observed across genetic disorders. These profiles, however, can change throughout development and, thus, the same genetic syndromes are outlined in the following sections in adulthood.

Down Syndrome

Down syndrome in adulthood is complicated by comorbidities, including depression (Collacott, Cooper, & McGrother, 1992; Myers & Pueschel, 1995) and the high risk for developing Alzheimer-related dementia, especially after the age of 40 (Holland, Hon, Huppert, & Stevens, 2000). An increasing amount of studies are now attempting to identify early markers for dementia by examining cognitive, neuropsychological, and adaptive profiles, among other factors. For instance, working memory impairments have been identified as early markers for dementia, as have personality and behavioral changes (Holland et al., 2000; Nelson, Orme, Osann, & Lott, 2001).

Studies on adaptive behavior profiles in Down syndrome have been variable. Some studies have found lower adaptive scores in adults with Down syndrome who also have dementia compared to those without, as well as worsening adaptive skills with age (Burt, Loveland, & Lewis, 1992; Cosgrave, Tyrrell, McCarron, Gill, & Lawlor, 1999). However, another study that examined adaptive behavior as a potential marker for dementia found no differences in Vineland scores between adults with Down syndrome with early cognitive deterioration compared to those without cognitive deterioration, despite significant decreases in executive functioning for the early sample (Adams & Oliver, 2010). Yet another study that stratified adults with Down syndrome by genetic polymorphisms in the genes coding for either the catechol-O-methyltransferase or dopamine transporter found that the catechol-O-methyltransferase group showed poorer adaptive skills and was at higher risk for early dementia than the dopamine group (Del Hoyo et al., 2016). Though the jury may still be out on whether adaptive deficits can predict dementia in Down syndrome, adaptive behavior appears to be vulnerable in these adults. Moreover, the well-documented symptoms of depression are of concern, as are the associations between depression and poorer adaptive skills, which raises the question as to whether adaptive deficits in Down syndrome are more related to the psychiatric and medical comorbidities than to the disorder itself (Määttä, Tervo-Määttä, Taanila, Kaski, & Iivanainen, 2006). This highlights the need for improved mental health management in these adults.

CAUTION

Significant adaptive deficits observed in individuals with Down syndrome may be related more to comorbid conditions such as depression and dementia than to the disorder itself.

Fragile X Syndrome

In fragile X syndrome, adaptive skills have been found to increase in adolescence and then stabilize into adulthood (Smith, Hong, Greenberg, & Mailick, 2016). Family environment factors play a role in outcome in that high levels of warmth and low levels of criticism are associated with higher adaptive abilities. Recent research has also been investigating sex differences in adults with fragile X syndrome, noting that independent living in males is associated with stronger adaptive personal, domestic, and communication skills, whereas age and interpersonal skills are more predictive of independent living in females (Hartley et al., 2011).

Similar to what is observed in adults with autism spectrum disorder (ASD—see following section), very few adults with fragile X syndrome end up living independently—as few as only 10% (Hartley et al., 2011). The behavioral and medical challenges become extremely burdensome to the individuals, as well as to parents and caregivers, with lifetime costs for males with fragile X syndrome approaching $1 million and for females over $500,000 (Chevreul et al., 2016). Additionally, if significant behavioral problems are present, there can also be higher levels of parental stress, anxiety, and depression (Bailey et al., 2012; Chevreul et al., 2016). Adaptive skills then become all the more critical to foster in children with fragile X syndrome so that they can grow to be more functional and independent adults.

DON'T FORGET

Frequently, in adults with various genetic disorders, their adaptive deficits change over time and can hamper their ability to be independent adults. As such, monitoring these skills throughout the life span is essential.

Williams Syndrome

As noted in Chapter 4, cognitive functioning in Williams syndrome is relatively stable from childhood to adulthood, whereas adaptive behavior trajectories are more variable depending on the research. One of the most recent studies found decreasing scores in adaptive communication and daily living skills, and a trend for a decrease in socialization skills (Fisher, Lense, & Dykens, 2016). The decrease in standard scores, however, was assumed to be a plateau in the acquisition of new adaptive skills rather than a regression or loss of previously acquired skills. Although there may not be a well-defined adaptive behavior profile in adults with Williams syndrome, the observed delays in cognition and adaptive behavior should be monitored and treated over time.

ADAPTIVE BEHAVIOR PROFILES IN ADULTS WITH AUTISM SPECTRUM DISORDER

In contrast to the relative dearth of research on adaptive behavior in adults with many other disabilities, there is actually a great deal of research of adaptive behavior in adults with autism spectrum disorder (ASD). Although the majority of research on adaptive functioning in ASD to date has studied children, studies on adults with ASD are showing that adaptive deficits extend into adulthood and often substantially impede independent functioning. Unfortunately, services for adults with autism—especially those who do not meet eligibility criteria for ID—often do not appropriately address health, vocational, residential, and community needs (Shattuck, Wagner, Narendorf, Sterzing, & Hensley, 2011). Medical costs are significantly higher for adults compared to children with ASD, as are emergency room visits, and adults with ASD do not feel that they have effective communication with their primary care physicians about their physical or mental health needs (Buescher, Cidav, Knapp, & Mandell, 2014; Mandell, 2013). Recent estimates of the lifetime financial burdens associated with ASD reach as high as $2 to $3 million, with higher costs for more cognitively impaired individuals (Buescher et al., 2014; Ganz, 2007; Howlin, Moss, Savage, & Rutter, 2013).

DON'T FORGET

Adaptive behavior is often a better predictor of optimal outcome for adults with ASD than intact cognition and language alone.

One of the greatest barriers to positive outcomes in adulthood is limited practical and independent life skills. As with school-age children, adults with ASD exhibit significant deficits in adaptive skills compared to chronological age and IQ (Kraper, Kenworthy, Popal, Martin, & Wallace, 2017; Matson, Rivet, Fodstad, Dempsey, & Boisjoli, 2009; Matthews et al., 2015). Deficits in all areas of adaptive functioning have been found in adults with ASD despite having average cognition, with adaptive socialization scores typically being the most delayed (Kraper et al., 2017; Matthews et al., 2015). Studies that have examined subdomain scores of, for instance, the Vineland Adaptive Behavior Scales domains, found written skills to be the highest area of ability, whereas interpersonal skills were the lowest (Matthews et al., 2015). The high written score is likely due to the affinity for numbers, letters, reading, and writing that is often observed in ASD, even in childhood. That is, regardless of IQ, adaptive written or rote visual skills tend to be areas of relative strength.

The significant discrepancy between cognition and adaptive behavior has also been observed in adults with ASD (Kraper et al., 2017). Of primary concern is that the greater this gap, the greater the likelihood of comorbid psychopathology, such as anxiety and depression. Although there is an observed gap between cognition and adaptive behavior in older versus younger individuals, this does not necessarily indicate that individuals are regressing or losing previously acquired adaptive skills but rather their gains are not keeping pace with chronological development. Individuals with ASD often acquire new adaptive skills over time, just at a slower rate than their cognitive development.

Some studies, however, do show a plateau in adaptive development in adulthood (e.g., Kraper et al., 2017). Longitudinal studies can shed light on what factors might influence stronger rates of gain. For instance, a 10-year study following 152 children from age 5 to 15 found that although children improved in their adaptive social and communicative functioning, gains were preserved primarily for those without cognitive impairment (Baghdadli et al., 2012). Poorer progress was noted in children with low cognitive and language skills, those with seizures, and those with high levels of autism symptomatology. Similarly, in a longitudinal study by Farley and colleagues (2009), a sample of 41 individuals with ASD was followed from age 7 to 32 years. Although IQ was associated with positive social functioning at outcome, all Vineland scores—but particular Daily Living skills—had the strongest correlations with social functioning. In fact, individuals with higher cognition that had lower Daily Living skills failed to achieve as good an outcome due to those limited practical skills. This was one of the first studies to highlight the importance of adaptive skills instruction in intervention programs during early development in order to foster independence into adulthood.

Research also shows that independent employment, living, and relationships are problematic for adults with ASD (Billstedt, Gillberg, Gillberg, & Gillberg, 2005; Eaves & Ho, 2008; Howlin, Goode, Hutton, & Rutter, 2004). As early as 1985, a study by Rumsey, Rapoport, and Sceery (1985) revealed that 14 adult men with autism without cognitive impairment fared worse in vocational adjustment and independent living when their adaptive socialization scores were a relative weakness (Rumsey et al., 1985). Seminal studies conducted by Howlin and colleagues (2004, 2013) followed adults with autism who were diagnosed as having average nonverbal intelligence as children over 20 years of adulthood. They defined successful outcome by levels of vocational success, independent living, and positive social relationships. During the first study, only 24% of adults with ASD and average intelligence fell within the "good/very good" outcome range (Howlin et al., 2004). Twenty years later, only 18% of these adults had this high level of outcome, suggesting that independence was deteriorating with age (Howlin et al., 2013).

Oftentimes, it is not solely adaptive behavior, cognition, or severity of autism symptomatology that impedes functional independence but also the many comorbid challenges that adults with ASD can face, such as anxiety, depression, ADHD, and psychotic features in some cases (Hofvander et al., 2009; Saulnier & Klin, 2007). One study examined severity of adaptive and cognitive deficits in adults with ASD in comparison to adults with ID without ASD and to adults with ASD with comorbid Axis 1 psychopathology (Matson et al., 2009). They found that the most severe deficits were in the group of adults with ASD and psychopathology, followed by adults with ASD and ID. Those adults with ID without comorbidity had the strongest adaptive skills. Farley et al. (2009) also noted a subsample of participants with high IQ and high practical skills that still failed to be independent given significant levels of anxiety—raising yet another confounding factor to successful outcome. Consequently, adults with ASD receiving vocational rehabilitation services are likely to be rejected services due to the severity of their disability (Lawer, Brusilovskiy, Salzer, & Mandell, 2009). When they are fortunate enough to obtain services, the cost of the needed services is often prohibitive (Cimera & Cowan, 2009; Lawer et al., 2009).

CAUTION

Comorbid psychopathology—especially anxiety and depression but even some psychotic features—can significantly affect individuals with ASD and their ability to function independently in adulthood, even if they have intact cognition and strong practical skills.

To summarize, adults with ASD are not buffered by their high IQ. Having strong cognitive skills is not sufficient for achieving levels of independence into adulthood in the absence of direct instruction to foster practical and functional skills. Moreover, poorer adaptive functioning regardless of cognition puts adults at risk for a host of comorbid conditions, including anxiety, depression, ADHD, and even psychosis. Yet, many educational programs fail to provide even the mandated services for preparing for adulthood (e.g., Landmark & Zhang, 2013), let alone the dearth of services actually afforded to these individuals once they enter into adulthood. Therefore, awareness needs to be raised about the impact of limited functional skills on adult outcome in ASD, or we are going to fail to actualize on the great potential that adults with autism have to offer in every community.

ADULTS WITH LANGUAGE IMPAIRMENTS

Though many early speech and language delays resolve themselves during childhood, there are certainly language impairments that sustain through adulthood. Psychosocial outcomes were studied in adults with specific language impairment (SLI), pragmatic language impairment (PLI), and ASD (Whitehouse, Watt,

Line, & Bishop, 2009). The PLI sample fared the best, obtaining higher levels of education and being employed in skilled professions. Adults with SLI required vocational training and jobs that did not have heavy language expectations. However, the PLI and SLI groups fared better than adults with ASD. With the sheer number of alternative and augmentative communication strategies and devices available in this day and age, even those adults who are minimally or nonverbal should be afforded alternative means for expressing themselves.

ASSESSMENT FOR INTELLECTUAL DISABILITY IN PRISONERS

The inclusion of prisoners in this chapter is of importance given the need for determining whether or not someone who is incarcerated also has ID. This issue became particularly controversial after the United States Supreme Court ruled in *Atkins v. Virginia* (2002) that it is unconstitutional to execute individuals with ID. Therefore, appropriate assessment of IQ and adaptive functioning in prisoners is critical.

Unlike IQ, which can be directly assessed with the individual, the assessment of a prisoner's adaptive behavior can be quite challenging if an appropriate third-party respondent is not available who can provide accurate information on a prisoner's current adaptive skills (McBrien, 2003). Depending on the length of incarceration, close family members or friends might not be knowledgeable of the individual's current behavioral performance, if these sources exist at all. In many cases, this leaves correctional staff members as the designated respondents. However, most measures of adaptive functioning reflect behaviors expected of individuals living in the community (e.g., shopping, driving or traveling, making medical appointments, etc.) rather than those behaviors relevant to a prison environment. It is then a point of debate if one can infer functioning in the community from functioning in the highly restricted and structured environment of a prison (Macvaugh & Cunningham, 2009; Stevens & Price, 2006; Widaman & Siperstein, 2009). Even if a prisoner can perform a particular behavior in the highly structured setting, it is not necessarily the case that he or she can also perform the same task in a more dynamic and complex environment in the real world.

CAUTION

One of the major challenges to assessing adaptive behavior in prisoners is finding an appropriate third-party respondent.

There can also be ulterior motives for presenting information in a particular light in that a respondent can report that individuals perform either better or worse than they do in actuality to make their case. For example, if arguing that an individual should be deemed incompetent to stand trial, it might be worth a respondent underreporting the individual's true adaptive skills. Conversely, if a respondent is motivated to show that an individual can be self-sufficient on release from prison, there might be an overrepresentation of the individual's true skill base.

This phenomenon is not limited to respondents who are either family members or friends of the prisoner. There is controversy surrounding biases in correctional officers, as well. Despite correctional officers having knowledge about a prisoner's current functioning, the officers might have biases such as pro-prosecution (i.e., biases based on the prisoner's history) or they may never have observed the prisoner in a community setting (Olley & Cox, 2008). One study directly compared responses on the Adaptive Behavior Assessment System, Second Edition (ABAS-2) between correctional officers and other respondents (Boccaccini et al., 2016). In their study, they found large discrepancies between informants with correctional staff members rating prisoners particularly low. Interestingly, none of the officers indicated that they guessed on various responses despite not having had direct knowledge of, for example, true community living skills. Consequently, forensic experts have been concerned about the reliability of correctional officers' reporting of adaptive behavior.

CAUTION

When using correctional officers as the informant for adaptive behavior in a prisoner, be cautious of pro-prosecution bias (i.e., biases based on the prisoner's history rather than true adaptive performance).

There is some evidence to suggest that self-report administration of some of the measures of adaptive behavior may be reliable, thus eliminating the need for a third-party respondent (Sparrow, Cicchetti, & Balla, 2005; Voelker et al., 1990). However, in a study using self-report of adaptive behavior (Herrington, 2009), none of the prisoners assessed had adaptive behavior composites below 69 despite just over 10% having an overall IQ of less than 69. The mean overall adaptive behavior composite in their sample was 10 points below the standardized norm of 100; however, on average, the prisoners performed better on their adaptive behavior skills than would be predicted given their cognitive functioning.

In looking at subscale scores, prisoners showed the greatest weakness on the Daily Living Skills domain. Average mean Daily Living Skills were 86.3, compared to Communication scores of 93.2 and Socialization scores of 97.7. Even in those with lower IQ, the same adaptive behavior profile remained. This suggests that prisoner self-report administration may inflate true adaptive abilities.

Malingering or intentional exaggeration of "symptoms" can also be a factor in self-reporting. Research on forensic cases has shown that when a prisoner, for example, is coached (e.g., by family, friends, attorneys, etc.), the prisoner can present as having a disability such as ID when, in fact, this is not the case (Feldstein, Durham, Keller, Kelebe, & Davis, 2000). The measure used could help disentangle false reporting. One study examined two measures of adaptive behavior to compare malingering effects: the Adaptive Behavior Assessment System, Second Edition (ABAS-II) and the Scales of Independent Behavior, Revised (SIB-R) (Doane & Salekin, 2009). Results favored the SIB-R in detecting intentional malingering, whereas the ABAS-II was found to be susceptible to believable malingering—that is, independent raters could not distinguish true cases of ID based on ABAS-II ratings alone.

CAUTION

If resorting to self-report measures of adaptive functioning when assessing for ID in prisoners, be cautious of potential malingering, exaggeration of symptoms, or minimization of symptoms in an attempt to manipulate the results.

Given these aforementioned challenges in assessing adaptive behavior in prisoners, there is ongoing debate as to the prevalence of ID in incarcerated individuals (Hellenbach, Karatzias, & Brown, 2017; Olley & Cox, 2008). One survey conducted on nearly 12,000 prisoners across four different countries estimated the prevalence of ID in prisoners to be between .5% and 1.5% (Fazel, Xenitidis, & Powell, 2008). Few prisoners, however, seem to fall in the moderate or severe range of ID. Rather, most show mild or borderline deficits, making the diagnosis of ID all the more challenging (Brooke, Taylor, Gunn, & Maden, 1996; Gunn, Maden, & Swinton, 1991).

Taken collectively, these extreme limitations in the accurate assessment of cognition and adaptive behavior in prisoners raise many concerns regarding the outcome of incarcerated individuals with ID. More likely than not, hundreds of thousands of individuals will fail to receive appropriate intervention and rehabilitation services that will enable release from prison and prevention of future re-incarceration.

THE RELATIONSHIP BETWEEN ADAPTIVE BEHAVIOR AND RESIDENTIAL AND VOCATIONAL SUCCESS

Given the historical pairing of cognitive impairment with adaptive deficits for a diagnosis of ID, fostering adaptive living skills is essential to successful residential placement. An individual's lack of independent functioning typically results in the need for more intensive supports across residential, vocational, and community care. Moreover, adults with ID with poorer adaptive skills are more likely to live with relatives or in nursing homes compared to partial or fully independent community settings (Heller, Miller, & Hsieh, 2002; Woodman et al., 2014). To the contrary, adults with stronger adaptive skills—even those with moderate ID—are more likely to be independent at home and at work (Woolf, Woolf, & Oakland, 2010). Thus, for individuals with ID, adaptive behavior is one of the largest predictors of successful residential placement and employment (Su, Lin, Wu, & Chen, 2008; Woodman et al., 2014; Woolf et al., 2010) and is actually a better predictor of positive outcome than cognition alone, especially for vocational success (Soenen, Van Berckelaer-Onnes, & Scholte, 2009).

Additional factors other than adaptive behavior certainly play a role in successful residential placement. These include family support and involvement, income, and emotional stability, as well as the presence of strong social networks (Woodman et al., 2014). An adult with ID, for instance, who experiences high family conflict, has lower family income, or who has limited adult relationships, is more likely to experience multiple residential transitions, resulting in less stability in life. Longitudinal research has also shown adaptive skills to be stronger at follow-up when adults with disabilities are provided with opportunities to make choices in their living environment and when the environment is physically attractive (Heller et al., 2002).

DON'T FORGET

Factors that are associated with successful residential placement include family support and involvement and having a higher income, better emotional stability, and strong social networks.

Comorbid psychopathology is another major factor that impedes good outcomes in adults with neurodevelopmental disorders. Research is extremely varied on the prevalence of psychopathologies in ID, likely due in part to the type of comorbidity (e.g., anxiety, depression, ADHD, psychosis, disruptive behavior disorders, substance abuse, epilepsy, etc.). However, the negative impact of psychopathology on adaptive functioning is clear (Matson et al., 2009; Smith & Matson, 2010). Identifying the various influences on adaptive behavior, and when these factors come into play, is of utmost importance for optimizing adult outcome.

For school-age children with disabilities, the Individuals with Disabilities Education Act (IDEA 2004) states that the needs of the child must demonstrate an inability or impairment to access the general curriculum, which incorporates social and adaptive functioning in addition to academic. In this regard, adaptive functioning can be part of an intervention program (i.e., with goals and objectives on the individualized education program) on eligibility for services. Unfortunately, this is not often the case. In fact, many school programs begin to consider addressing adaptive skills only when planning for the transition out of the educational system into the "real world," whether this be into postsecondary education, the workforce, or community living. The IDEA stipulates that transition planning must begin before the student turns 16, but this is far too late to begin teaching practical, real-life skills. Opportunities to foster functional skills really need to start *at diagnosis of the disability.*

DON'T FORGET

Adaptive skills should be explicitly taught and part of any treatment or intervention programming on diagnosis of the disability!

Focusing on the acquisition and advancement of adaptive behavior in an educational program does not need to be at the detriment of academic focus. However, depending on the financial climate of a school district, nonacademic courses that focus on basic skills instruction can often be cut in favor of those that are required for graduation. It can then become a struggle for families and school providers to weigh the pros and cons of choosing highly modified or nonacademic courses in favor of those requisites needed for graduation (Bateman, 1995), which is all the more reason that practical skills should be taught early on and embedded throughout academic programming. The IDEA does suggest using an individual's strengths and interests to cultivate adaptive and vocational skills. However, in ASD, the presence of circumscribed and perseverative behaviors can often interfere with social and daily functioning if they are all-consuming. Therefore, when using these intense interests as a potential vocational skill, it is important to consider intervention strategies to ensure that the individual with ASD can be easily redirected from fixations as needed and that the negative impact of their intrusive interests does not outweigh the benefits of honing an area of strength.

CAUTION

Although the IDEA suggests using an individual's interests and areas of strength to cultivate vocational skills, the circumscribed and perseverative interests in some adults with ASD may become all-consuming and interfere with the adult's ability to successfully perform the job or navigate the workplace.

SUMMARY

In summary, adaptive deficits persist into adulthood across most disabilities, regardless of cognitive impairment. Moreover, adaptive deficits are often associated with poorer outcome in residential and vocational placements, and they can be negatively affected by social, emotional, and behavioral challenges. Available jobs and housing are limited, as are treatment and intervention services. In addition, access to health care professionals who have a good understanding of the needs of adults with disabilities is extremely variable. These sobering statistics elucidate the innumerable challenges that parents, caregivers, family members, and adults with disabilities themselves endure throughout the life span. If there is any take-home message here, it is to embed functional, practical skills into every aspect of an individual's life as early as vulnerabilities are identified.

🪶 TEST YOURSELF 🪶

1. **What is the most common comorbid psychiatric disorder that adults with ID also suffer from?**
   a. Anxiety
   b. Depression
   c. Bipolar disorder
   d. Schizophrenia
2. **True or false? Third-party respondents are more likely to endorse more affective and cognitive depressive symptoms of individuals with ID than the individual themselves.**
3. **True or false? In addition to typical depressive symptomatology, adults with ID can also display depression symptoms including aggression, regression of skills, and behavior disruption.**

4. **Name three risk factors for obesity in adults with ID.**

5. **True or false? Family environmental factors do not play a role in outcome in individuals with fragile X syndrome.**

6. **What is the best predictor of optimal outcome for adults with ASD?**

   a. Language
   b. Cognition
   c. Motor abilities
   d. Adaptive behavior

7. **Which subdomain on the Vineland Adaptive Behavior Scales was the highest and lowest respectively for adults with ASD?**

   a. Interpersonal; Fine Motor
   b. Interpersonal; Written
   c. Written; Interpersonal
   d. Written; Receptive Language

8. **What is a major barrier of assessing adaptive behaviors in prisoners?**

   a. Finding an appropriate third-party respondent
   b. Biases in correctional officers
   c. Ulterior motives from respondent
   d. All of the above

9. **Name three of the factors that are associated with successful residential placement.**

10. **When should teaching adaptive skills become part of an individual's treatment or intervention plan?**

    a. At diagnosis of disability
    b. When the individual turns 16
    c. When the individual moves into his or her own home
    d. At the first job placement

Answers: (1) b; (2) False. Individuals with ID are more likely to endorse more affective and cognitive depressive symptoms than third-party respondents; (3) True; (4) Possible answers include being female, having milder cognitive deficits, having Down syndrome, being older in age, consuming antipsychotic medications, lacking physical exercise, living in less-restricted environments; (5) False. Family environmental factors do play a role in outcome in that high levels of warmth and low levels or criticism are associated with higher adaptive skills; (6) d; (7) c; (8) d; (9) Possible answers include family support and involvement, having a higher income, having better emotional stability, and having strong social networks; (10) a.

Eight

THE ROLE OF ADAPTIVE BEHAVIOR IN TREATMENT AND INTERVENTION

The previous chapters in this book highlight the overwhelming evidence that having limited practical, "real-life" skills impedes an individual's ability to be independent in everyday activities throughout the life span. The primary consideration for treatment therefore should be the development of skills needed to promote age-appropriate independence to meet life's demands. These skills are, by nature, modifiable; therefore, they are perfect targets for treatment—all the more reason that home, school, and early intervention programs need to focus on adaptive behavior skills as early as possible, beginning at diagnosis or detection of vulnerabilities.

DON'T FORGET
Because adaptive behavior is modifiable, these skills are perfect targets for treatment and intervention programs.

Within the educational system, goals and objectives for adaptive behavior intervention are typically included in an individualized education program (IEP) for children with the most severe disabilities (or in the individualized family service plan [IFSP] prior to age 3). But oftentimes, particularly when children's academic or developmental skills are on par with their grade level, adaptive behavior is either not addressed or not adequately addressed, even when there are significant delays or deficits in adaptive functioning. This could be the case because children without cognitive impairments who are integrated into mainstream classrooms are either faring well academically, despite their adaptive delays (and therefore do not receive eligibility and any services) or their intervention is targeted to areas specific to their disability. It has been emphasized throughout this book that far too many individuals with neurodevelopmental disorders are not achieving levels of independence into adulthood in the areas of work, residential placement, community involvement, self-care, and social competency—even those with the cognitive capacity to do so. This calls to action the urgency for including targeted interventions for adaptive functioning at every level of development.

FACTORS TO CONSIDER IN DEVELOPING AN INTERVENTION PLAN

When developing treatment goals for adaptive behavior deficits, it is important to consider the individual's age, disability, gender, grade, cultural expectations, and community standards. The hierarchy of behaviors to address should be selected, agreed on, and executed by all individuals working and caring for the individual. Consistency of approach across people and contexts will more likely result in a successful intervention, as will addressing adaptive behaviors as they occur naturally. For instance, fine motor impairments not only impede an individual's ability to perform fine-motor tasks, such as writing, cutting, and so on, they also negatively affect adaptive daily living skills such as dressing, grooming, and eating. However, occupational therapy that typically addresses fine-motor delays is often given the least amount of focus in intervention programs—perhaps only once or twice a month for some individuals with significant disabilities. This is not sufficient intensity to address adaptive behaviors that are demanded daily. Thus, the recommendation should be that these skills are addressed throughout the individual's day by all teachers, professionals, and caregivers working with the individual.

DON'T FORGET

Treatment of adaptive behaviors should be embedded into naturally occurring contexts and routines and should be addressed by everyone working with the individual so as to ensure consistency of approach.

Another consideration when developing a treatment plan is the extent that the environment is contributing to the adaptive deficit. Oftentimes, the significant impairments that come with respective disabilities are prioritized by caregivers and families. Parents, for example, may understandably do more for their child with a disability than they might for a typically developing child, such as dressing, feeding, bathing, and cleaning up after them given that the demands of the disability require their efforts in other ways. Treatment in this case should begin with parent training and awareness before directly intervening with the individual—otherwise, treatment efforts could be futile after the individual returns home. The environment in which the skill needs to be performed also should be considered so that intervention can ensure that the behavior can be practiced and reinforced. This is especially important for daily life skills that tend to occur outside of the school environment (e.g., bathing, conducting household chores, shopping and managing money, and so forth). Special education programs are increasingly creating experiential facilities to learn and practice real-life skills, such as kitchens, laundry rooms, fully equipped bathrooms, and even stores and restaurants, because being taught these skills in a didactic manner rarely generalizes to naturalistic settings.

CAUTION

Never assume that intervention for adaptive deficits should only be conducted with the individual with a disability. Environmental factors always need to be considered and assessed and then appropriately addressed when present.

Cultural and socioeconomic factors are also imperative to consider when developing a treatment plan. This begins with confirmation that these factors were also considered during the evaluation that identified adaptive delays. If, for example, a Latino child whose primary language in the home is Spanish was identified as having intellectual disability (ID) based on standardized measures of IQ and adaptive behavior that were normed on English-speaking children, the results should be interpreted with caution if at all. Once test results are deemed valid, the next step is to consider the home and community environments. For example, although a teacher, clinician, or evaluator might think a particular treatment strategy is indicated, the targeted behavior might not be culturally appropriate or accepted, or there might not be available resources in the environment to access the treatment. For this reason, family members should always be included in the discussions regarding treatment programming.

DON'T FORGET

Family members and caregivers should be included in discussions regarding treatment programming.

IDENTIFYING ADAPTIVE BEHAVIORS TO TARGET IN INTERVENTION

The first step in determining target areas for intervention is to conduct the appropriate measure of adaptive behavior (see Chapter 3) in order to identify delays or deficits. Recommendations for treatment and intervention can be derived from the general adaptive areas denoted in broad domain standard scores, from specific adaptive areas denoted in subdomain scaled scores and most importantly from individual items within a given measure. These items link to explicit behaviors that can be directly translated into recommendations for early intervention, educational, vocational, residential, or community programming based on skills that the individual should be demonstrating but is not.

Most standardized measures now include automated intervention reports within their respective computerized scoring programs that will generate these targeted areas for treatment. For instance, the Vineland Adaptive Behavior Scales, Third Edition (Vineland-3) has an Intervention Guidance that identifies clusters of behaviors by topic area (e.g., pre-reading skills; toileting skills) based on low-performing scores. The Adaptive Behavior Assessment System, Third Edition (ABAS-3) similarly has an Intervention Planner that generates recommendations based on item ratings. Even in the absence of using these programs, examiners can analyze scoring profiles to identify behaviors that are most salient to the individual's needs. Commercial resources are even available that offer specific suggestions in terms of goals and objectives that can be directly used in report recommendations or IEP development. For example, the Adaptive Behavior Intervention Manuals 4–12 Years (McCarney, McCain, & Bauer, 2006a) and 13–18 Years (McCarney, McCain, & Bauer, 2006b) were specifically developed to offer treatment suggestions for the most common adaptive behavior deficits identified by educators. These manuals focus on goals, objectives, and interventions for 55 adaptive behavior problems. These types of interventions can then be used to help write IEP goals. Though these were developed in conjunction with the Adaptive Behavior Evaluation Scales, the strategies can be used independent of the standardized measure.

Once a profile of strengths and weaknesses is obtained, priorities can be set with regards to structuring the intervention. As a general ballpark, in each area where the individual scored one standard deviation or more below the mean, the specific items should be examined to determine which ones constitute primary concerns across the various environments (e.g., home, school, work, community). Parents, caregivers, teachers, interventionists, vocational trainers, and so on are encouraged to work together to prioritize adaptive behaviors that are most critical to address—and only a few at a time. For many individuals with significant disabilities, the list of behaviors that are automatically generated from computerized reports can be overwhelming, and addressing too many behaviors simultaneously will likely not be beneficial.

CAUTION

Only a few adaptive behaviors should be addressed simultaneously. Attempting to target the entire list of behaviors that are delayed will likely not result in any progress. Less is more! Additional behaviors can always be added to the intervention program on acquisition and mastery of skills.

Progress monitoring is another way to identify target areas for intervention for individuals that are followed over time. Again, many standardized measures have automated metrics for tracking change across multiple administrations of the same measure. Change over time can be evaluated at the global, domain, subdomain, and even item level in order to identify specific behaviors that have been acquired or lost during the course of intervention. Item-level analysis is particularly important because observations of standard score change over time does not necessarily inform whether or not gains or losses have occurred. For instance, an individual's standard scores can decrease over the course of a year, but the individual still could have made gains in adaptive behavior—just not at the pace commensurate with chronological development. Some measures offer growth scale values (GSVs; e.g., Vineland-3) that provide a metric for tracking performance across test administrations. GSVs increase or decrease along with raw scores and offer an indication of absolute change.

CAUTION

Changes in standard scores over time do not necessarily indicate regression or loss of skills! An individual can still be acquiring new skills over time but at a slower pace than expected based on chronological age. Therefore, analyzing changes in growth scale values (GSVs) or age-equivalent scores can better determine true progress.

Defining how data will be collected is also important to the development of a treatment plan. If an adaptive skill is defined too broadly in an IEP, it cannot be measured and, consequently, this can be detrimental to the individual with the disability and to all treatment providers. Take, for example, a case in which an individual failed to receive credit for conversation items. The intervention team decides that this is a priority for intervention so the following goal is developed for his IEP: "Johnny will improve his conversational skills." This is unlikely to result in any progress because the goal is too broadly defined to be accurately measurable and it is not time-delineated. A better goal would be, "Johnny will initiate a conversation with his peers twice per day every day," because this behavior can be observed and monitored for progress. If progress is not made within several months, then the goal should be reevaluated and possibly modified. A red flag for any intervention program should be when an IEP does not show any progress made over an extended period of time—especially when goals are carried over multiple years. Every individual—regardless of disability—is capable of learning when intervention is appropriately targeted to his or her level of functioning.

CAUTION

A red flag for any treatment program is lack of progress over an extended period of time. This suggests that the targets or metrics need to be modified so as to facilitate progress. Every individual is capable of making gains in adaptive behavior!

Mastery of a skill also needs to be explicitly defined. For instance, what is the frequency of the targeted behavior at baseline? If the behavior is performed *sometimes,* under what circumstances is it successfully performed versus not, and what is the ultimate goal of success—100% or somewhat less? The goal for toileting, for example, is often 100%. Talking without interrupting, however, may be a lower percentage (e.g., 80%) dependent on the hierarchy of needs of the individual. Once frequency is determined, the team can then define the metrics for mastery across time, people, and contexts. For example, "Johnny will initiate a conversation with his peers twice per day every day for 5 consecutive days with three different people across three different contexts."

DON'T FORGET

Adaptive skills to target in intervention need to be explicitly defined, measurable, and time-delineated.

Finally, a good rule of thumb when determining which behaviors to target in intervention is to identify those behaviors that will be meaningful to and functional for the individual's life.

To ensure a behavior is meaningful, teach adaptive skills in the context that they will be naturally applied, using already learned vocabulary, and having a hands-on component or highly familiar context such as pictures of the individual's actual environment. Individuals are more likely to learn and retain a skill that is highly meaningful, salient, or rewarding to them. Examples can include teaching number concepts with actual materials (i.e., rather than paper and pencil), fractions with cooking, and counting change when in a store purchasing a preferred item (Dykens, Hodapp, & Finucane, 2000).

DON'T FORGET

When prioritizing skills to teach, focus on ones that use an individual's strengths and are important to an individual's daily routines.

When prioritizing skills to explicitly teach, focus also on those skills that will be functional to the individual's daily routines. Take, for instance, a child with Williams syndrome with significant fine-motor and graphomotor weaknesses. Rather than focusing on printing and writing skills, a more functional (and ultimately successful) approach would be to facilitate use of computers and other keyboarding skills, calculators, and audio taping to help individuals show his or her true capabilities. Similarly, when transitioning an adolescent or adult into the workplace, focus on skills that will be required on the job, including social communication and interaction skills in addition to vocational skills.

≡ Rapid Reference 8.1

Steps to consider when identifying target adaptive behaviors for intervention:

- Conduct an appropriate measure of adaptive behavior.
- Analyze profiles of strengths and weaknesses to see what is affecting the child the most.
- Work with parents, caregivers, teachers, interventionists, vocational trainers, and so on to prioritize the most-critical adaptive behaviors.
- Monitor progress and determine if intervention is working or needs to be tweaked.
- Define how the behavior is going to be measurable, time-delineated, and mastered.
- Ensure the behavior is meaningful and functional.

EVIDENCED-BASED PRACTICES FOR TREATING ADAPTIVE BEHAVIOR

Though adaptive behavior assessments are now considered standard practice in diagnostic evaluations for many neurodevelopmental disorders, they are far less used as outcome measures to examine the efficacy of treatment and intervention methods. When intervention studies have done so, the evidence is positive in that individuals are able to acquire new functional skills with targeted treatment even if gains are not at the rate expected by chronological development.

Treatment research on adaptive behavior has historically focused on specific adaptive skills, such as daily living or practical skills needed within vocational or residential placements, for individuals with ID. For instance, interventions have proven to be successful in teaching a range of tasks including, but not limited to, appropriate mealtime behaviors (O'Brien, Bugle, & Azrin, 1972; Wilson, Reid, Phillips, & Burgio, 1984), pedestrian safety (Page, Iwata, & Neef, 1976), independent walking (Gruber, Reeser, & Reid, 1979), purchasing skills and ordering meals in restaurants (Haring, Kennedy, Adams, & Pitts-Conway, 1987), and money concepts such as counting change (Lowe & Cuvo, 1976; Miller, Cuvo, & Borakove, 1977).

However, as adaptive behavior has become more of a focus on outcome for individuals with neurodevelopmental disorders, research has expanded to include a wide range of skills assessed across a multitude of intervention methods. In the next sections we provide an overview of specific methodologies as well as current research on the efficacy of addressing certain adaptive behaviors across disabilities. Yet, we need to caution that there is no one method that applies to treating adaptive behavior more generally. Rather, all intervention for individuals with developmental disabilities should be individualized based on the specific needs of the person.

DON'T FORGET

When designing intervention programs and determining methodology for teaching, there is no one method that works for everyone. It is imperative that interventions are designed and individualized based on the specific needs of the individual you are working with.

Applied Behavior Analysis (ABA)

Applied behavior analysis (ABA) is a treatment methodology that can be extremely helpful in teaching adaptive behavior skills. ABA is based on principles of operant conditioning in which behaviors can be shaped and taught through repetition and reinforcement. Once skill deficits are identified, a task analysis can be conducted to break down complex tasks into smaller components (Haring & Kennedy, 1988). The behavior can then be shaped into its full form by reinforcing approximations of the behavior until the full behavior is produced. Chaining, similar to shaping, is a process in ABA that helps to determine which tasks to teach first and then how to link the steps together to have the individual complete the entire sequence of events leading to a particular task. Use of reinforcers is often helpful to teach skills that an individual does not have internal motivation to complete independently—with the goal that through familiarity and mastery, intrinsic motivation will be established.

A great deal of intervention research that has addressed adaptive behavior has been conducted using principles of ABA, and because ABA is one of the evidenced-based treatments for autism spectrum disorder (ASD), the majority of research in this regard has been in the field of ASD. Some of the earliest studies involved discrete trial therapy (DTT), a form of ABA that focuses on skill acquisition using repetition in one-to-one or small-group instruction, and found DTT to be effective in improving IQ and adaptive skills (e.g., Lovaas, 1981; McEachin, Smith, & Lovaas, 1993). As the focus of intervention broadened to include very young children with ASD, studies began to focus on early intensive behavioral interventions (EIBIs). In one study on preschoolers with ASD who underwent EIBI, gains in adaptive daily living skills as measured by the Vineland were stronger for the EIBI sample compared to a control sample. Although standard scores actually decreased over time, suggesting a slowed rate of acquisition, gains were still made (Magiati, Charman, & Howlin, 2007).

Optimal outcomes studies, or studies on children with ASD who were diagnosed as toddlers but later lost their diagnosis due to very limited or no residual symptomatology, have reported that many of the children who obtained this optimal outcome had received early behavioral treatments (Fein et al., 2013; Sutera et al., 2007). In addition to losing their autism symptomatology, many of the children in these studies had cognitive and adaptive skills in the average range. Though it has been well established in ASD that cognition alone does not predict optimal outcome, it is very promising that these children had acquired age-appropriate adaptive skills that they were independently applying to their daily lives. Moreover, they were fully integrated into mainstream classrooms with their same-aged peers. Future research is certainly needed to follow up with these children as they reach adulthood to see if, in fact, these skills were sustained over time.

Gains in adaptive skills have also been observed in treatments using ABA methods in conjunction with medication to target problem behaviors in ASD.

In a clinical trial comparing the use of Risperidone or a manualized parent training program to address serious behavioral problems in children with ASD ages 4 to 13 years, both treatments resulted in improved adaptive socialization and overall Vineland Adaptive Behavior Composite scores, though the greatest improvement was observed when both treatments were combined for a duration of 24 weeks (Scahill et al., 2012). When the same manualized parent training protocol was downward-extended to preschool-age children with ASD and behavioral problems, gains in adaptive daily living skills on the Vineland were observed even in the absence of medication (Scahill et al., 2016). In the latter study, one module of the 16-week protocol actually targeted adaptive behavior, which highlights that if adaptive skills are directly addressed within an intervention program, gains can be observed even within as short a time frame as 4 months.

DON'T FORGET

When adaptive behavior skills are targeted in intervention programs improvements can be seen in as little as 4 months!

Some of the major criticisms of early research on ABA techniques have included the intensity of intervention required to show efficacy as well as limited generalizability and maintenance of skills learned (Koegel, 1995). For this reason, training parents to implement the strategies has been incorporated into many programs to maximize intensity as well as address generalizability. A comprehensive review of parent training methods within ABA programs for treating children with ASD suggested that multiple formats of parent training can enhance treatment effectiveness while also being cost effective, including individualized or group training; use of manuals, curriculums, or video; and use of live instruction (Matson, Mahan, & LoVullo, 2009).

Part of what makes ABA strategies successful is the use of predictability and routine. As behaviors become second nature or automatic, it is easier for individuals to apply them as needed. In addition, individuals who are prone to anxiety in novel or unpredictable situations are more behaviorally regulated when they have clear expectations about their day. Use of visual schedules can therefore be helpful in enhancing predictability by providing visual cues (i.e., in the form of pictures, line drawings, printed words, etc.) for each activity, task, or event. In a study on adults with fragile X syndrome, for instance, the greatest vocational success was observed in programs that had a predictable routine, a slower-paced work program, and when interactions were needed with only a few people (Dykens et al., 2000). Understanding these basic principles can be extremely effective when teaching adaptive skills.

DON'T FORGET

Individuals likely learn best with structure and routine and when behaviors are well practiced. In this way, they are more automatic and can be called on more easily as life expectations demand them.

Naturalistic Developmental Behavioral Interventions (NDBIs)

Blended developmental and behavioral approaches such as naturalistic developmental behavioral interventions (NDBIs) can also be helpful in teaching adaptive skills. NDBIs are becoming increasingly more used in the field of ASD and neurodevelopmental disorders in which intervention is happening as early as the toddler years and even infancy in some cases. NDBIs allow for more child-initiated activities based on the child's interests and what is motivating to him or her (as opposed to the more adult-initiated approach of ABA). Some of the most common NDBIs are pivotal response training (PRT), which incorporates ABA techniques with the use of naturalistic reinforcers in naturalistic environments (Koegel, Koegel, Yoshen, & McNerney, 1999); incidental teaching (McGee, Morrier, & Daly, 1999), which involves systematic behavioral instruction within naturalistic contexts; Early Start Denver model (ESDM), which is a comprehensive early intervention model that blends behavioral and developmental techniques when treating toddlers (Dawson et al., 2010); joint attention, symbolic play, engagement, and regulation (JASPER), which focuses on joint attention and interactive play (Kasari, Freeman, & Paparella, 2006); and early social interaction (ESI), which is a parent coaching model for teaching transactional supports to enhance social communication skills with infants and toddlers in their naturalistic daily routines (Wetherby et al., 2014).

Research conducted on many of the NDBIs has shown improvements in adaptive functioning. Using ESDM, significant gains in adaptive and developmental skills have been found when treating preschoolers with ASD (Dawson et al., 2010), and these gains were sustained after a 2-year follow-up (Estes et al., 2015). Using ESI, which involved coaching parents to use transactional supports to keep their toddlers with ASD actively engaged during naturalistic routines and activities for at least 25 hours per week also found significant improvements in adaptive communication, socialization, and daily living skills after a 9-month treatment protocol (Wetherby et al., 2014). Given that this early intervention research is relatively new to the field, it will be important to conduct longer-term follow-up studies on these children in their teenage and adult years to see how gains in adaptive behavior were maintained over time.

Similar to ABA, one of the criticisms of well-controlled NDBI trials is that some of the interventions fail to be replicated by community-based programs and if they do, they are not financially viable. One quasi-experimental study examined the impact of an inclusive toddler program for children with ASD ages 2 to 3 over the course of 8 months (Stahmer, Akshoomoff, & Cunningham, 2011). The program used a blend of NDBIs, including PRT techniques among others, and results showed significant improvements in adaptive communication, daily living skills, and socialization skills on the Vineland on exit of the program. Increases in developmental skills were also observed. Of notable importance, 31% of the 102 children studied were functioning at age level on completion of the program.

DON'T FORGET

Although there is still work to do in achieving community and financial viability, research on NDBIs has shown promising improvements in all areas of adaptive behavior.

Social Communication Approaches

Treatment approaches that focus on enhancing social communication and interaction skills have also become very effective for enhancing adaptive behavior, as well as in reducing maladaptive or problem behaviors (National Research Council, 2001). Teaching functional communication strategies to individuals who are minimally verbal or nonverbal is also vital for behavioral regulation. When individuals cannot express themselves through speech, gestures, or other means, they will resort to expressing themselves through aberrant behaviors, including hitting, screaming, biting, aggression, self-injury, and behavioral dysregulation. In this regard, *behavior equals communication*. Using behavioral strategies to extinguish or minimize the aberrant behaviors will not be effective unless an alternative, functional communication strategy is taught and used in its place. There are numerous alternative and augmentative communication strategies to choose from that meet the needs of most individuals with speech, language, and communication challenges. These include use of sign language, gestures, voice output systems, augmentative devices, tablets, apps, and so on. The use of any alternative or augmentative strategy does not hinder the development of speech. To the contrary, increasing functional communication skills will actually help other adaptive areas such as coping, behavior regulation, and social skills.

There are an increasing number of interventions focusing on functional social communication and interaction skills, including but not limited to more contemporary ABA techniques and the NDBIs. The following strategies have been found to be effective when intervening with young children who have social communication and interaction vulnerabilities (Woods & Wetherby, 2003): (1) modifying the environment to elicit spontaneous initiations for social interaction; (2) using naturalistic reinforcers that are meaningful to the context, such as access to, or elimination of, preferred objects or activities; (3) using time delay or the withholding of a preferred item to elicit a desired response; and (4) using contingent imitation, or immediately imitating a child's actions, to promote engagement.

≡ *Rapid Reference 8.2*

In designing intervention programs for young children with social communication vulnerabilities, the following strategies have been found effective:

- Modifying the environment to elicit spontaneous initiations for social interaction
- Using naturalistic reinforcers
- Using time delay and withholding strategies
- Using contingent imitation

There is also increasing evidence in support of using peer training when treating children with neurodevelopmental disorders. Peer interventions can consist of reverse inclusion (i.e., bringing typical peers into a 1:1 or small-group treatment session to teach specific social skills), working with peers within inclusion settings, use of peers as "buddies" or companions to integrate into social contexts, or inclusion of peers within social skills groups or special-interest groups to facilitate skills. Peer training has been found to be effective for enhancing a host of adaptive behaviors (e.g., Garfinkle & Schwartz, 2002; Pierce & Schreibman, 1997a, 1997b). Using peers in intervention is more effective, however, when the peers are adequately trained to know the child with whom they are working and become familiar with the disability (Barron & Foot, 1991; Campbell, Ferguson, Herzinger, Jackson, & Marino, 2004; Kamps et al., 2002).

The SCERTS model, which stands for social communication, emotional regulation, and transactional supports, is a school-based intervention for children with ASD and communication disorders, though the principles can certainly be applied to children across disabilities (Prizant, Wetherby, Rubin, Laurent, & Rydell, 2006). Using a classroom measure of active engagement as part of a study evaluating SCERTS in young school-age children with ASD, results indicated that children with ASD were not actively engaged in their classrooms and that they spent less than half of their time in a well-regulated state (Sparapani, Morgan, Reinhardt, Schatschneider, & Wetherby, 2016). As such, a cluster randomized trial was conducted to evaluate the efficacy of a classroom SCERTS intervention (CSI) in comparison to autism training modules in 129 classrooms with 197 students with ASD. Results of the trial indicated that CSI was effective in significantly increasing the students' active engagement in the classroom, with additional improvements noted in adaptive behavior, social skills and executive functioning (Morgan et al., in preparation).

COMMERCIAL PRODUCTS

There are a host of commercial products that target adaptive behavior, though few have been scientifically studied to provide evidence for their efficacy. Nevertheless, because adaptive skills are necessary for survival, practical strategies that are derived from common sense (e.g., teach children who cannot dress themselves to dress themselves) can be just as effective for many individuals as evidenced-based practices. When teaching skills, however, be cognizant of what strategies are and are not effective and modify as needed. Again, take an individualized approach.

DON'T FORGET

Although evidenced-based practices are ideal for formalized interventions, commercial products can certainly be helpful in teaching practical skills that are common, everyday behaviors. Just be sure to monitor progress and adjust treatments accordingly.

Toilet training, for instance, is a common adaptive deficit for many individuals with neurodevelopmental disorders, let alone many typically developing children. For some, acquiring independent toileting skills may be extremely challenging and require intensive intervention strategies such as those within ABA.

But for others, strategies that are common practice for toilet training in, for example, homes, day cares, and preschools can certainly be effective regardless of the methodology. These include the use of consistency, frequent trips to the bathroom, reinforcement charts, visual schedules, and so on. Commercial products can be very helpful in teaching these basic strategies, especially when they are developed by trained professionals (see, for example, *Toilet Training Success* by Frank Cicero [2012], a board-certified behavior analyst).

Similarly, commercial books and programs that address a variety of adaptive issues can be effective, including sleep problems (e.g., *Sleep Better!,* Durand, 2014), behavioral problems (e.g., *Solving Behavior Problems in Autism,* Hodgdon, 1999), and social communication and interaction skills (e.g., The Social Express, www.thesocialexpress.com; Model Me Kids, www.modelmekids.com). Video modeling using commercial products or even simple video-recording techniques (e.g., cameras, phones, tablets) have also proven to be effective in increasing targeted social skills, functional communication skills, conversational skills, and play skills (Bellini & Akulian, 2007).

Comprehensive programs for addressing practical skills are also available commercially. The *Adaptive Living Skills Curriculum* (Bruininks, Morreau, Gilman, & Anderson, 1991), for example, is a comprehensive curriculum that addresses specific adaptive skills in the following areas: personal care (including sexuality), home living (including residential placements), community living (including social interaction, travel, and money management), and employment skills for ages infancy through 40+ years. The curriculum provides goals and training objectives that are measurable with performance standards, and there are suggestions for the most natural settings and materials in which to teach the skills. Similarly, the *Steps to Independence* guidebook was developed by Baker and Brightman in 1997 and is now in its fourth edition (Baker & Brightman, 2004). It was developed for children ages 3 through young adulthood and focuses on teaching individuals the life skills they will need in order to live as independently as possible. It is designed as a tool for parents. The program provides easy-to-follow steps for teaching the following seven types of skills: get ready, self-help, toilet training, play, self-care, home care, and information-gathering skills. In addition, the program offers information on managing problem behaviors, using a functional behavior analysis approach.

SUMMARY

Despite that fact that there is no single treatment to address adaptive behavior, there are an increasing number of evidence-based and commercially based methods that effectively target the various skills associated with adaptive behavior deficits in individuals with neurodevelopmental disabilities. Once adaptive behaviors are identified, the collectively agreed on behaviors to target in intervention need to be consistently targeted across people and contexts and then generalized and maintained over time. When adaptive skills are systematically addressed, research is showing enhancement of functional communication, social interaction and play, behavioral regulation and coping, self-care, safety, and community and vocational skills within relatively short periods of time that result in increased independence. This is because adaptive behavior is modifiable and is the common thread between disabilities that determines optimal outcome.

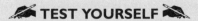

TEST YOURSELF

1. **What is the appropriate action plan for a high-functioning child who has significant deficits in adaptive behavior?**
   a. Support development of cognitive skills and assume that adaptive skills will follow
   b. Target those adaptive behavior deficits through intervention
   c. Do nothing because the child is on par with typically developing peers academically
   d. Move the child into a classroom with other children with developmental delays
2. **True or false? Adaptive behavior intervention, for example, development of fine-motor skills, should only be targeted in the specific context in which the individual displayed the deficit, that is, cutting and writing.**
3. **Who should be involved in the treatment of adaptive behavior skills?**
   a. Therapists, such as physical therapists, speech therapists, and occupational therapists
   b. Parents
   c. Teachers
   d. All of the above
4. **Why is it important to consider the environment and the inclusion of family members and caregivers when developing treatments to targeting adaptive behavior skills?**
5. **Looking at an adaptive behavior report, what is an operational definition for "domains of adaptive behaviors that necessitate treatment"?**
6. **True or false? Multiple adaptive behaviors should be targeted at once, because they emerge simultaneously in typically developing children.**
7. **List the six considerations to targeting adaptive behaviors for intervention.**

8. **True or false? Adaptive behavior measures are often used as outcome measures.**

9. **Which of the following is *not* a treatment methodology in applied behavior analysis (ABA)?**
   a. Shaping
   b. Chaining
   c. Baiting
   d. Reinforcement

10. **List three naturalistic developmental behavioral intervention (NDBI) models.**

Answers: (1) b; (2) False. Adaptive behavior skills should be targeted in all naturally occurring contexts, that is, in writing and cutting but also dressing and grooming; (3) d; (4) Because skills must be generalizable in all contexts, meaning that must be promoted in multiple settings such as at school, at home, in the community, and so on, and the skills must be culturally appropriate or accepted; (5) The domains in which an individual falls below one standard deviation or more from the mean; (6) False. Adaptive behaviors should be targeted one-by-one and attempting to target multiple adaptive behaviors at once will likely not result in any progress; (7) Conduct appropriate measures of adaptive behavior, analyze strengths and weaknesses, work with all individuals who interact with the child to identify appropriate and generalizable goals, monitor progress and determine if goals should be changed, operationally define the behavior, ensure behavior is both meaningful and functional; (8) False. They are most often used as a part of diagnostic evaluations; (9) c; (10) Answers include PRT, incidental teaching, ESDM, JASPER, and ESI.

Nine

CASE SAMPLES

T he following case samples are provided to exemplify how adaptive behavior test results can be interpreted within a written report and how recommendations for enhancing adaptive skills can be provided. These reports are fictional samples, although they are based on real cases of a variety of disorders in which adaptive behavior can be affected. Sample recommendation strategies are provided for each case based on age and level of functioning; however, clinicians should bear in mind that recommendations always need to be individualized for every person and his or her unique situation.

The three case samples provided in this chapter describe how adaptive behavior can be affected in three distinct conditions:

- An individual with intellectual disability
- An individual with autism spectrum disorder (ASD) and cognitive functioning within the average range
- An individual with attention deficit/hyperactivity disorder

The reports also offer a way to think about profiles across different measures of adaptive functioning. In these cases, we provide samples of the Vineland Adaptive Behavior Scales, Second Edition, and the Adaptive Behavior Assessment Scale, Third Edition, but focus should be more on the profiles of scores and how to interpret them rather than on the measure itself. These case samples are not comprehensive but instead provide enough information to gather the specific diagnostic information and associated strengths and weaknesses across adaptive profiles.

CASE SAMPLE 1: INDIVIDUAL WITH INTELLECTUAL DISABILITY

Child: Johnny Jones
Age: 13 years, 2 months
Diagnosis: Intellectual disability

Tests Administered
Wechsler Intelligence Scale for Children, Fourth Edition (WISC-IV)
Vineland Adaptive Behavior Scales, Second Edition, Survey Form
(Vineland-II)

Results

Cognitive Assessment
Johnny's intellectual skills were measured using the Wechsler Intelligence Scale
for Children, Fourth Edition (WISC-IV). The WISC-IV provides a general measure of intellectual functioning, along with index scores that assess cognitive skills
in four areas of functioning. Johnny's Full Scale IQ and Index scores on the
WISC-IV are listed here (Standard Scores have a mean of 100 and standard deviation of 15).

Index	Composite Score	Confidence Interval (90%)	Percentile	Qualitative Description
Verbal Comprehension	55	52–63	<1	Mild Impairment
Perceptual Reasoning	67	63–76	1	Mild Impairment
Working Memory	59	56–69	<1	Mild Impairment
Processing Speed	78	73–88	7	Borderline
Full Scale	*56*	*53–61*	*<1*	*Mild Impairment*

Johnny's scores on the WISC-IV reveal a variable cognitive profile, with his
Full Scale IQ of 56 falling within the mild range of intellectual disability. His
Index scores ranged from mild impairment to the Borderline range of function-
ing, with a 23-point discrepancy between his lowest and highest Index score.
Due to this significant variability between Johnny's Index scores, his Full Scale
IQ should be interpreted with caution because it represents an average of highly
discrepant scores.

Johnny received a Verbal Comprehension Index score of 55, reflecting verbal
reasoning skills in the mild range of impairment. Johnny's Perceptual Reasoning
Index score of 67 reflects mildly impaired abilities in the area of nonverbal
reasoning and visual spatial processing. His score of 59 on the Working Memory
Index also fell in the mildly impaired range. Johnny's Processing Speed Index
score of 78 fell in the Borderline range. This profile denotes areas of relative
strength in nonverbal reasoning skills and most notably in speed of mental and
graphomotor processing.

Adaptive Behavior Assessment

Johnny's mother provided information necessary for completing the Vineland Adaptive Behavior Scales, Second Edition, Survey Form (Vineland-II). The Vineland-II is an individual assessment of adaptive behavior, which can be defined as day-to-day activities necessary to take care of oneself and get along with others. Adaptive behavior reflects what a child *actually* does in an independent manner (i.e., without prompts or supports) as opposed to what the child is *capable* of doing. This is in contrast to standardized cognitive or language measures that assess capabilities or potential under highly structured and supportive conditions. The Vineland-II covers four adaptive behavior domains: Communication, Daily Living Skills, Socialization, and Motor Skills (however, the Motor Skills domain is not administered to children over the age of 6 years). It also provides an Adaptive Behavior Composite score. Standard scores have a mean of 100 and standard deviation of 15. V-scaled scores have a mean of 15 and standard deviation of 3. Johnny's current scores on the Vineland-II are provided here.

Subdomain/ Domain	Standard/ V-scale Score	Age Equivalent (years-months)	Percentile Rank	Adaptive Level
Receptive	9	3–5		Low
Expressive	8	2–9		Low
Written	9	6–11		Low
Communication	**65**		**1**	**Low**
Personal	9	5–2		Low
Domestic	12	8–0		Moderately Low
Community	6	3–2		Low
Daily Living Skills	**66**		**1**	**Low**
Interpersonal	8	2–11		Low
Play/Leisure Time	9	5–3		Low
Coping	8	2–5		Low
Socialization	**58**		**1**	**Low**
Adaptive Behavior Composite	**64**		**1**	**Low**

The Vineland-II interview with Johnny's mother yielded an Adaptive Behavior Composite score of 64, which is ranked at the 1st percentile and classified in the Low range compared to the standardization sample of individuals his age. Based on his mother's report, Johnny shows delays across the domains of Communication, Daily Living Skills, and Socialization. However, it is important to note that his adaptive skills in some areas actually fall slightly above what would be expected given his cognitive level, suggesting that he is learning and applying functional and practical skills to his daily routines.

Within the domain of Communication, Johnny's standard score of 65 falls in the Low range compared to other individuals his age. Receptively, Johnny listens to a story, but not an informational talk, for at least 30 minutes. Expressively, he sometimes reports on routine experiences in simple sentences but does not yet recount a story. In regard to written expression, he reads simple stories but does not yet write short sentences.

Within the domain of Daily Living Skills, Johnny shows a relative strength in his moderately low domestic skills, including assisting with cleaning multiple rooms at home, using the microwave, and putting away his clothes. By contrast, he has a relative weakness in applying his skills within the community. He does not yet understand the function of money or telling time on a clock.

Within the domain of Socialization, Johnny demonstrates similar skills across interpersonal relationships, play and leisure time, and coping. He appropriately takes turns without being asked, says "please" and "thank you," and sometimes answers when familiar adults make small talk. He does not yet use words to express his emotions or go places with friends during the day with adult supervision.

Sample Recommendations for Treatment of Adaptive Behavior

Based on results of the adaptive behavior assessment, the following areas of adaptive functioning should be directly addressed within Johnny's treatment and intervention program:

- **Enhancing Communication Skills.** Gradually increase the amount of time that Johnny is able to listen to talks. Start by taking him to lectures that may be more interesting to him, such as talks at a museum. Ones that have associated visual effects can also help him realize the value in attending for the duration of a talk. Expressively, help Johnny to break down a story so that he will be able to retell it. Use of picture cues can help him sequence and thus elaborate on his experiences. With regard to written skills, help him to write sentences, using either pen and paper or a computer. He can start by dictating sentences and then copying them so that he does not get frustrated.
- **Enhancing Daily Living Skills.** Help teach Johnny the purpose of money and when it is used. When he goes to a store, have him give the money to the cashier and talk to him about change. At a store, explore different brands of the same product and discuss the differences in cost. The purpose

would be to make money more explicit so that he starts to understand the value of it. Once value is understood, teach him the various coins and bills and their values. With regard to telling time, if analog clocks have been taught and he has had difficulty learning, teach using a digital clock. Teach vocabulary concepts to go with the time such as quarter to an hour and the like.

- **Enhancing Socialization Skills.** Teach Johnny how to express his feelings across various situations. Enrolling Johnny in a social skills group that targets social skills and emotional development can also be helpful. Also, play dates outside of the house, such as to a restaurant or a movie, would be recommended.

CASE SAMPLE 2: INDIVIDUAL WITH AUTISM SPECTRUM DISORDER

Child: Jane Smith
Age: 9 years, 0 months
Diagnosis: Autism spectrum disorder

Tests Administered

Wechsler Intelligence Scale for Children, Fourth Edition (WISC-IV)
Vineland Adaptive Behavior Scales, Second Edition, Survey Form (Vineland-II)

Results

Cognitive Assessment

Jane's intellectual skills were measured using the Wechsler Intelligence Scale for Children, Fourth Edition (WISC-IV). The WISC-IV provides a general measure of intellectual functioning, along with Index scores that assess cognitive skills in four areas of functioning. Jane's Full Scale IQ and Index scores on the WISC-IV are listed here (Standard Scores have a mean of 100 and standard deviation of 15).

Index	Composite Score	Confidence Interval (90%)	Percentile	Qualitative Description
Verbal Comprehension	93	88–99	32	Average
Perceptual Reasoning	92	86–99	30	Average
Working Memory	80	75–88	9	Low Average
Processing Speed	78	73–88	7	Borderline
Full Scale	*83*	*79–88*	*13*	*Low Average*

Jane's performance on the WISC-IV yielded a Full Scale IQ of 83, which falls in the Low Average range for her age. Jane's Verbal Comprehension and Perceptual Reasoning Index scores fell in the Average range and significantly above her Working Memory Index score, which fell in the Low Average range, and her Processing Speed Index score, which fell in the Borderline range of impairment. Given these differences, her Full Scale IQ should be interpreted with caution, because it represents an average of discrepant scores.

Adaptive Behavior Assessment

Jane's mother provided information necessary for completing the Vineland Adaptive Behavior Scales, Second Edition, Survey Form (Vineland-II). The Vineland-II is an individual assessment of adaptive behavior, defined as day-to-day activities necessary to take care of oneself and get along with others. Adaptive behavior reflects what a child *actually* does in an independent manner (i.e., without prompts or supports) as opposed to what the child is *capable* of doing. The Vineland-II covers four adaptive behavior domains: Communication, Daily Living Skills, Socialization, and Motor Skills (though the Motor Skills domain is not administered to children over the age of 6 years). It also provides an Adaptive Behavior Composite score. Standard scores have a mean of 100 and standard deviation of 15. V-scaled scores have a mean of 15 and standard deviation of 3. Jane's scores on the Vineland-II are provided here.

Subdomain/ Domain	Standard/ V-scale Score	Age Equivalent (years-months)	Percentile Rank	Adaptive Level
Receptive	11	3–11		Moderately Low
Expressive	9	3–11		Low
Written	12	7–10		Moderately Low
Communication	**75**		**5**	**Moderately Low**
Personal	10	4–11		Moderately Low
Domestic	11	5–5		Moderately Low
Community	9	6–0		Low
Daily Living Skills	**71**		**3**	**Moderately Low**
Interpersonal	7	1–1		Low
Play/Leisure Time	7	2–1		Low
Coping	7	0–10		Low
Socialization	**57**		**<1**	**Low**
Adaptive Behavior Composite	**67**		**67**	**Low**

The results of the Vineland-II indicate that Jane's overall adaptive skills as measured by her Adaptive Behavior Composite score of 67 fall within the Low range for her age. Given the significant discrepancies between her domain scores, her overall Adaptive Behavior Composite score should be interpreted with caution. It should be noted that Jane's standard scores on the Vineland-II are below what would be expected given her age and cognitive abilities. This suggests that she is having difficulty independently applying her repertoire of skills to daily contexts and routines with independence.

Jane's Communication standard score of 75 falls within the Moderately Low range for her age. Her Expressive Communication Skills fall below her Receptive and Written Skills. In terms of Receptive Communication Skills, Jane may follow instructions if she is not distracted or involved in a preferred activity. Her mother reported that she likes to be read to and may listen for 20 to 30 minutes. She prefers nonfiction and tends to take what she reads and hears very literally. Her mother is concerned that if she is teased, she may not realize it. Jane's reading comprehension is also not on par with her peers.

Expressively, Jane occasionally mixes up her pronouns, and she may make some mistakes with irregular verbs or verb tenses. Jane can tell the basic parts of a simple story but may focus on nonsalient aspects and details of the experiences. She may use scripts from songs or repeat things she thinks are funny. In regards to her Written Skills, Jane can read simple sentences, but writing is difficult for her. She can print but has difficulty with cursive writing.

Jane's Daily Living Skills standard score of 71 falls within the Moderately Low range. With regard to personal care, Jane showers and dresses herself, and handles buttons and snaps well. She may need help with hooking zippers and tying shoes. She needs help with brushing her teeth and taking care of her hair. Domestically, Jane will help with chores she enjoys, such as sweeping or cooking, but she can resist chores at times as well. In regards to her Community Skills, Jane has a basic understanding of money, although she does not understand that some things cost more than others. She understands the concept of time and can tell time on a digital clock. She is learning to tell time with an analog clock. With regard to safety, Jane is not likely to be mindful of her surroundings; she may not look both ways when crossing a street or keep in mind other safety rules. Her mother described that she does not let Jane out of her sight. Jane is quite dependent on her mother and can seem quite anxious at times. Until recently, she slept with her parents, but has graduated to her own bed where she sleeps with the light on.

Jane's adaptive Socialization Skills are an area of significant deficit, with her standard score of 57 falling in the Low range and below her age and her other adaptive abilities. Interpersonally, Jane has some interest in the idea of interacting with other children, but she generally does not do so. She can be rude, although she is not likely aware that her behavior is perceived in this way. She is unlikely to do things to please other people or show concern for others. She does not approach other children and may or may not respond when others greet her or make a comment. When her mother sets limits, Jane may respond dramatically by saying, "I'm extinct" or "Send me away to an orphanage." In regards to Play/Leisure Skills, Jane has trouble playing cooperatively with other children, although she will join an active game such as tag. She is not likely to follow rules in other games or take turns cooperatively. She may enjoy a simple board game but is likely to try to change the rules. Jane's Coping Skills are also an area of weakness. Her behavior can be consistently challenging for her parents and she is not coping with changes and task demands as one would expect of a 9-year-old child. Her mother described that she has a short fuse and may be defiant, physically aggressive to others, or bite herself.

Sample Recommendations for ASD Educational Programming and Adaptive Behavior

- **Educational Programming.** We recommend that Jane receive an intervention program that is appropriate for children with ASDs. Given her solid repertoire of cognitive skills, we recommend that her social and adaptive behavior curriculum be the core emphasis within her educational program. Specifically, we recommend that she receive specialized instruction for social communication, interaction, behavioral regulation, and adaptive development by professionals who are trained in and knowledgeable of ASDs. We also strongly recommend that Jane have frequent access to typically developing peers so she can practice using her learned skills with highly supported and facilitated instruction. As such, we recommend that her educational programming take place within a structured and supported school setting where Jane can be immersed in an environment with her typical peers.
- **Enhancement of Adaptive Skills.** Jane's adaptive skills are delayed relative to same age peers. We strongly recommend that a formal intervention be constructed to address these delays, because research is showing that adaptive functioning more accurately predicts success in school, work, and the community than does cognitive functioning, alone. A behaviorist can be engaged to design the intervention plan and help Jane's parents measure her progress.

- Based on results of the adaptive behavior assessment, the following areas of adaptive functioning should be directly addressed within Jane's treatment and intervention program:
  - **Enhancing Daily Living Skills.** Improve on Jane's self-care skills such as teaching her to tie her shoes, dress herself completely, and brush her teeth and her hair. Establish routine chores for Jane at home with clear expectations and appropriate reinforcements (tailored to what is motivating for her).
  - **Enhancing Safety Awareness.** Develop a safety plan for Jane in which specific rules for making sure she is safe when out and about are described and written down. Teach Jane each rule and practice each scenario repeatedly, again, with appropriate reinforcement for compliance.
  - **Enhancing Coping Skills.** Teach Jane skills for coping with frustration, anger, and other complex and unpleasant emotions. Jane will need direct instruction on how to manage and self-regulate her emotions and behavior and opportunities to practice. However, this cannot be accomplished unless Jane is motivated to learn these skills. We recommend a functional behavioral assessment of her biting, hitting, and other aggressive behaviors, including tantrumming and refusing to cooperate.

CASE SAMPLE 3: INDIVIDUAL WITH ATTENTION DEFICIT HYPERACTIVITY DISORDER

Child: Jennifer Pratt
Age: 6 years, 9 months
Diagnosis: Attention deficit/hyperactivity disorder

Tests Administered
Differential Ability Scales, Second Edition (DAS-II), Early Years Battery
Conners Rating Scale, Third Edition (Conners 3)
Adaptive Behavior Assessment System, Third Edition (ABAS-3)

Results

Cognitive Assessment
Jennifer was administered the Differential Ability Scales, Second Edition (DAS-II), in order to assess her cognitive abilities. This test assesses cognitive skills in three domains: Verbal Reasoning, Nonverbal Reasoning, and Spatial Reasoning. In addition, a General Conceptual Ability score (GCA) is reported.

The results are reported in standard scores that have an average of 100 and standard deviation of 15. Subtest scores are reported as T-scores with an average of 50 and standard deviation of 10. Jennifer's scores on the DAS-II are provided here.

	Standard Score	T-Score	Percen-tile	95% Confidence Interval	Age Equivalent
Verbal	147		99.9	133–151	
Verbal Comprehension		90	>99.9		>8 years, 10 months
Naming Vocabulary		64	92		>8 years, 10 months
Nonverbal Reasoning	127		96	114–133	
Picture Similarities		71	98		>8 years, 10 months
Matrices		60	84		8 years, 10 months
Spatial	109		73	102–115	
Pattern Construction		50	50		6 years, 10 months
Copying		61	86		>8 years, 10 months
General Conceptual Ability	134		99	126–139	

Results of the DAS-II indicate that Jennifer's overall cognitive abilities fall within the Very Superior range compared to other children her age, with her General Conceptual Ability (GCA) score of 134 falling at the 99th percentile. However, her Verbal and Nonverbal Reasoning domain scores are significantly higher than her Spatial domain score, which indicates that the overall GCA score is not the best summary of her abilities. It is more informative to focus on Jennifer's specific abilities within each domain, which are described next.

Assessment of Attention, Hyperactivity, and Impulsivity
The Conners Rating Scale, Third Edition (Conners 3), was completed by Jennifer's mother and classroom teacher. This questionnaire is used to obtain observations about the child's behavior that relate to inattention, hyperactivity, and other problems. Results are reported in T-scores that have a mean of 50 and standard deviation of 10. Scores above 65 are considered to fall in the Elevated range, and scores higher than 70 are Very Elevated compared to other children of the same age. Jennifer's scores on the Conners 3 are provided here.

Content Scale	Parent T-Score/ Interpretation	Teacher T-Score/ Interpretation
Inattention	83/Very Elevated	62/Normal Range
Hyperactivity/Impulsivity	68/Elevated	61/Normal Range
Learning Problems	73/Very Elevated	67/Elevated
Executive Functioning	87/Very Elevated	59/Normal Range
Defiance/Aggression	60/Normal Range	46/Normal Range
Peer Relations	43/Normal Range	44/Normal Range
Symptom Scale	Parent T-Score/ Interpretation	Teacher T-Score/ Interpretation
Attention Deficit/Hyperactivity Disorder, Inattentive Type	84/Very Elevated	64/Normal Range
Attention Deficit/Hyperactivity Disorder, Hyperactive-Impulsive Type	67/Elevated	62/Normal Range
Conduct Disorder	45/Normal Range	46/Normal Range
Oppositional Defiant Disorder	75/Very Elevated	52/Normal Range

Jennifer's mother's ratings on the Connors 3 led to several scores in the Very Elevated range in the areas of Inattention, Learning Problems, Executive Functioning, ADHD-Inattentive Type, and Oppositional Defiant Disorder, and scores in the Elevated range in Hyperactivity/Impulsivity, and ADHD Hyperactive-Impulsive Type. Although her teacher's ratings did not lead to any scores in the Very Elevated range, ratings on the Learning Problems scale led to a score in the Elevated range.

Additionally, Jennifer's mother noted that Jennifer's problems very frequently affect her academic functioning, often affect her functioning in the home setting, and occasionally affect her functioning in social settings.

Adaptive Behavior Assessment
Jennifer's mother completed the Adaptive Behavior Assessment System, Third Edition, Parent/Primary Caregiver Form, for Ages 5–21 years (ABAS-3) in order to provide information on Jennifer's adaptive behaviors in home, school, and community or other settings. The ABAS-3 measures adaptive behavior in three broad domains of Conceptual, Practical, and Social Skills as well as in overall adaptive functioning with a General Adaptive Composite (GAC), which have standard scores with a mean of 100 and standard deviation of 15. Ten adaptive skill areas are provided in scaled scores with a mean of 10 and standard deviation of 3. Jennifer's scores on the ABAS-3 are provided here.

Skill Area/ Domain	Standard/ Scaled Score	Confidence Interval (95%)	Percentile Rank	Adaptive Level
Communication	7			Below Average
Functional Academics	8			Average
Self-Direction	6			Below Average
Conceptual	**83**	**77–89**	**13**	**Below Average**
Leisure	9			Average
Social	6			Below Average
Social	**86**	**80–92**	**18**	**Below Average**
Community Use	7			Below Average
Home Living	6			Below Average
Health and Safety	9			Average
Self-Care	8			Average
Practical	**85**	**79–91**	**16**	**Below Average**
General Adaptive Composite (GAC)	**83**	**79–87**	**13**	**Below Average**

Jennifer's scores on the ABAS-3 resulted in an overall General Adaptive Composite of 83, which falls in the Below Average range for her age. It should be noted that given Jennifer's superior cognitive skills, her adaptive skills are lower than would be expected for her cognition.

Jennifer's Conceptual skills fall in the Below Average range. In the area of Communication, Jennifer tells her parents about her favorite activities, speaks clearly and with correct grammar, but she has trouble listening for long periods of time and engaging in conversations without interrupting others. Her Functional Academics Skills fall in the Average range. She is beginning to read and write, and she is learning to tell time, but she cannot answer simple questions about what she has read. Her Self-Direction Skills are an area of weakness. She cannot work independently, is extremely restless, and has difficulty controlling her temper when her feelings are hurt or she does not get her way.

Jennifer's Social Skills fall in the Below Average range. Her Leisure Skills are an area of strength and in the Average range. She engages in a variety of activities, takes turns, and invites others to play. Her adaptive Social Skills, however, are an area of weakness, falling in the Below Average range. Though she identifies friends, these relationships are not always reciprocated due to her impulsivity and emotional dysregulation.

Jennifer's Practical Skills fall in the Below Average range, though her skill areas within this domain range from Below Average to Average. Her Community Skills are varied. She sometimes forgets to look both ways when crossing the street, and she is not fully independent in ordering her own meals or finding restrooms when out in public. Jennifer's Home Living Skills are an area of weakness. Her impulsivity results in making a mess at home, frequently spilling food and drinks and having her clothing and bedroom in disarray. Her Health and Safety Skills are average. She buckles her car seat, is careful around scissors and dangerous objects, and tests hot foods before eating them. Her Self-Care Skills are also average. She can dress and bathe herself and she is fully toilet trained.

In summary, Jennifer's adaptive skills are variable, with relative strengths in her Functional Academics, Leisure, Health and Safety Skills, and Self-Care Skills. However, she has numerous areas of vulnerability that are not commensurate with her extremely strong cognitive abilities. For this reason, it will be important to provide Jennifer with support in applying her skills to daily contexts and routines with complete independence.

Sample Recommendations for Treatment of Adaptive Behavior

Based on results of the adaptive behavior assessment, Jennifer's adaptive skills are delayed relative to same-age peers. We strongly recommend that a formal intervention be constructed to address these delays, because research is showing that adaptive functioning more accurately predicts success in school, work, and the community than does cognitive functioning alone. A behaviorist can be engaged to design the intervention plan and help Jennifer's parents measure her progress.

- **Enhancing Conceptual Skills.** Improve on Jennifer's ability to listen and engage in conversations. Jennifer might need visual cues to help her know when it is her turn to speak. Using clear signals, such as red and green lights for stop and go, might help her to know when it is appropriate for her to take her conversational turn.
- **Enhancing Functional Academic Skills.** Working on her ability to retell something she has read is also important. Checking her comprehension after shorter reading chunks could be helpful. She should follow a pattern of checking for comprehension in which initially, after every paragraph, she should try and retell what she has read. As she improves, checking for comprehension can be done at the end of every chapter.
- **Enhancing Self-Direction Skills.** Jennifer has a very difficult time working independently and coping with her emotions. Strategies and rewards for increasing time on task and independence should be implemented. If her behavior is disruptive to the classroom then a behavior plan should be implemented to more specifically target these behaviors.

- **Improving Social Skills.** Secondary to Jennifer's impulsivity, her friendships are struggling. A social skills group or lunch bunch can be beneficial in helping her learn how to engage appropriately with her peers and better learn how her behaviors are contributing to her difficulties with peer relations.
- **Enhancing Practical Skills.** Jennifer's impulsivity is also leading to significant safety issues. Breaking tasks down and working on slowing her down before she crosses a street is imperative so that she does not get injured. Providing clear visual spots for her to place her belongings is also recommended. For example, a placemat can be used with designated places for her plate and cup so that she is not constantly putting her cup down and then knocking it over. Helping her to order her own meals in restaurants, practicing first at a fast food restaurant with more limited menu options, can be beneficial.

SUMMARY

In summary, when writing up the results of adaptive behavior assessments, keep the following in mind:

- If there is any indication that the results are not valid, make a validity statement. Many measures have estimated or guessing options, and if a respondent provides too many, the measure becomes invalid. Make note of these instances.
- Provide an overview of global, standard, and domain scores.
- If there is significant variability among domain scores, then add a cautionary statement about interpreting the overall composite score, because it would be averaging highly discrepant scores and therefore be less meaningful.
- Identify significant and relative areas of strength and weakness. Again, if there is significant variability within domain scores, use cautionary statements about the more general score.
- Make a comparison statement of the adaptive scores to age and cognitive scores and if these are commensurate or not. If not, elaborate on any concerns. For instance, if adaptive scores are falling substantially below age and cognitive expectations, then there is evidence that the individual is struggling to apply skills that he or she has to daily contexts and routines with independence—that is, the individual has the capacity to perform the adaptive behavior but is not when life demands it. If adaptive skills are

higher than age expectations, then this might also be of concern because adaptive skills ideally should be age (or mental age) appropriate.

- When describing subdomain results, provide examples of behaviors that the individual should be performing with independence but did not receive credit (focus on behaviors that are most relevant to his or her needs). If no credit was given for behaviors in the ceiling range, there is no need to focus on them if they are above the person's capacity.

- If this is a readministration of the same measure over time, provide comparison statements to prior results. Elaborate on areas of progress, areas of stagnation, and especially highlight any potential loss of previously acquired skills.

- If there are multiple respondents (e.g., a parent and a teacher), compare findings across raters and provide explanations for any potential discrepancies. Remember that behavior often differs across contexts; thus, just because an individual has a behavior at home, for example, but not school, this does not mean that one respondent is wrong. There are often reasons to justify these differences (e.g., more consistency at school or more familiarity at home, and so forth).

- Use the results to generate recommendations for adaptive behavior that are most pertinent to the needs of the individual. These recommendations will be informed by all aspects of the evaluation and not just the adaptive behavior assessment.

References

CHAPTER ONE

American Association on Mental Retardation. (1992). *Mental retardation: Definition, classification, and systems of support* (9th ed.). Washington, DC: Author.

American Association on Mental Retardation. (2002). *Mental retardation: Definition, classification, and systems of supports; Workbook*. Washington, DC: Author.

American Psychiatric Association (APA). (1952). *Diagnostic and statistical manual of mental disorders*. Washington, DC: Author.

American Psychiatric Association (APA). (1968). *Diagnostic and statistical manual of mental disorders* (2nd ed.). Washington, DC: Author.

American Psychiatric Association (APA). (1980). *Diagnostic and statistical manual of mental disorders* (3rd ed.). Washington, DC: Author.

American Psychiatric Association (APA). (1987). *Diagnostic and statistical manual of mental disorders* (3rd ed., rev.). Washington, DC: Author.

American Psychiatric Association (APA). (1994). *Diagnostic and statistical manual of mental disorders* (4th ed.). Washington, DC: Author.

American Psychiatric Association (APA). (2000). *Diagnostic and statistical manual of mental disorders* (4th ed., text rev.). Washington, DC: Author.

American Psychiatric Association (APA). (2013). *Diagnostic and statistical manual of mental disorders* (5th ed.) Arlington, VA: Author.

Brockley, J. A. (1999). History of mental retardation: An essay review. *History of Psychology, 2*(1), 25–36.

Bruininks, R. H., Woodcock, R. W., Weatherman, R. F., & Hill, B. K. (1985). *Scales of independent behavior*. Allen, TX: DLM Teaching Resources.

Doll, E. A. (1917). *Clinical studies in feeble-mindedness*. Boston, MA: The Gorham Press.

Doll, E. A. (1936). Idiot, imbecile, and moron. *Journal of Applied Psychology, 20*(4), 427–437. http://doi.org/10.1037/h0056577

Doll, E. A. (1941). The essentials of an inclusive concept of mental deficiency. *American Journal of Mental Deficiency, 46*, 214–219.

Doll, E. A. (1953). *The measurement of social competence: A manual for the Vineland Social Maturity Scale*. Minneapolis, MN: Educational Test Bureau.

Gelb, S. A. (1999). Spilled religion: The tragedy of Henry H. Goddard. *Mental Retardation, 37*(3), 240–243. http://doi.org/10.1352/0047-6765

Goddard, H. H. (1908). The Binet and Simon Tests of Intellectual Capacity. *Training School, 5*, 3–9.

Goddard, H. H. (1912). *The Kallikak family: A study in the heredity of feeble-mindedness*. New York, NY: Macmillan.

Goddard, H. H. (1914). *Feeble-mindedness: Its causes and consequences*. New York, NY: Macmillan.

Grossman, H. J. (1973). *Manual on terminology in mental retardation*. Washington, DC: American Association on Mental Deficiency.

Grossman, H. J. (1977). *Manual on terminology in mental retardation*. Washington, DC: American Association on Mental Deficiency.

Grossman, H. J. (1983). *Classification in mental retardation*. Washington, DC: American Association on Mental Deficiency.

Harrison, P. L., & Oakland, T. (2000). *Adaptive behavior assessment system*. San Antonio, TX: The Psychological Corporation.

Harrison, P. L., & Oakland, T. (2003). *Adaptive behavior assessment system* (2nd ed.). San Antonio, TX: Pearson.

Heber, R. (1959). A manual on terminology and classification in mental retardation. *American Journal of Mental Deficiency, Suppl 64*(2), 1–111.

Heber, R. A. (1961). *A manual on terminology and classification in mental retardation: Monograph supplement to the American Journal of Mental Deficiency* (2nd ed.). Springfield, IL: American Association on Mental Deficiency.

Luckasson, R., Coulter, D., Polloway, E. A., Reiss, S., Schalock, R. L., Snell, M. E., . . . & Stark, J. A. (1992). *Mental retardation: Definition, classification, and systems of supports*. Washington, DC: American Association on Mental Retardation.

Nihira, K., Foster, R., Shellhaas, M., & Leland, H. (1974). *AAMD adaptive behavior scale*. Washington, DC: Author.

Reilly, P. R. (1987). Involuntary sterilization in the United States: A surgical solution. *The Quarterly Review of Biology, 62*(2), 153–70.

Reschly, D. J., Myers, T. G., Hartel, C. R., & National Research Council. (2002). *Mental retardation: Determining eligibility for social security benefits*. Washington, DC: National Academies Press.

Richards, S. B., Brady, M. P., & Taylor, R. L. (2015). Definition and classification of cognitive/intellectual disabilities. *Cognitive and intellectual disabilities: Historical perspectives, current practices, and future directions* (2nd ed., pp. 38–62). New York, NY: Routledge.

Schalock, R. L., Borthwick-Duffy, S. A., Bradley, V. J., Buntinx, W. H. E., Coulter, D. L., Craig, E. M., . . . & Yeager, M. H. (2010). *Intellectual disability: Definition, classification, and systems of supports* (11th ed.). Washington, DC: American Association on Intellectual and Developmental Disabilities.

Sparrow, S. S., Balla, D., & Cicchetti, D. V. (1984). *Vineland adaptive behavior scales* (Expanded). Circle Pines, MN: American Guidance Service.

Sparrow, S. S., Cicchetti, D. V., & Saulnier, C. A. (2016). *Vineland adaptive behavior scales* (3rd ed.). Bloomington, MN: NCS Pearson.

Zenderland, L. (2001). *Measuring Minds: Henry Herbert Goddard and the Origins of American Intelligence Testing*. Cambridge University Press.

CHAPTER TWO

Adams, G. L. (2000). *CTAB-R and NABC-R technical manual*. Seattle, WA: Educational Achievement Systems.

Boyle, C. A., Yeargin-Allsopp, M., Doernberg, N. S., Holmgreen, P., Murphy, C. C., & Schendel, D. E. (1996). Prevalence of selected developmental disabilities in children 3–10 years of age: The metropolitan Atlanta developmental disabilities surveillance program, 1991. *Morbidity and Mortality Weekly Report, 45*(2), 1–14.

Bruininks, R. H., Woodcock, R. W., Weatherman, R. F., & Hill, B. K. (1996). *SIB-R: Scales of independent behavior* (rev.) Chicago, IL: Riverside Publishing.

Bryant, B. R., Bryant, D. P., & Chamberlain, S. (1999). Examination of gender and race factors in the assessment of adaptive behavior. In R. L. Schalock & D. L. Braddock (Eds.), *Adaptive behavior and its measurement: Implications for the field of mental retardation* (pp. 141–160). Washington, DC: American Association on Mental Retardation.

Craig, E. M., & Tasse, M. J. (1999). Cultural and demographic group comparisons in adaptive behavior. In R. L. Schalock & D. L. Braddock (Eds.), *Adaptive behavior and its measurement: Implications for the field of mental retardation* (pp. 119–140). Washington, DC: American Association on Mental Retardation.

Doll, E. A. (1953). *The measurement of social competence: A manual for the Vineland Social Maturity Scale*. Minneapolis, MN: Educational Test Bureau.

Doucette, J., & Freedman, R. (1980). *Progress tests for the developmentally disabled: An evaluation*. Cambridge, MA: Abt Books.

Harrison, P., & Oakland, T. (2003). *Adaptive behavior assessment system* (2nd ed.). San Antonio, TX: Pearson.

Hutton, J. B., Dubes, R., & Muir, S. (1992). Assessment practices of school psychologists: Ten years later. *School Psychology Review, 21*(2), 271–284.

Jacobson, J. W., & Mulick, J. A. (1996). *Manual of diagnosis and professional practice in mental retardation*. Washington, DC: American Psychological Association.

Kamphaus, R. W. (1987). Conceptual and psychometric issues in the assessment of adaptive behavior. *Journal of Special Education, 21*(1), 27–35.

National Research Council. (2002). *Mental retardation*. Washington, DC: National Academies Press.

Neisser, U., Boodoo, G., Bouchard, T. J., Boykin, A. W., Brody, N., Cici, S. J., . . . & Urbina, S. (1996). Intelligence: Knowns and unknowns. *American Psychologist, 51*(2), 77–101.

Ochoa, S. H., Powell, M. P., & Robles-Pina, R. (1996). School psychologists' assessment practices with bilingual and limited-English-proficient students. *Journal of Psychoeducational Assessment, 14*(3), 250–275.

Sparrow, S. S., Balla, D., & Cicchetti, D. V. (1984). *Vineland adaptive behavior scales* (Expanded). Circle Pines, MN: American Guidance Service.

Sparrow, S. S., Cicchetti, D. V., & Balla, D. A. (2005). *Vineland adaptive behavior scales* (2nd ed.). San Antonio, TX: Pearson.

Sparrow, S. S., Cicchetti, D. V., & Saulnier, C. A. (2016). *Vineland adaptive behavior scales* (3rd ed.). Bloomington, MN: NCS Pearson.

Spreat, S. (1999). Psychometric standards for adaptive behavior assessment. In R. L. Schalock (Ed.), *Adaptive behavior and its measurement: Implications for the field of mental retardation* (pp. 103–108). Washington, DC: American Association on Mental Retardation.

Stinnett, T. A., Havey, J. M., & Oehler-Stinnett, J. (1994). Current test usage by practicing school psychologists: A national survey. *Journal of Psychoeducational Assessment, 12*(4), 331–350.

Thompson, F. R., McGrew, K. S., & Bruininks, R. H. (1999). Adaptive and maladaptive behavior: Functional and structural characteristics. In R. L. Schalock (Ed.), *Adaptive behavior and its measurement: Implications for the field of mental retardation* (pp. 15–42). Washington, DC: American Association on Mental Retardation.

Watkins, C. E., Campbell, V. L., Nieberding, R., & Hallmark, R. (1995). Contemporary practice of psychological assessment by clinical psychologists. *Professional Psychology: Research and Practice, 26*(1), 54–60.

CHAPTER THREE

American Psychiatric Association [APA]. (2000). *Diagnostic and statistical manual of mental disorders* (4th ed., text rev.). Washington, DC: Author.

American Psychiatric Association [APA]. (2013). *Diagnostic and statistical manual of mental disorders* (5th ed.). Arlington, VA: Author.

Bayley, N. (2006). *Bayley scales of infant and toddler development* (3rd ed.). San Antonio, TX: Harcourt Assessment.

Bruininks, R. H., Woodcock, R. W., Weatherman, R. F., & Hill, B. K. (1996). *SIB-R: Scales of independent behavior–Revised*. Chicago, IL: Houghton Mifflin Harcourt Publishing.

Doll, E. A. (1953). *The measurement of social competence: A manual for the Vineland Social Maturity Scale*. Minneapolis, MN: Educational Test Bureau.

Givens, T., & Ward, C. L. (1982). Stability of the AAMD Adaptive Behavior Scale, Public School Version. *Psychology in the Schools, 19*(2), 166–169.

Harrison, P. L., & Oakland, T. (2000). *Adaptive behavior assessment system*. San Antonio, TX: The Psychological Corporation.

Harrison, P., & Oakland, T. (2003). *Adaptive behavior assessment system* (2nd ed.). San Antonio, TX: Pearson.

Harrison, P., & Oakland, T. (2015). *Adaptive behavior assessment system* (3rd ed.). Torrance, CA: Western Psychological Services.

Heber, R. (1959). A manual on terminology and classification in mental retardation. *American Journal of Mental Deficiency, Suppl 64*(2), 1–111.

Lambert, N. (1981). *AAMD adaptive behavior scale, school edition: Diagnostic and technical manual*. Monterey, CA: Publishers Test Service.

Lambert, N., Nihira, K., & Leland, H. (1993). *AAMR adaptive behavior scale–school* (2nd ed.). Austin, TX: PRO-ED.

Lambert, N., Windmiller, M., Cole, L., & Figueroa, R. (1975). *Manual: AAMD adaptive behavior scale, public school version (1974 revision)*. Washington, DC: American Association on Mental Deficiency.

McCarney, S. B., & Arthaud, T. J. (2006). *Adaptive behavior evaluation scale* (2nd ed., rev). Columbia, MO: Hawthorne Educational Services.

McCarney, S. B., & House, S. N. (2017). *Adaptive behavior evaluation scale* (3rd ed.). Columbia, MO: Hawthorne Educational Services.

Newborg, J. (2016). *Battelle developmental inventory: Normative update* (2nd ed.). Boston, MA: Houghton Mifflin Harcourt.

Nihira, K., Leland, H., & Lambert, N. M. (1993). *ABS-RC:2: AAMR adaptive behavior scale: Residential and community*. Austin, TX: American Association on Mental Retardation.

Sattler, J. M. (2002). *Assessment of children: Behavioral and clinical applications*. San Diego, CA: Author.

Schalock, R. L., Borthwick-Duffy, S. A. Bradley, V. J., Buntinx, W. H. E., Coulter, D. L., Craig, E. M., Gomez, S. C., . . . & Yeager, M. H. (2010). *Intellectual disability: Definition, classification, and systems of support* (11th ed.). Washington, DC: American Association on Intellectual and Developmental Disabilities.

Sparrow, S. S., Balla, D. A., & Cicchetti, D. V. (1985). *The Vineland adaptive behavior scales: Classroom edition*. Circle Pines, MN: American Guidance Service.

Sparrow, S. S., Balla, D., & Cicchetti, D. V. (1984). *Vineland adaptive behavior scales* (Expanded). Circle Pines, MN: American Guidance Service.

Sparrow, S. S., Cicchetti, D. V., & Balla, D. A. (2005a). *Vineland adaptive behavior scales: Teacher rating form manual* (2nd ed.). San Antonio, TX: NCS Pearson.

Sparrow, S. S., Cicchetti, D. V., & Balla, D. A. (2005b). *Vineland adaptive behavior scales* (2nd ed.). San Antonio, TX: Pearson.

Sparrow, S. S., Cicchetti, D. V., & Balla, D. A. (2008). *Vineland adaptive behavior scales: Expanded interview form manual* (2nd ed.). San Antonio, TX: NCS Pearson.

Sparrow, S. S., Cicchetti, D. V., & Saulnier, C. A. (2016). *Vineland adaptive behavior scales* (3rd ed.). Bloomington, MN: NCS Pearson.

Stinnett, T. A. (1997). Book review: AAMR Adaptive Behavior Scale–School (2nd ed.). *Journal of Psychoeducational Assessment, 15*(4), 361–372. http://doi.org/10.1177/073428299701500409

Stinnett, T. A., Fuqua, D. R., & Coombs, W. T. (1999). Construct validity of the AAMR Adaptive Behavior Scale–School:2. *School Psychology Review, 28*(1), 31–43.

Tassé, M. J., Schalock, R. L., Balboni, G., Bersani, H., Borthwick-Duffy, S. A., & Spreat, S. (2018). *Diagnostic adaptive behavior scale: User's manual*. Washington, DC: American Association on Intellectual and Developmental Disabilities.

Tassé, M. J., Schalock, R. L., Balboni, G., Spreat, S., & Navas, P. (2016). Validity and reliability of the Diagnostic Adaptive Behavior Scale. *Journal of Intellectual Disability Research, 60,* 80–88.

Tsujii, M., Murakami, T., Kuroda, M., Ito, H., Someki, F., & Hagiwara, T. (2015). *The Japanese Vineland Adaptive Behavior Scales* (2nd ed.). Tokyo, Japan: Nihon Bunka Kagakusha.

CHAPTER FOUR

Abbeduto, L., & McDuffie, A. (2010). Genetic syndromes associated with intellectual disabilities. *Handbook of medical neuropsychology: Applications of cognitive neuroscience* (pp. 193–221). New York, NY: Springer.

American Psychiatric Association. (2013). *Diagnostic and statistical manual of mental disorders* (5th ed.). Arlington, VA: Author.

Annaz, D., Hill, C. M., Ashworth, A., Holley, S., & Karmiloff-Smith, A. (2011). Characterisation of sleep problems in children with Williams syndrome. *Research in Developmental Disabilities, 32,* 164–169.

Australian Institute of Health and Welfare. (2007). *Disability support services 2004–2005 CSTDA NMDS service user data*. Canberra, Australia: Author.

Axelsson, E. L., Hill, C. M., Sadeh, A., & Dimitrou, D. (2013). Sleep problems and language development in toddlers with Williams syndrome. *Research in Developmental Disabilities, 34,* 3988–3996.

Bailey, D. B., Mesibov, G. B., Hatton, D. D., Clark, R. D., Roberts, J. E., & Mayhew, L. (1998). Autistic behavior in young boys with fragile X syndrome. *Journal of Autism and Developmental Disorders, 28*(6), 499–508.

Bayley, N. (1969). *Bayley scales of infant development*. New York, NY: Harcourt Assessment.

Bellugi, U., Lichtenberger, L., Mills, D., Galaburda, A., & Korenberg, J. R. (1999). Bridging cognition, the brain and molecular genetics: Evidence from Williams syndrome. *Trends in Neuroscience, 22,* 197–207.

Beuren, A. J., Aptiz, J., & Harmjanz, D. (1962). Supravalvular aortic stenosis in association with mental retardation and a certain facial appearance. *Circulation, 26,* 1235–1240.

Boer, H., Holland, A., Whittington, J., Butler, J., Webb, T., & Clarke, D. (2002). Psychotic illness in people with Prader-Willi syndrome due to chromosome 15 maternal uniparental disomy. *The Lancet, 359*(9301), 135–136.

Brawn, G., & Porter, M. (2014). Adaptive functioning in Williams syndrome and its relation to demographic variables and family environment. *Research in Developmental Disabilities, 35,* 3606–3623.

Buckley, S., Broadley, I., MacDonald, J., & Laws, G. (1995). Long-term maintenance of memory skills taught to children with Down syndrome. *Down Syndrome Research and Practice, 3*(3), 103–109.

Buiting, K., Saitoh, S., Gross, S., Dittrich, B., Schwartz, S., Nicholls, R. D., & Horsthemke, B. (1995). Inherited microdeletions in the Angelman and Prader-Willi syndromes define an imprinting centre on human chromosome 15. *Nature Genetics, 9*(4), 395–400.

Carpentieri, S., & Morgan, S. B. (1996). Adaptive and intellectual functioning in autistic and nonautistic retarded children. *Journal of Autism and Developmental Disorders, 26*(6), 611–620.

Chapman, R. S., & Hesketh, L. J. (2001). Language, cognition, and short-term memory in individuals with Down syndrome. *Down's Syndrome, Research and Practice: The Journal of the Sarah Duffen Centre, 7*(1), 1–7.

Clayton-Smith, J., & Pembrey, M. E. (1992). Angelman syndrome. *Journal of Medical Genetics, 29*(6), 412–415.

Coe, D. A., Matson, J. L., Russell, D. W., Slifer, K. J., Capone, G. T., Baglio, C., & Stallings, S. (1999). Behavior problems of children with Down syndrome and life events. *Journal of Autism and Developmental Disorders, 29*(2), 149–156.

Cohen, I. L., Vietze, P. M., Sudhalter, V., Jenkins, E. C., & Brown, W. T. (1989). Parent-child dyadic gaze patterns in fragile X males and in non-fragile X males with autistic disorder. *Journal of Child Psychology and Psychiatry, and Allied Disciplines, 30*(6), 845–856.

Colley, A. F., Leversha, M. A., Voullaire, L. E., & Rogers, J. G. (1990). Five cases demonstrating the distinctive behavioral features of chromosome deletion 17 (p11.2) (Smith-Magenis syndrome). *Journal of Paediatrics and Child Health, 26*, 17–21.

Connolly, J. A. (1978). Intelligence levels of Down syndrome children. *American Journal of Mental Deficiency, 83*, 183–196.

Cowley, A., Holt, G., Bouras, N., Sturmey, P., Newton, J. T., & Costello, H. (2004). Descriptive psychopathology in people with mental retardation. *The Journal of Nervous and Mental Disease, 192*, 232–237.

Crocker, N., Vaurio, L., Riley, E. P., & Mattson, S. N. (2009). Comparison of adaptive behavior in children with heavy prenatal alcohol exposure or attention-deficit hyperactivity disorder. *Alcoholism: Clinical and Experimental Research, 33*(11), 2015–2023.

Davies, M., Udwin, O., & Howlin, P. (1998). Adults with Williams syndrome: Preliminary study of social, emotional, and behavioural difficulties. *British Journal of Psychiatry, 172*, 273–276.

Davis, A. S. (2008). Children with Down syndrome: Implications for assessment and intervention in the school. *School Psychology Quarterly, 23*(2), 271–281.

Denmark, J. L., Feldman, M. A., & Holden, J. J. (2003). Behavioral relationship between autism and fragile X syndrome. *American Journal of Mental Retardation, 108*(5), 314–326.

Dimitropoulos, A., Ho, A. Y., Klaiman, C., Koenig, K., & Schultz, R. T. (2009). A comparison of behavioral and emotional characteristics in children with autism, Prader-Willi syndrome, and Williams syndrome. *Journal of Mental Health Research in Intellectual Disabilities, 2*(3), 220–243.

Di Nuovo, S., & Buono, S. (2011). Behavioral phenotypes of genetic syndromes with intellectual disability: Comparison of adaptive profiles. *Psychiatry Research, 189*(3), 440–445.

Dykens, E. M. (1995). Measuring behavioral phenotypes: Provocation from the "new genetics." *American Journal of Mental Retardation, 99*, 522–532.

Dykens, E. M. (1999). Direct effects of genetic mental retardation syndromes: Maladaptive behavior and psychopathology. *International Review of Research in Mental Retardation, 22*, 1–26.

Dykens, E. M., & Hodapp, R. M. (2001). Research in mental retardation: Toward an etiologic approach. *Journal of Child Psychology and Psychiatry, 42*, 49–71.

Dykens, E. M., Hodapp, R. M., & Evans, D. W. (2006). Profiles and development of adaptive behavior in children with Down syndrome. *Down's Syndrome, Research and Practice: The Journal of the Sarah Duffen Centre, 9*(3), 45–50.

Dykens, E. M., Hodapp, R. M., & Finucane, B. M. (2000). *Genetics and mental retardation syndromes: A new look at behavior and interventions.* Baltimore, MD: Brookes.

Dykens, E. M., Hodapp, R. M., Ort, S. I., & Leckman, J. F. (1993). Trajectory of adaptive behavior in males with fragile X syndrome. *Journal of Autism and Developmental Disorders, 23*(1), 135–145.

Dykens, E. M., Hodapp, R. M., Walsh, K., & Nash, L. J. (1992). Adaptive and maladaptive behavior in Prader-Willi syndrome. *Journal of the American Academy of Child and Adolescent Psychiatry, 31*(6), 1131–1136.

Dykens, E. M., & Kasari, C. (1997). Maladaptive behavior in children with Prader-Willi syndrome, Down syndrome, and nonspecific mental retardation. *American Journal on Mental Retardation, 102*(3), 228.

Dykens, E. M., Lee, E., & Roof, E. (2011). Prader-Willi syndrome and autism spectrum disorders: An evolving story. *Journal of Neurodevelopmental Disorders, 3*(3), 225–237.

Dykens, E., Ort, S., Cohen, I., Finucane, B., Spiridigliozzi, G., Lachiewicz, A., . . . & O'Connor, R. (1996). Trajectories and profiles of adaptive behavior in males with fragile X syndrome: Multicenter studies. *Journal of Autism and Developmental Disorders, 26*(3), 287–301.

Dykens, E. M., & Roof, E. (2008). Behavior in Prader-Willi syndrome: Relationship to genetic subtypes and age. *Journal of Child Psychology and Psychiatry, 49*(9), 1001–1008.

Dykens, E. M., Roof, E., & Hunt-Hawkins, H. (2017). Cognitive and adaptive advantages of growth hormone treatment in children with Prader-Willi syndrome. *Journal of Child Psychology and Psychiatry, 58*(1), 64–74.

Elison, S., Stinton, C., & Howlin, P. (2010). Health and social outcomes in adults with Williams syndrome: Findings from cross-sectional and longitudinal cohorts. *Research in Developmental Disabilities, 31*(2), 587–599.

Ewart, A. K., Morris, C. A., Atkinson, D., Jin, W., Sternes, K., Spallone, P., . . . & Keating, M. T. (1993). Hemizygosity at the elastin locus in a developmental disorder, Williams syndrome. *Nature Genetics, 5*, 11–16.

Fagerlund, A., Autti-Ramo, I., Kalland, M., Santtila, P., Hoyme, E. H., Mattson, S. N., & Korkman, M. (2012). Adaptive behavior in children and adolescents with fetal alcohol spectrum disorders: A comparison with specific learning disability and typical development. *European Child & Adolescent Psychiatry, 21*, 221–231.

Feinstein, C., & Reiss, A. L. (1998). Autism: The point of view from fragile X studies. *Journal of Autism and Developmental Disorders, 28*(5), 393–405.

Fernell, E., & Ek, U. (2010). Borderline intellectual functioning in children and adolescents—insufficiently recognized difficulties. *Act Paediatrica, 99*, 748–753.

Fidler, D. J., Hepburn, S., & Rogers, S. (2006). Early learning and adaptive behaviour in toddlers with Down syndrome: Evidence for an emerging behavioural phenotype? *Down's Syndrome, Research and Practice: The Journal of the Sarah Duffen Centre, 9*(3), 37–44.

Fidler, D., Most, D., & Philofsky, A. (2009). The Down syndrome behavioural phenotype: Taking a developmental approach. *Down Syndrome Research and Practice, 12*(3), 37–44.

Finucane, B. M., Lusk, L., Arkilo, D., Chamberlain, S., Devinsky, O., Dindot, S., . . . & Cook, E. H. (1993). 15q duplication syndrome and related disorders. *GeneReviews(®)*. University of Washington, Seattle.

Fisch, G. S., Carpenter, N., Holden, J. J., Howard-Peebles, P. N., Maddalena, A., Borghgraef, M., . . . & Fryns, J. P. (1999). Longitudinal changes in cognitive and adaptive behavior in fragile X females: A prospective multicenter analysis. *American Journal of Medical Genetics, 83*(4), 308–312.

Fisch, G. S., Carpenter, N., Howard-Peebles, P. N., Holden, J. J. A., Tarleton, J., Simensen, R., & Battaglia, A. (2012). Developmental trajectories in syndromes with intellectual disability, with a focus on Wolf-Hirschhorn and its cognitive-behavioral profile. *American Journal on Intellectual and Developmental Disabilities, 117*(2), 167–179.

Fisch, G. S., Simensen, R. J., & Schroer, R. J. (2002). Longitudinal changes in cognitive and adaptive behavior scores in children and adolescents with the fragile X mutation or autism. *Journal of Autism and Developmental Disorders, 32*(2), 107–114.

Fisher, M. H., Lense, M. D., & Dykens, E. M. (2016). Longitudinal trajectories of intellectual and adaptive functioning in adolescents and adults with Williams syndrome. *Journal of Intellectual Disability Research, 60*(10), 920–932.

Fjørtoft, T., Grunewaldt, K. H., Løhaugen, G. C. C., Mørkved, S., Skranes, J., & Evensen, K. A. I. (2015). Adaptive behavior in 10–11 year old children born preterm with a very low birth weight (VLBW). *European Journal of Paediatric Neurology, 19*(2), 162–169.

Flint, J., & Yule, W. (1994). Behavioral phenotypes. In M. Rutter, E. Taylor, & L. Hersov (Eds.), *Child and adolescent psychiatry* (pp. 666–687). Oxford, UK: Blackwell Scientific.

Freund, L. S., Peebles, C. D., Aylward, E., & Reiss, A. L. (1995). Preliminary report on cognitive and adaptive behaviors of preschool-aged males with fragile X. *Developmental Brain Dysfunction, 8*, 242–251.

Fu, T. J., Lincoln, A. J., Bellugi, U., & Searcy, Y. M. (2015). The association of intelligence, visual-motor functioning, and personality characteristics with adaptive behavior in individuals with Williams syndrome. *American Journal on Intellectual and Developmental Disabilities, 120*(4), 273–288.

Gibson, D. (1978). *Down's syndrome: The psychology of mongolism.* Cambridge, UK: Cambridge University Press.

Glass, H. C., Costarino, A. T., Stayer, S. A., Brett, C. M., Cladis, F., & Davis, P. J. (2015). Outcomes for extremely premature infants. *Anesthesia and Analgesia, 120*(6), 1337–1351.

Greenberg, F., Guzzetta, V., de Oca-Luna, R. M., Magenis, R. E., Smith, A. C. M., Richter, S. F., . . . & Lupski, J. R. (1991). Molecular analysis of the Smith-Magenis syndrome: A possible continguous-gene syndrome associated with del(17) (p11.2). *American Journal of Human Genetics, 4*, 1207–1218.

Greer, M. K., Brown, F. R. I., Pai, G., Choudry, S. H., & Klein, A. J. (1997). Cognitive, adaptive, and behavioral characteristics of Williams syndrome. *American Journal of Medical Genetics, 74*, 521–525.

Grieco, J., Pulsifer, M., Seligsohn, K., Skotko, B., & Schwartz, A. (2015). Down syndrome: Cognitive and behavioral functioning across the lifespan. *American Journal of Medical Genetics Part C: Seminars in Medical Genetics, 169*(2), 135–149.

Griffith, G. M., Hastings, R. P., Nash, S., & Hill, C. (2010). Using matched groups to explore child behavior problems and maternal well-being in children with Down syndrome and autism. *Journal of Autism and Developmental Disorders, 40*(5), 610–619.

Grossman, H. J. (1983). *Classification in mental retardation.* Washington, DC: American Assocation on Mental Deficiency.

Hack, M., Taylor, H. G., Drotar, D., Schluchter, M., Cartar, L., Andreias, L., . . . & Klein, N. (2005). Chronic conditions, functional limitations, and special health care needs of school-aged children born with extremely low-birth-weight in the 1990s. *JAMA, 294*(3), 318.

Hagerman, R. J., & Jackson, A. W. (1985). Autism or fragile X syndrome? *Journal of the American Academy of Child Psychiatry, 24*(2), 239–240.

Hahn, L. J., Brady, N. C., Warren, S. F., & Fleming, K. K. (2015). Do children with fragile X syndrome show declines or plateaus in adaptive behavior? *American Journal on Intellectual and Developmental Disabilities, 120*(5), 412–432.

Harries, J., Guscia, R., Nettelbeck, T., & Kirby, N. (2009). Impact of additional disabilities on adaptive behavior and support profiles for people with intellectual disabilities. *American Journal on Intellectual and Developmental Disabilities, 114*(4), 237–253.

Harrison, P., & Oakland, T. (2003). *Adaptive behavior assessment system* (2nd ed.). San Antonio, TX: Pearson.

Hatton, D. D., Wheeler, A. C., Skinner, M. L., Bailey, D. B., Sullivan, K. M., Roberts, J. E., . . . & Clark, R. D. (2003). Adaptive behavior in children with fragile X syndrome. *American Journal of Mental Retardation, 108*(6), 373–390.

Hodapp, R. M. (1997). Direct and indirect behavioral effects of different genetic disorders of mental retardation. *American Journal of Mental Retardation, 102*, 67–79.

Hodapp, R. M. (2006). Total versus partial specificity in the behaviour of persons with Down syndrome. In J. Rondal & J. Perera (Eds.), *Down syndrome: Neurobehavioral specificity*. Hoboken, NJ: Wiley.

Howe, T. H., Sheu, C. F., Hsu, Y.W., Wang, T. N., & Wang, L. W. (2016). Predicting neurodevelopmental outcomes at preschool age for children with very low birth weight. *Research in Developmental Disabilities, 48,* 231–241.

Howlin, P., Elison, S., Udwin, O., & Stinton, C. (2010). Cognitive, linguistic and adaptive functioning in Williams syndrome: Trajectories from early to middle adulthood. *Journal of Applied Research in Intellectual Disabilities, 23*(4), 322–336.

Jobling, A. (1998). Motor development in school-aged children with Down syndrome: A longitudinal perspective. *International Journal of Disability, Development and Education, 45*(3), 283–293.

Kalberg, W. O., Provost, B., Tollison, S. J., Tabachnick, B. G., Robinson, L. K., Eugene Hoyme, H., . . . & May, P. A. (2006). Comparison of motor delays in young children with fetal alcohol syndrome to those with prenatal alcohol exposure and with no prenatal alcohol exposure. *Alcoholism: Clinical and Experimental Research, 30*(12), 2037–2045.

Kaufmann, W. E., Cortell, R., Kau, A. S., Bukelis, I., Tierney, E., Gray, R. M., . . . & Stanard, P. (2004). Autism spectrum disorder in fragile X syndrome: Communication, social interaction, and specific behaviors. *American Journal of Medical Genetics Part A, 129A*(3), 225–234.

Key, A. P., Jones, D., & Dykens, E. M. (2013). Social and emotional processing in Prader-Willi syndrome: Genetic subtype differences. *Journal of Neurodevelopmental Disorders, 5*(1), 7.

King, B. H., Toth, K. E., Hodapp, R. M., & Dykens, E. M. (2009). Intellectual disability. In B. J. Sadock, V. A. Sadock, & P. Ruiz (Eds.), *Comprehensive textbook of psychiatry* (pp. 3444–3474). Philadelphia, PA: Lippincott Williams & Wilkins.

Klaiman, C., Quintin, E.-M., Jo, B., Lightbody, A. A., Hazlett, H. C., Piven, J., . . . & Reiss, A. L. (2014). Longitudinal profiles of adaptive behavior in fragile X syndrome. *Pediatrics, 134*(2), 315–324.

Kover, S. T., Pierpont, E. I., Kim, J.-S., Brown, W. T., & Abbeduto, L. (2013). A neurodevelopmental perspective on the acquisition of nonverbal cognitive skills in adolescents with fragile X syndrome. *Developmental Neuropsychology, 38*(7), 445–460.

Lauteslager, P., Vermeer, A., Helders, P., & Mazer, B. (1998). Disturbances in the motor behaviour of children with Down's syndrome: The need for a theoretical framework. *Physiotherapy, 84*(1), 5–13.

Leonard, H., & Wen, X. (2002). The epidemiology of mental retardation: Challenges and opportunities in the new millenium. *Mental Retardation and Developmental Disabilities Research Reviews, 8,* 1117–1134.

Loveland, K. A., & Kelley, M. L. (1991). Development of adaptive behavior in preschoolers with autism or Down syndrome. *American Journal of Mental Retardation, 96*(1), 13–20.

Madduri, N., Peters, S. U., Voigt, R. G., Llorente, A. M., Lupski, J. R., & Potocki, L. (2006). Cognitive and adaptive behavior profiles in Smith-Magenis syndrome. *Journal of Developmental & Behavioral Pediatrics, 27*(3), 188–192.

Maloney, E. S., & Larrivee, L. S. (2007). Limitations of age-equivalence scores in reporting results of norm-referenced tests. *Contemporary Issues in Communication Sciences and Disorders, 34,* 86–93.

Marchal, J. P., Maurice-Stam, H., Houtzager, B. A., Rutgers van Rozenburg-Marres, S. L., Oostrom, K. J., Grootenhuis, M. A., & van Trotsenburg, A. S. P. (2016). Growing up with Down syndrome: Development from 6 months to 10.7 years. *Research in Developmental Disabilities, 59,* 437–450.

Mascari, M. J., Gottlieb, W., Rogan, P. K., Butler, M. G., Waller, D. A., Armour, J. A. L., . . . & Nicholls, R. D. (1992). The frequency of uniparental disomy in Prader-Willi syndrome. *New England Journal of Medicine, 326*(24), 1599–1607.

Maulik, P. K., Mascarenhas, M. N., Mathers, C. D., Dua, T., & Saxena, S. (2011). Prevalence of intellectual disability: A meta-analysis of population-based studies. *Research in Developmental Disabilities, 32*(2), 419–436.

Mazzocco, M. M., & Holden, J. A. (1996). Neuropsychological profiles of three sisters homozygious for the fragile X mutation. *American Journal of Medical Genetics, 64*, 323–328.

McKenzie, K., Milton, M., Smith, G., & Ouellette-Kuntz, H. (2016). Systematic review of the prevalence and incidence of intellectual disabilities: Current trends and issues. *Current Developmental Disorders Reports, 3*, 104–115.

Mervis, C. B., & Bertrand, J. (1997). Developmental relations between cognition and language: Evidence from Williams syndrome. In L. B. Adamson & M. A. Romski (Eds.), *Communication and language acquisition: Discoveries from atypical development* (pp. 75–106). Baltimore, MD: Brookes.

Mervis, C. B., & John, A. E. (2010). Cognitive and behavioral characteristics of children with Williams syndrome: Implications for intervention approaches. *American Journal of Medical Genetics Part C: Seminar in Medical Genetics, 2*, 229–248.

Mervis, C. B., & Klein-Tasman, B. P. (2000). Williams syndrome: Cognition, personality, and adaptive behavior. *Mental Retardation Developmental Disabilities Research Review, 6*, 148–158.

Mervis, C. B., & Klein-Tasman, B. P. (2004). Methodological issues in group-matching designs: Alpha levels for control variable comparisons and measurement characteristics of control and target variables. *Journal of Autism and Developmental Disorders, 34*(1), 7–17.

Mervis, C. B., Klein-Tasman, B. P., & Mastin, M. E. (2001). Adaptive behavior of 4- through 8-year-old children with Williams syndrome. *American Journal on Mental Retardation, 106*(1), 82.

Mervis, C. B., & Pitts, C. H. (2015). Children with Williams syndrome: Developmental trajectories for intellectual abilities, vocabulary abilities, and adaptive behavior. *American Journal of Medical Genetics Part C: Seminar in Medical Genetics, 169*(2), 158–171.

Meyers, C. E., Nihira, K., & Zetlin, A. (1979). *The measurement of adaptive behavior.* In N. R. Ellis (Ed.), *Handbook of mental deficiency. Psychological theory and research* (2nd ed.). Hillsdale, NJ: Erlbaum.

Miny, P., Basaran, S., Kuwertz, E., Holzgreve, W., Pawlowitzki, I.-H., Claussen, U., . . . & Courchesne, E. (1986). Inv dup (15): Prenatal diagnosis and postnatal follow-up. *Prenatal Diagnosis, 6*(4), 303–306.

Mircher, C., Toulas, J., Cieuta-Walti, C., Marey, I., Conte, M., González Briceño, L., . . . & Ravel, A. (2017). Anthropometric charts and congenital anomalies in newborns with Down syndrome. *American Journal of Medical Genetics Part A, 173*(8), 2166–2175.

Morris, C. A. (2006). The dysmorphology, genetics, and natural history of Williams-Beuren syndrome. In C. A. Morris, H. M. Lenhoff, & P. P. Wang (Eds.), *Williams-Beuren syndrome: Research, evaluation, and treatment* (pp. 3–17). Baltimore, MD: Johns Hopkins University Press.

Morris, C. A. (2010). Introduction: Williams syndrome. *American Journal of Medical Genetics Part C: Seminar in Medical Genetics, 154C*, 203–208.

Murphy, C. C., Yeargin-Allsopp, M., Decoufle, P., & Drews, C. D. (1995). The adminstrative prevalence of mental retardation in 10-year-old children in metropolitan Atlanta. *American Journal of Public Health, 85*, 319–323.

Myers, B. A., & Pueschel, S. M. (1991). Psychiatric disorders in persons with Down syndrome. *The Journal of Nervous and Mental Disease, 179*(10), 609–613.

National Research Council: Reschly, D.J., Myers, T.G., & Hartel, C.R. (Eds.) (2002). *Mental retardation: Determining eligibility for social security benefits.* Washington, DC: National Academies Press.

Nicholls, R. D., Knoll, J. H. M., Butler, M. G., Karam, S., & Lalande, M. (1989). Genetic imprinting suggested by maternal heterodisomy in non-deletion Prader-Willi syndrome. *Nature, 342*(6247), 281–285.

Patterson, T., Rapsey, C. M., & Glue, P. (2013). Systematic review of cognitive development across childhood in Down syndrome: Implications for treatment interventions. *Journal of Intellectual Disability Research, 57*(4), 390–392.

Philofsky, A., Hepburn, S. L., Hayes, A., Hagerman, R. J., & Rogers, S. J. (2004). Linguistic and cognitive functioning and autism symptoms in young children with fragile X syndrome. *American Journal on Mental Retardation, 109*(3), 208–218.

Piek, J., Dawson, L., Smith, L., & Gasson, N. (2008). The role of early fine and gross motor development on later motor and cogntiive ability. *Human Movement Science, 2*(5), 668–684.

Prader, A., Labhart, A., & Willi, A. (1956). Ein syndrom von aidositas, kleinwuchs, kryptorchismus und oligophrenie nach myotonieartigm zustand im neugeborenenalter [A syndrome of obesity, hypogonadism, and learning disability, with hypotonia during the neonatal period]. *Schweizerische Medizinische Wochenschrift, 86*, 1260–1261.

Reiss, A. L., Freund, L., Abrams, M. T., Boehm, C., & Kazazian, H. (1993). Neurobehavioral effects of the fragile X premutation in adult women: A controlled study. *American Journal of Human Genetics, 52*, 884–894.

Reschly, D., Grimes, J., & Ross-Reynolds, J. (1981). *Report: State norms for IQ, adaptive behavior, and sociocultural status: Implications for nonbiased assessment.* Des Moines, IA: Iowa State Department of Public Instruction.

Richards, S. B., Brady, M. P., & Taylor, R. L. (2015). Definition and classification of cognitive/intellectual disabilities. *Cognitive and intellectual disabilities: Historical perspectives, current practices, and future directions* (2nd ed., pp. 38–62). New York, NY: Routledge.

Robinson, W. P., Bottani, A., Xie, Y. G., Balakrishman, J., Binkert, F., Mächler, M.,...& Schinzel, A. (1991). Molecular, cytogenetic, and clinical investigations of Prader-Willi syndrome patients. *American Journal of Human Genetics, 49*(6), 1219–1234.

Rondal, J., Perera, J., & Nadel, L. (1999). *Down syndrome: A review of current knowledge.* Hoboken, NJ: Wiley.

Rosenbaum, P., Saigal, S., Szatmari, P., & Hoult, L. (1995). Vineland Adaptive Behavior Scales as a summary of functional outcome of extremely low-birthweight children. *Developmental Medicine and Child Neurology, 37*(7), 577–586.

Rush, K. S., Bowman, L. G., Eidman, S. L., Toole, L. M., & Mortenson, B. P. (2004). Assessing psychopathology in individuals with developmental disabilities. *Behavior Modification, 28*, 621–637.

Saitoh, S., Buiting, K., Cassidy, S. B., Conroy, J. M., Driscoll, D. J., Gabriel, J. M.,...& Nicholas, R. D. (1997). Clinical spectrum and molecular diagnosis of Angelman and Prader-Willi syndrome imprinting mutation patients. *American Journal of Medical Genetics, 68*, 195–206.

Silverman, W. (2007). Down syndrome: Cognitive phenotype. *Mental Retardation and Developmental Disabilities Research Reviews, 13*(3), 228–236.

Simon, E. W., & Finucane, B. M. (1996). Facial emotion identification in males with fragile X syndrome. *American Journal of Medical Genetics, 67*(1), 77–80.

Smith, J. C. (2001). Angelman syndrome: Evolution of the phenotype in adolescents and adults. *Developmental Medicine and Child Neurology, 43*(7), 476–480.

Soenen, S., Van Berckelaer-Onnes, I., & Scholte, E. (2009). Patterns of intellectual, adaptive and behavioral functioning in individuals with mild mental retardation. *Research in Developmental Disabilities, 30*(3), 433–444.

Sparrow, S. S., Balla, D., & Cicchetti, D. V. (1984). *Vineland adaptive behavior scales* (Expanded). Circle Pines, MN: American Guidance Service.

Summers, J. A., & Feldman, M. A. (1999). Distinctive pattern of behavioral functioning in Angelman syndrome. *American Journal on Mental Retardation, 104*(4), 376.

Taylor, R., & Partenio, I. (1983). *Florida norms for the SOMPA.* Tallahassee, FL: Bureau of Education for Exceptional Students.

Tremblay, K. N., Richer, L., Lachance, L., & Côté, A. (2010). Psychopathological manifestations of children with intellectual disabilities according to their cognitive and adaptive behavior profile. *Research in Developmental Disabilities, 31*(1), 57–69.

Tsao, R., & Kindelberger, C. (2009). Variability of cognitive development in children with Down syndrome: Relevance of good reasons for using the cluster procedure. *Research in Developmental Disabilities, 30*(3), 426–432.

Turk, J., & Cornish, K. (1998). Face recognition and emotion perception in boys with fragile X syndrome. *Journal of Intellectual Disability Research, 42*(Pt 6), 490–499.

Turner, G., Webb, T., Wake, S., & Robinson, H. (1996). Prevalence of fragile X syndrome. *American Journal of Medical Genetics, 64*, 197.

Valencia, R. R., & Suzuki, L. A. (2001). *Intelligence testing and minority students: Foundations, performance factors and assessment issues.* Thousand Oaks, CA: Sage.

Van Duijn, G., Dijkxhoorn, Y., Scholte, E. M., & Van Berckelaer-Onnes, I. A. (2010). The development of adaptive skills in young people with Down syndrome. *Journal of Intellectual Disability Research, 54*(11), 943–954.

van Isterdael, C. E. D., Stilma, J. S., Bezemer, P. D., & Tijmes, N. T. (2006). 6220 institutionalised people with intellectual disability referred for visual assessment between 1993 and 2003: Overview and trends. *British Journal of Ophthamology, 90*, 1297–1303.

Verkerk, A. J., Pieretti, M., Sutcliffe, J. S., Fu, Y. H., Kuhi, D. P., Pizzuit, A., ... & Warren, S. T. (1991). Identification of a gene (FMR-1) containing a CHGG repeat coincident with a breakpoint cluster region exhibiting length variation in fragile X syndrome. *Cell, 65*, 905–914.

Vicari, S. (2006). Motor development and neuropsychological patterns in persons with Down syndrome. *Behavior Genetics, 36*(3), 355–364.

Vig, S., & Jedrysek, E. (1995). Adaptive behavior of young urban children with developmental disabilities. *Mental Retardation, 33*(2), 90–98.

Volman, M. J. M., Visser, J. J. W., & Lensvelt-Mulders, G. J. L. M. (2007). Functional status in 5- to 7-year-old children with Down syndrome in relation to motor ability and performance mental ability. *Disability and Rehabilitation, 29*(1), 25–31.

Wadell, P. M., Hagerman, R. J., & Hessl, D. R. (2013). Fragile X syndrome: Psychiatric manifestations, assessment and emerging therapies. *Current Psychiatry Reviews, 9*(1), 53–58.

Ware, A. L., Glass, L., Crocker, N., Deweese, B. N., Coles, C. D., Kable, J. A., ... & CIFASD. (2014). Effects of prenatal alcohol exposure and ADHD on adaptive functioning. *Alcoholism: Clinical and Experimental Research, 38*(5), 1439–1447.

Warren, S. F., Brady, N., Fleming, K. K., & Hahn, L. J. (2017). The longitudinal effects of parenting on adaptive behavior in children with fragile X syndrome. *Journal of Autism and Developmental Disorders, 47*(3), 768–784.

Weeland, M. M., Nijhof, K. S., Otten, R., Vermaes, I. P. R., & Buitelaar, J. K. (2017). Beck's cognitive theory and the response style theory of depression in adolescents with and without mild to borderline intellectual disability. *Research in Developmental Disabilities, 69*, 39–48.

Whittington, J., Holland, A., Webb, T., Butler, J., Clarke, D., & Boer, H. (2004). Academic underachievement by people with Prader-Willi syndrome. *Journal of Intellectual Disability Research, 48*(2), 188–200.

Williams, J. C., Barrett-Boyes, B. G., & Lowe, J. B. (1961). Supravalvular aortic stenosis. *Circulation, 24*, 1311–1318.

CHAPTER FIVE

Anderson, D. K., Oti, R. S., Lord, C., & Welch, K. (2009). Patterns of growth in adaptive social abilities among children with autism spectrum disorders. *Journal of Abnormal Child Psychology, 37*(7), 1019–1034.

Bal, V. H., Kim, S.-H., Cheong, D., & Lord, C. (2015). Daily living skills in individuals with autism spectrum disorder from 2 to 21 years of age. *Autism: The International Journal of Research and Practice, 19*(7), 774–784.

Balboni, G., Tasso, A., Muratori, F., & Cubelli, R. (2016). The Vineland-II in preschool children with autism spectrum disorders: An item content category analysis. *Journal of Autism and Developmental Disorders, 46*(1), 42–52.

Blanche, E. I., Diaz, J., Barretto, T., & Cermak, S. A. (2015). Caregiving experiences of Latino families with children with autism spectrum disorder. *The American Journal of Occupational Therapy, 69*(5), 1–11.

Carter, A., Volkmar, F. R., Sparrow, S. S., Wang, J. J., Lord, C., Dawson, G., . . . & Schopler, E. (1998). The Vineland Adaptive Behavior Scales: Supplementary norms for individuals with autism. *Journal of Autism and Developmental Disorders, 28*(4), 287–302.

Christensen, D. L., Baio, J., Braun, K. V. N., Bilder, D., Charles, J., Constantino, J. N., . . . & Yeargin-Allsopp, M. (2016). Prevalence and characteristics of autism spectrum disorder among children aged 8 years: Autism and developmental disabilities monitoring network, 11 sites, United States, 2012. *MMWR Surveillance Summaries, 65*(3), 1–23.

Cuccaro, M. L., Brinkley, J., Abramson, R. K., Hall, A., Wright, H. H., Hussman, J. P., . . . & Pericak-Vance, M. A. (2007). Autism in African American families: Clinical-phenotypic findings. *American Journal of Medical Genetics Part B: Neuropsychiatric Genetics, 144B*(8), 1022–1026.

Durkin, M. S., Maenner, M. J., Meaney, J., Levy, S. E., DiGuiseppi, C., Nicholas, J. S., . . . & Schieve, L. A. (2010). Socioeconomic inequality in the prevalence of autism spectrum disorder: Evidence from a U.S. cross-sectional study. *PLOS ONE, 5*(7), e11551.

Fenton, G., D'Ardia, C., Valente, D., Del Vecchio, I., Fabrizi, A., & Bernabei, P. (2003). Vineland Adaptive Behavior profiles in children with autism and moderate to severe developmental delay. *Autism: The International Journal of Research and Practice, 7*(3), 269–287.

Frazier, T. W., Georgiades, S., Bishop, S. L., & Hardan, A. Y. (2014). Behavioral and cognitive characteristics of females and males with autism in the Simons Simplex Collection. *Journal of the American Academy of Child and Adolescent Psychiatry, 53*(3), 329–340.

Freeman, B. J., Del'Homme, M., Guthrie, D., & Zhang, F. (1999). Vineland Adaptive Behavior Scale scores as a function of age and initial IQ in 210 autistic children. *Journal of Autism and Developmental Disorders, 29*(5), 379–384.

Frost, K. M., Hong, N., & Lord, C. (2017). Correlates of adaptive functioning in minimally verbal children with autism spectrum disorder. *American Journal on Intellectual and Developmental Disabilities, 122*(1), 1–10.

Garland, A. F., Lau, A. S., Yeh, M., McCabe, K. M., Hough, R. L., & Landsverk, J. A. (2005). Racial and ethnic differences in utilization of mental health services among high-risk youths. *American Journal of Psychiatry, 162*(7), 1336–1343.

Gotham, K., Pickles, A., & Lord, C. (2012). Trajectories of autism severity in children using standardized ADOS scores. *Pediatrics, 130*(5), e1278–e1284.

Ijalba, E. (2016). Hispanic immigrant mothers of young children with autism spectrum disorders: How do they understand and cope with autism? *American Journal of Speech-Language Pathology, 25*(2), 200–213.

Kanne, S. M., Gerber, A. J., Quirmbach, L. M., Sparrow, S. S., Cicchetti, D. V, & Saulnier, C. A. (2011). The role of adaptive behavior in autism spectrum disorders: Implications for functional outcome. *Journal of Autism and Developmental Disorders, 41*(8), 1007–1018.

Kenworthy, L., Case, L., Harms, M. B., Martin, A., & Wallace, G. L. (2010). Adaptive behavior ratings correlate with symptomatology and IQ among individuals with high-functioning autism spectrum disorders. *Journal of Autism and Developmental Disorders, 40*(4), 416–423.

Klin, A., Saulnier, C. A., Sparrow, S. S., Cicchetti, D. V, Volkmar, F. R., & Lord, C. (2007). Social and communication abilities and disabilities in higher functioning individuals with autism spectrum disorders: The Vineland and the ADOS. *Journal of Autism and Developmental Disorders, 37*(4), 748–759.

Liss, M., Harel, B., Fein, D., Allen, D., Dunn, M., Feinstein, C., ... & Rapin, I. (2001). Predictors and correlates of adaptive functioning in children with developmental disorders. *Journal of Autism and Developmental Disorders, 31*(2), 219–230.

Liss, M., Saulnier, C., Fein, D., & Kinsbourne, M. (2006). Sensory and attention abnormalities in autistic spectrum disorders. *Autism: The International Journal of Research and Practice, 10*(2), 155–172.

Lord, C., & Schopler, E. (1985). Differences in sex ratios in autism as a function of measured intelligence. *Journal of Autism and Developmental Disorders, 15*(2), 185–193.

Loveland, K. A., & Kelley, M. L. (1991). Development of adaptive behavior in preschoolers with autism or Down syndrome. *American Journal of Mental Retardation, 96*(1), 13–20.

Magaña, S., Lopez, K., Aguinaga, A., & Morton, H. (2013). Access to diagnosis and treatment services among Latino children with autism spectrum disorders. *Intellectual and Developmental Disabilities, 51*(3), 141–153.

Mandell, D. S., Wiggins, L. D., Carpenter, L. A., Daniels, J., DiGuiseppi, C., Durkin, M. S., ... & Kirby, R. S. (2009). Racial/ethnic disparities in the identification of children with autism spectrum disorders. *American Journal of Public Health, 99*(3), 493–498.

Mandic-Maravic, V., Pejovic-Milovancevic, M., Mitkovic-Voncina, M., Kostic, M., Aleksic-Hil, O., Radosavljev-Kircanski, J., ... & Lecic-Tosevski, D. (2015). Sex differences in autism spectrum disorders: Does sex moderate the pathway from clinical symptoms to adaptive behavior? *Scientific Reports, 5*(1), 10418.

Mandy, W., Chilvers, R., Chowdhury, U., Salter, G., Seigal, A., & Skuse, D. (2012). Sex differences in autism spectrum disorder: Evidence from a large sample of children and adolescents. *Journal of Autism and Developmental Disorders, 42*(7), 1304–1313.

Parish, S., Magaña, S., Rose, R., Timberlake, M., & Swaine, J. G. (2012). Health care of Latino children with autism and other developmental disabilities: Quality of provider interaction mediates utilization. *American Journal on Intellectual and Developmental Disabilities, 117*(4), 304–315.

Paul, R., Loomis, R., & Chawarska, K. (2014). Adaptive behavior in toddlers under two with autism spectrum disorders. *Journal of Autism and Developmental Disorders, 44*(2), 264–270.

Paul, R., Miles, S., Cicchetti, D., Sparrow, S., Klin, A., Volkmar, F., ... & Booker, S. (2004). Adaptive behavior in autism and pervasive developmental disorder–not otherwise specified: Microanalysis of scores on the Vineland Adaptive Behavior Scales. *Journal of Autism and Developmental Disorders, 34*(2), 223–228.

Perry, A., Flanagan, H. E., Dunn Geier, J., & Freeman, N. L. (2009). Brief report: The Vineland Adaptive Behavior Scales in young children with autism spectrum disorders at different cognitive levels. *Journal of Autism and Developmental Disorders, 39*(7), 1066–1078.

Ratto, A. B., Anthony, B. J., Kenworthy, L., Armour, A. C., Dudley, K., & Anthony, L. G. (2016). Are non-intellectually disabled Black youth with ASD less impaired on parent report than their White peers? *Journal of Autism and Developmental Disorders, 46*(3), 773–781.

Ray-Subramanian, C. E., Huai, N., & Ellis Weismer, S. (2011). Brief report: Adaptive behavior and cognitive skills for toddlers on the autism spectrum. *Journal of Autism and Developmental Disorders, 41*(5), 679–684.

Rogers, S. J., Hepburn, S., & Wehner, E. (2003). Parent reports of sensory symptoms in toddlers with autism and those with other developmental disorders. *Journal of Autism and Developmental Disorders, 33*(6), 631–642.

Saulnier, C. A., & Klin, A. (2007). Brief report: Social and communication abilities and disabilities in higher functioning individuals with autism and Asperger syndrome. *Journal of Autism and Developmental Disorders, 37*(4), 788–793.

Schatz, J., & Hamdan-Allen, G. (1995). Effects of age and IQ on adaptive behavior domains for children with autism. *Journal of Autism and Developmental Disorders, 25*(1), 51–60.

Schopler, E., Andrews, C. E., & Strupp, K. (1979). Do autistic children come from upper-middle-class parents? *Journal of Autism and Developmental Disorders, 9*(2), 139–152.

Szatmari, P., Bryson, S. E., Boyle, M. H., Streiner, D. L., & Duku, E. (2003). Predictors of outcome among high functioning children with autism and Asperger syndrome. *Journal of Child Psychology and Psychiatry, and Allied Disciplines, 44*(4), 520–528.

Szatmari, P., Liu, X.-Q., Goldberg, J., Zwaigenbaum, L., Paterson, A. D., Woodbury-Smith, M., . . . & Thompson, A. (2012). Sex differences in repetitive stereotyped behaviors in autism: Implications for genetic liability. *American Journal of Medical Genetics Part B: Neuropsychiatric Genetics, 159B*(1), 5–12.

Tomanik, S. S., Pearson, D. A., Loveland, K. A., Lane, D. M., & Bryant Shaw, J. (2007). Improving the reliability of autism diagnoses: Examining the utility of adaptive behavior. *Journal of Autism and Developmental Disorders, 37*(5), 921–928.

Valicenti-McDermott, M., Hottinger, K., Seijo, R., & Shulman, L. (2012). Age at diagnosis of autism spectrum disorders. *The Journal of Pediatrics, 161*(3), 554–556.

Ventola, P. E., Saulnier, C. A., Steinberg, E., Chawarska, K., & Klin, A. (2014). Early-emerging social adaptive skills in toddlers with autism spectrum disorders: An item analysis. *Journal of Autism and Developmental Disorders, 44*(2), 283–293.

Volkmar, F. R., Carter, A., Sparrow, S. S., & Cicchetti, D. V. (1993). Quantifying social development in autism. *Journal of the American Academy of Child and Adolescent Psychiatry, 32*(3), 627–632.

Volkmar, F. R., Sparrow, S. S., Goudreau, D., Cicchetti, D. V, Paul, R., & Cohen, D. J. (1987). Social deficits in autism: An operational approach using the Vineland Adaptive Behavior Scales. *Journal of the American Academy of Child and Adolescent Psychiatry, 26*(2), 156–161.

Volkmar, F. R., Szatmari, P., & Sparrow, S. S. (1993). Sex differences in pervasive developmental disorders. *Journal of Autism and Developmental Disorders, 23*(4), 579–591.

Wells, K., Condillac, R. A., Perry, A., & Factor, D. C. (2009). Comparison of three adaptive behaviour measures in autism in relation to cognitive level and severity of autism. *Journal on Developmental Disabilities, 15*(3), 55–63.

White, E. I., Wallace, G. L., Bascom, J., Armour, A. C., Register-Brown, K., Popal, H. S., . . . & Kenworthy, L. (2017). Sex differences in parent-reported executive functioning and adaptive behavior in children and young adults with autism spectrum disorder. *Autism Research, 10*(10), 1653–1662.

Wing, L. (1980). Childhood autism and social class: A question of selection? *The British Journal of Psychiatry: The Journal of Mental Science, 137*, 410–417.

Yang, S., Paynter, J. M., & Gilmore, L. (2016). Vineland Adaptive Behavior Scales II: Profile of young children with autism spectrum disorder. *Journal of Autism and Developmental Disorders, 46*(1), 64–73. http://doi.org/10.1007/s10803-015-2543-1

Zuckerman, K. E., Lindly, O. J., Reyes, N. M., Chavez, A. E., Macias, K., Smith, K. N., & Reynolds, A. (2017). Disparities in diagnosis and treatment of autism in Latino and non-Latino White families. *Pediatrics, 139*(5), e20163010.

CHAPTER SIX

American Psychiatric Association. (2013). *Diagnostic and statistical manual of mental disorders.* Washington, DC: Author.

American Speech-Language-Hearing Association (ASHA). (2006). *Guidelines for speech language pathologists in diagnosis, assessment, and treatment of autism spectrum disorders across the life span.* Rockville, MD: Author.

Aram, D. M., Morris, R., & Hall, N. E. (1993). Clinical and research congruence in identifying children with specific language impairment. *Journal of Speech and Hearing Research, 36*(3), 580–591.

Arciuli, J., Stevens, K., Trembath, D., & Simpson, I. C. (2013). The relationship between parent report of adaptive behavior and direct assessment of reading ability in children with autism spectrum disorder. *Journal of Speech, Language, and Hearing Research, 56*(6), 1837–1844.

Balboni, G., & Ceccarani, P. (2003). Sensorimotor disorder: Assessment of disability. In B. G. Cook, M. Tankersley, & T. J. Landrum (Eds.), *Advances in learning and behavioral disabilities* (Vol. 16, pp. 191–204). West Yorkshire, UK: Emerald Group Publishing Limited.

Balboni, G., Incognito, O., Belacchi, C., Bonichini, S., & Cubelli, R. (2017). Vineland-II Adaptive Behavior profile of children with attention-deficit/hyperactivity disorder or specific learning disorders. *Research in Developmental Disabilities, 61*, 55–65.

Balboni, G., Pedrabissi, L., Molteni, M., & Villa, S. (2001). Discriminant validity of the Vineland Scales: Score profiles of individuals with mental retardation and a specific disorder. *American Journal of Mental Retardation, 106*(2), 162–172.

Barkley, R. A., Fischer, M., Edelbrock, C. S., & Smallish, L. (1990). The adolescent outcome of hyperactive children diagnosed by research criteria: I. An 8-year prospective follow-up study. *Journal of the American Academy of Child & Adolescent Psychiatry, 29*(4), 546–557.

Bautista, R. E. D. (2017). Understanding the self-management skills of persons with epilepsy. *Epilepsy & Behavior, 69*, 7–11.

Beer, J., Harris, M. S., Kronenberger, W. G., Holt, R. F., & Pisoni, D. B. (2012). Auditory skills, language development, and adaptive behavior of children with cochlear implants and additional disabilities. *International Journal of Audiology, 51*(6), 491–498.

Beitchman, J. H., Wilson, B., Brownlie, E. B., Walters, H., & Lancee, W. (1996). Long-term consistency in speech/language profiles: I. Developmental and academic outcomes. *Journal of the American Academy of Child & Adolescent Psychiatry, 35*(6), 804–814.

Berg, A. T., Smith, S. N., Frobish, D., Beckerman, B., Levy, S. R., Testa, F. M., & Shinnar, S. (2004). Longitudinal assessment of adaptive behavior in infants and young children with newly diagnosed epilepsy: Influences of etiology, syndrome, and seizure control. *Pediatrics, 114*(3).

Bradford, A., & Dodd, B. (1994). The motor planning abilities of phonologically disordered children. *European Journal of Disorders of Communication, 29*(4), 349–369.

Bradford, A., & Dodd, B. (1996). Do all speech disordered children have motor deficits? *Clinical Linguistics & Phonetics, 10,* 77–101.

Brown, L., & Leigh, J. (1986). *Adaptive behavior inventory.* Austin, TX: PRO-ED.

Buelow, J. M., Perkins, S. M., Johnson, C. S., Byars, A. W., Fastenau, P. S., Dunn, D. W., & Austin, J. K. (2012). Adaptive functioning in children with epilepsy and learning problems. *Journal of Child Neurology, 27*(10), 1241–1249.

Carter, A. S., O'Donnell, D. A., Schultz, R. T., Scahill, L., Leckman, J. F., & Pauls, D. L. (2000). Social and emotional adjustment in children affected with Gilles de la Tourette's syndrome: Associations with ADHD and family functioning. *Journal of Child Psychology and Psychiatry, and Allied Disciplines, 41*(2), 215–223.

Clark, C., Prior, M., & Kinsella, G. (2002). The relationship between executive function abilities, adaptive behaviour, and academic achievement in children with externalising behaviour problems. *Journal of Child Psychology and Psychiatry, 43*(6), 785–796.

Coffey, B. J., & Park, K. S. (1997). Behavioral and emotional aspects of Tourette syndrome. *Neurologic Clinics, 15*(2), 277–289.

Crocker, N., Vaurio, L., Riley, E. P., & Mattson, S. N. (2009). Comparison of adaptive behavior in children with heavy prenatal alcohol exposure or attention-deficit hyperactivity disorder. *Alcoholism: Clinical and Experimental Research, 33*(11), 2015–2023.

Daneshi, A., & Hassanzadeh, S. (2007). Cochlear implantation in prelingually deaf persons with additional disability. *The Journal of Laryngology & Otology, 121*(7), 635–638.

Dawda, Y., & Ezewuzie, N. (2010). Epilepsy: Clinical features and diagnosis. *Clinical Pharmacist, 2,* 86–88.

de Bildt, A., Kraijer, D., Sytema, S., & Minderaa, R. (2005). The psychometric properties of the Vineland Adaptive Behavior Scales in children and adolescents with mental retardation. *Journal of Autism and Developmental Disorders, 35*(1), 53–62.

Dewey, D., Roy, E. A., Square-Storer, P. A., & Hayden, D. (1988). Limb and oral praxic abilities of children with verbal sequencing deficits. *Developmental Medicine and Child Neurology, 30,* 743–751.

Donaldson, A. I., Heavner, K. S., & Zwolan, T. A. (2004). Measuring progress in children with autism spectrum disorder who have cochlear implants. *Archives of Otolaryngology–Head & Neck Surgery, 130*(5), 666.

Dunlap, W. R., & Sands, D. I. (1990). Classification of the hearing impaired for independent living using the Vineland Adaptive Behavior Scale. *American Annals of the Deaf, 135*(5), 384–388.

Dykens, E., Leckman, J., Riddle, M., Hardin, M., Schwartz, S., & Cohen, D. (1990). Intellectual, academic, and adaptive functioning of Tourette syndrome children with and without attention deficit disorder. *Journal of Abnormal Child Psychology, 18*(6), 607–615.

Eggink, H., Kuiper, A., Peall, K. J., Contarino, M. F., Bosch, A. M., Post, B., . . . & de Koning, T. J. (2014). Rare inborn errors of metabolism with movement disorders: A case study to evaluate the impact upon quality of life and adaptive functioning. *Orphanet Journal of Rare Diseases, 9*(1), 177.

Erhardt, D., & Hinshaw, S. P. (1994). Initial sociometric impressions of attention-deficit hyperactivity disorder and comparison boys: Predictions from social behaviors and from nonbehavioral variables. *Journal of Consulting and Clinical Psychology, 62*(4), 833–842.

Fagerlund, A., Autti-Ramo, I., Kalland, M., Santtila, P., Hoyme, E. H., Mattson, S. N., & Korkman, M. (2012). Adaptive behavior in children and adolescents with fetal alcohol spectrum disorders: A comparison with specific learning disability and typical development. *European Child & Adolescent Psychiatry, 21,* 221–231.

Farmer, M., Echenne, B., Drouin, R., & Bentourkia, M. H. (2017). Insights in developmental coordination disorder. *Current Pediatric Reviews, 13.*

Flament, M. F., Whitaker, A., Rapoport, J. L., Davies, M., Berg, C. Z., Kalikow, K., . . . & Shaffer, D. (1988). Obsessive compulsive disorder in adolescence: An epidemiological study. *Journal of the American Academy of Child & Adolescent Psychiatry, 27*(6), 764–771.

García-Cazorla, A., Wolf, N. I., Serrano, M., Pérez-Dueñas, B., Pineda, M., Campistol, J., . . . & Hoffmann, G. F. (2009). Inborn errors of metabolism and motor disturbances in children. *Journal of Inherited Metabolic Disease, 32*(5), 618–629.

Geller, D. A., Coffey, B., Faraone, S., Hagermoser, L., Zaman, N. K., Farrell, C. L., . . . & Biederman, J. (2003). Does comorbid attention-deficit/hyperactivity disorder impact the clinical expression of pediatric obsessive-compulsive disorder? *CNS Spectrums, 8*(4), 259–264.

Green, S., Pring, L., & Swettenham, J. (2004). An investigation of first-order false belief understanding of children with congenital profound visual impairment. *British Journal of Developmental Psychology, 22,* 1–17.

Greenaway, R., Pring, L., Schepers, A., Isaacs, D. P., & Dale, N. J. (2017). Neuropsychological presentation and adaptive skills in high-functioning adolescents with visual impairment: A preliminary investigation. *Applied Neuropsychology. Child, 6*(2), 145–157.

Hall, N. E., & Segarra, V. R. (2007). Predicting academic performance in children with language impairment: The role of parent report. *Journal of Communication Disorders, 40*(1), 82–95.

Hall, P. K., Jordan, L., & Robin, D. (1993). *Developmental apraxia of speech: Theory and clinical practice.* Austin, TX: PRO-ED.

Hinshaw, S. P. (1992). Academic underachievement, attention deficits, and aggression: Comorbidity and implications for intervention. *Journal of Consulting and Clinical Psychology, 60*(6), 893–903.

Hinshaw, S. P. (2002). Intervention research, theoretical mechanisms, and causal processes related to externalizing behavior patterns. *Development and Psychopathology, 14*(4), 789–818.

Hobson, R. P., & Bishop, M. (2003). The pathogenesis of autism: Insights from congenital blindness. *Philosophical Transactions of the Royal Society of London Series B: Biological Sciences, 358*(1430), 335–344.

Hornsey, H., Banerjee, S., Zeitlin, H., & Robertson, M. (2001). The prevalence of Tourette syndrome in 13–14-year-olds in mainstream schools. *Journal of Child Psychology and Psychiatry, and Allied Disciplines, 42*(8), 1035–1039.

King, R. A., & Scahill, L. (2001). Emotional and behavioral difficulties associated with Tourette syndrome. *Advances in Neurology, 85,* 79–88.

Kjelgaard, M. M., & Tager-Flusberg, H. (2001). An investigation of language impairment in autism: Implications for genetic subgroups. *Language and Cognitive Processes, 16*(2–3), 287–308.

Ladd, G. W., & Burgess, K. B. (1999). Charting the relationship trajectories of aggressive, withdrawn, and aggressive/withdrawn children during early grade school. *Child Development, 70*(4), 910–929.

Leigh, J. (1987). Adaptive behavior of children with learning disabilities. *Journal of Learning Disabilities, 20*(9), 557–562.

Lindblad, I., Svensson, L., Landgren, M., Nasic, S., Tideman, E., Gillberg, C., & Fernell, E. (2013). Mild intellectual disability and ADHD: A comparative study of school-age children's adaptive abilities. *Acta Paediatrica, 102*(10), 1027–1031.

Meucci, P., Leonardi, M., Zibordi, F., & Nardocci, N. (2009). Measuring participation in children with Gilles de la Tourette syndrome: A pilot study with ICF-CY. *Disability and Rehabilitation, 31*(Sup1), S116–S120. http://doi.org/10.3109/09638280903317773

Newmeyer, A. J., Grether, S., Grasha, C., White, J., Akers, R., Aylward, C., . . . & deGrauw, T. (2007). Fine motor function and oral-motor imitation skills in preschool-age children with speech-sound disorders. *Clinical Pediatrics, 46*(7), 604–611.

Pijnacker, J., Vervloed, M. P. J., & Steenbergen, B. (2012). Pragmatic abilities in children with congenital visual impairment: An exploration of non-literal language and advanced theory of mind understanding. *Journal of Autism and Developmental Disorders, 42*(11), 2440–2449.

Rahi, J. S., Cable, N., & British Childhood Visual Impairment Study Group. (2003). Severe visual impairment and blindness in children in the UK. *Lancet, 362*(9393), 1359–1365.

Roizen, N. J., Blondis, T. A., Irwin, M., & Stein, M. (1994). Adaptive functioning in children with attention-deficit hyperactivity disorder. *Archives of Pediatrics & Adolescent Medicine, 148*(11), 1137–1142.

Shriberg, L. D., Aram, D. M., & Kwiatkowski, J. (1997). Developmental apraxia of speech: I. Descriptive and theoretical perspectives. *Journal of Speech, Language, and Hearing Research, 40*(2), 273–285.

Sparrow, S. S., Cicchetti, D. V., & Balla, D. A. (2005). *Vineland adaptive behavior scales* (2nd ed.). Circle Pines, MN: American Guidance Service.

Spencer, T., Biederman, J., Coffey, B., Geller, D., Faraone, S., & Wilens, T. (2001). Tourette disorder and ADHD. *Advances in Neurology, 85,* 57–77.

Stein, M. A., Szumowski, E., Blondis, T. A., & Roizen, N. J. (1995). Adaptive skills dysfunction in ADD and ADHD children. *Journal of Child Psychology and Psychiatry, and Allied Disciplines, 36*(4), 663–670.

Sukhodolsky, D. G., do Rosario-Campos, M. C., Scahill, L., Katsovich, L., Pauls, D. L., Peterson, B. S., . . . & Leckman, J. F. (2005). Adaptive, emotional, and family functioning of children with obsessive-compulsive disorder and comorbid attention deficit hyperactivity disorder. *American Journal of Psychiatry, 162*(6), 1125–1132.

Sukhodolsky, D. G., Scahill, L., Zhang, H., Peterson, B. S., King, R. A., Lombroso, P. J., . . . & Leckman, J. F. (2003). Disruptive behavior in children with Tourette's syndrome: Association with ADHD comorbidity, tic severity, and functional impairment. *Journal of the American Academy of Child and Adolescent Psychiatry, 42*(1), 98–105.

Swain, J. E., Scahill, L., Lombroso, P. J., King, R. A., & Leckman, J. F. (2007). Tourette syndrome and tic disorders: A decade of progress. *Journal of the American Academy of Child & Adolescent Psychiatry, 46*(8), 947–968.

Tan, S. S., Wiegerink, D. J. H. G., Vos, R. C., Smits, D. W., Voorman, J. M., Twisk, J. W. R., . . . PERRIN+ Study Group. (2014). Developmental trajectories of social participation in individuals with cerebral palsy: A multicentre longitudinal study. *Developmental Medicine & Child Neurology, 56*(4), 370–377.

Teverovsky, E. G., Bickel, J. O., & Feldman, H. M. (2009). Functional characteristics of children diagnosed with childhood apraxia of speech. *Disability and Rehabilitation, 31*(2), 94–102.

Tükel, Ş., Björelius, H., Henningsson, G., McAllister, A., & Eliasson, A. C. (2015). Motor functions and adaptive behaviour in children with childhood apraxia of speech. *International Journal of Speech-Language Pathology, 17*(5), 470–480.

Van Naarden, K., Decouflé, P., & Caldwell, K. (1999). Prevalence and characteristics of children with serious hearing impairment in metropolitan Atlanta, 1991–1993. *Pediatrics, 103*(3), 570–575.

van Schie, P. E. M., Siebes, R. C., Dallmeijer, A. J., Schuengel, C., Smits, D.-W., Gorter, J. W., & Becher, J. G. (2013). Development of social functioning and communication in school-aged (5-9 years) children with cerebral palsy. *Research in Developmental Disabilities, 34*(12), 4485–4494. http://doi.org/10.1016/j.ridd.2013.09.033

Villarreal, N. W., Riccio, C. A., Cohen, M. J., & Park, Y. (2014). Adaptive skills and somatization in children with epilepsy. *Epilepsy Research and Treatment, 2014*, 856735.

Visser, J. (2003). Developmental coordination disorder: A review of research on subtypes and comorbidities. *Human Movement Science, 22*(4–5), 479–493.

Vos, R. C., Dallmeijer, A. J., Verhoef, M., van Schie, P. E. M., Voorman, J. M., Wiegerink, D. J. H. G.,... & PERRIN+ Study Group. (2014). Developmental trajectories of receptive and expressive communication in children and young adults with cerebral palsy. *Developmental Medicine and Child Neurology, 56*(10), 951–959.

Winters, N. C., Collett, B. R., & Myers, K. M. (2005). Ten-year review of rating scales, VII: Scales assessing functional impairment. *Journal of the American Academy of Child and Adolescent Psychiatry, 44*(4), 309–338.

Zohar, A. H. (1999). The epidemiology of obsessive-compulsive disorder in children and adolescents. *Child and Adolescent Psychiatric Clinics of North America, 8*(3), 445–460.

Zwicker, J. G., Missiuna, C., Harris, S. R., & Boyd, L. A. (2012). Developmental coordination disorder: A review and update. *European Journal of Paediatric Neurology, 16*(6), 573–581.

CHAPTER SEVEN

Adams, D., & Oliver, C. (2010). The relationship between acquired impairments of executive function and behaviour change in adults with Down syndrome. *Journal of Intellectual Disability Research, 54*(5), 393–405.

American Association on Intellectual and Developmental Disabilities (AAIDD). (2017). *State of the states in intellectual and developmental disabilities*. Washington, DC: Author.

Baghdadli, A., Assouline, B., Sonié, S., Pernon, E., Darrou, C., Michelon, C.,... & Pry, R. (2012). Developmental trajectories of adaptive behaviors from early childhood to adolescence in a cohort of 152 children with autism spectrum disorders. *Journal of Autism and Developmental Disorders, 42*(7), 1314–1325.

Bailey, D. B., Raspa, M., Bishop, E., Mitra, D., Martin, S., Wheeler, A., & Sacco, P. (2012). Health and economic consequences of fragile X syndrome for caregivers. *Journal of Developmental & Behavioral Pediatrics, 33*(9), 705–712.

Bateman, B. D. (1995). *Writing individualized education programs (IEPs) for success*. Wrights Law. Learning Disabilities Association. Retrieved from http://wrightslaw.com/info/iep .success.bateman.htm

Belva, B. C., & Matson, J. L. (2013). An examination of specific daily living skills deficits in adults with profound intellectual disabilities. *Research in Developmental Disabilities, 34*(1), 596–604.

Bhaumik, S., Tyrer, F. C., McGrother, C., & Ganghadaran, S. K. (2008). Psychiatric service use and psychiatric disorders in adults with intellectual disability. *Journal of Intellectual Disability Research, 52*(11), 986–995.

Billstedt, E., Gillberg, I. C., Gillberg, C., & Gillberg, C. (2005). Autism after adolescence: Population-based 13- to 22-year follow-up study of 120 individuals with autism diagnosed in childhood. *Journal of Autism and Developmental Disorders, 35*(3), 351–360.

Boccaccini, M. T., Kan, L. Y., Rufino, K. A., Noland, R. M., Young-Lundquist, B. A., & Canales, E. (2016). Correspondence between correctional staff and offender ratings of adaptive behavior. *Psychological Assessment, 28*(12), 1608–1615.

Brooke, D., Taylor, C., Gunn, J., & Maden, A. (1996). Point prevalence of mental disorder in unconvicted male prisoners in England and Wales. *British Medical Journal, 313*, 1524–1527.

Buescher, A. V. S., Cidav, Z., Knapp, M., & Mandell, D. S. (2014). Costs of autism spectrum disorders in the United Kingdom and the United States. *JAMA Pediatrics*, *168*(8), 721.

Burt, D. B., Loveland, K. A., & Lewis, K. R. (1992). Depression and the onset of dementia in adults with mental retardation. *American Journal of Mental Retardation*, *96*(5), 502–511.

Chevreul, K., Gandré, C., Brigham, K. B., López-Bastida, J., Linertová, R., Oliva-Moreno, J., ... & BURQOL-RD Research Network. (2016). Social/economic costs and health-related quality of life in patients with fragile X syndrome in Europe. *The European Journal of Health Economic: Health Economics in Prevention and Care*, *17*(S1), 43–52.

Cimera, R. E., & Cowan, R. J. (2009). The costs of services and employment outcomes achieved by adults with autism in the US. *Autism: The International Journal of Research and Practice*, *13*(3), 285–302.

Collacott, R. A., Cooper, S. A., & McGrother, C. (1992). Differential rates of psychiatric disorders in adults with Down's syndrome compared with other mentally handicapped adults. *The British Journal of Psychiatry: The Journal of Mental Science*, *161*, 671–674.

Cosgrave, M. P., Tyrrell, J., McCarron, M., Gill, M., & Lawlor, B. A. (1999). Determinants of aggression, and adaptive and maladaptive behaviour in older people with Down's syndrome with and without dementia. *Journal of Intellectual Disability Research*, *43*(Pt 5), 393–399.

Del Hoyo, L., Xicota, L., Langohr, K., Sánchez-Benavides, G., de Sola, S., Cuenca-Royo, A., ... & TESDAD Study Group. (2016). VNTR-DAT1 and COMTVal158Met genotypes modulate mental flexibility and adaptive behavior skills in Down syndrome. *Frontiers in Behavioral Neuroscience*, *10*, 193.

Doane, B. M., & Salekin, K. L. (2009). Susceptibility of current adaptive behavior measures to feigned deficits. *Law and Human Behavior*, *33*(4), 329–343.

Eaves, L. C., & Ho, H. H. (2008). Young adult outcome of autism spectrum disorders. *Journal of Autism and Developmental Disorders*, *38*(4), 739–747.

Emerson, E. (2011). Health status and health risks of the "hidden majority" of adults with intellectual disability. *Intellectual and Developmental Disabilities*, *49*(3), 155–165.

Farley, M. A., McMahon, W. M., Fombonne, E., Jenson, W. R., Miller, J., Gardner, M., ... & Coon, H. (2009). Twenty-year outcome for individuals with autism and average or near-average cognitive abilities. *Autism Research*, *2*(2), 109–118.

Fazel, S., Xenitidis, K., & Powell, J. (2008). The prevalence of intellectual disabilities among 12000 prisoners: A systematic review. *International Journal of Law and Psychiatry*, *31*(4), 369–373.

Feldstein, S., Durham, R. L., Keller, F. R., Kelebe, K., & Davis, H. P. (2000). Classification of malingerers on a nondeclarative memory task as a function of coaching and task difficulty. *American Journal of Forensic Psychology*, *18*, 57–78.

Fisher, M. H., Lense, M. D., & Dykens, E. M. (2016). Longitudinal trajectories of intellectual and adaptive functioning in adolescents and adults with Williams syndrome. *Journal of Intellectual Disability Research*, *60*(10), 920–932.

Ganz, M. L. (2007). The lifetime distribution of the incremental societal costs of autism. *Archives of Pediatrics & Adolescent Medicine*, *161*(4), 343–349.

Gunn, J., Maden, A., & Swinton, M. (1991). Treatment needs of prisoners with psychiatric disorders. *British Medical Journal*, *303*, 338–341.

Hartley, S. L., Seltzer, M. M., Raspa, M., Olmstead, M., Bishop, E., & Bailey, D. B. (2011). Exploring the adult life of men and women with fragile X syndrome: Results from a national survey. *American Journal on Intellectual and Developmental Disabilities*, *116*(1), 16–35.

Hellenbach, M., Karatzias, T., & Brown, M. (2017). Intellectual disabilities among prisoners: Prevalence and mental and physical health comorbidities. *Journal of Applied Research in Intellectual Disabilities*, *30*(2), 230–241.

Heller, T., Miller, A. B., & Hsieh, K. (2002). Eight-year follow-up of the impact of environmental characteristics on well-being of adults with developmental disabilities. *Mental Retardation, 40*(5), 366–378.

Herrington, V. (2009). Assessing the prevalence of intellectual disability among young male prisoners. *Journal of Intellectual Disability Research, 53*(5), 397–410.

Hofvander, B., Delorme, R., Chaste, P., Nyden, A., Wentz, E., Stahlberg, O., . . . & Leboyer, M. (2009). Psychiatric and psychosocial problems in adults with normal-intelligence autism spectrum disorders. *BMC Psychiatry, 9*(35).

Holland, A. J., Hon, J., Huppert, F. A., & Stevens, F. (2000). Incidence and course of dementia in people with Down's syndrome: Findings from a population-based study. *Journal of Intellectual Disability Research, 44*(Pt 2), 138–146.

Howlin, P., Goode, S., Hutton, J., & Rutter, M. (2004). Adult outcome for children with autism. *Journal of Child Psychology and Psychiatry, and Allied Disciplines, 45*(2), 212–229.

Howlin, P., Moss, P., Savage, S., & Rutter, M. (2013). Social outcomes in mid- to later adulthood among individuals diagnosed with autism and average nonverbal IQ as children. *Journal of the American Academy of Child and Adolescent Psychiatry, 52*(6), 572–581.e1.

Kraper, C. K., Kenworthy, L., Popal, H., Martin, A., & Wallace, G. L. (2017). The gap between adaptive behavior and intelligence in autism persists into young adulthood and is linked to psychiatric co-morbidities. *Journal of Autism and Developmental Disorders.*

Landmark, L. J., & Zhang, D. (2013). Compliance and practices in transition planning. *Remedial and Special Education, 34*(2), 113–125.

Larson, S. A., Salmi, P., Smith, D., Anderson, L., & Hewitt, A. S. (2013). *Residential services for persons with intellectual or developmental disabilities: Status and trends through 2011.* Minneapolis, MN: University of Minnesota, Research and Training Center on Community Living, Institute on Community Integration.

Lawer, L., Brusilovskiy, E., Salzer, M. S., & Mandell, D. S. (2009). Use of vocational rehabilitative services among adults with autism. *Journal of Autism and Developmental Disorders, 39*(3), 487–494.

Määttä, T., Tervo-Määttä, T., Taanila, A., Kaski, M., & Iivanainen, M. (2006). Mental health, behaviour and intellectual abilities of people with Down syndrome. *Down's Syndrome, Research and Practice: The Journal of the Sarah Duffen Centre, 11*(1), 37–43.

Macvaugh, G., & Cunningham, M. D. (2009). Atkins v. Virginia: Implications and recommendations for forensic practice. *Journal of Psychiatry and Law, 37*(2–3), 125–130.

Mandell, D. S. (2013). Adults with autism: A new minority. *Journal of General Internal Medicine, 28*(6), 751–752.

Matson, J. L., Rivet, T. T., Fodstad, J. C., Dempsey, T., & Boisjoli, J. A. (2009). Examination of adaptive behavior differences in adults with autism spectrum disorders and intellectual disability. *Research in Developmental Disabilities, 30*(6), 1317–1325.

Matson, J. L., Rush, K. S., Hamilton, M., Anderson, S. J., Bamburg, J. W., Baglio, C. S., . . . & Kirkpatrick-Sanchez, S. (1999). Characteristics of depression as assessed by the Diagnostic Assessment for the Severely Handicapped-II (DASH-II). *Research in Developmental Disabilities, 20*(4), 305–313.

Matthews, N. L., Smith, C. J., Pollard, E., Ober-Reynolds, S., Kirwan, J., & Malligo, A. (2015). Adaptive functioning in autism spectrum disorder during the transition to adulthood. *Journal of Autism and Developmental Disorders, 45*(8), 2349–2360.

McBrien, J. A. (2003). Assessment and diagnosis of depression in people with intellectual disability. *Journal of Intellectual Disability Research, 47*(Pt 1), 1–13.

Mileviciute, I., & Hartley, S. L. (2015). Self-reported versus informant-reported depressive symptoms in adults with mild intellectual disability. *Journal of Intellectual Disability Research, 59*(2), 158–169.

Myers, B. A., & Pueschel, S. M. (1995). Major depression in a small group of adults with Down syndrome. *Research in Developmental Disabilities, 16*(4), 285–299.

Nelson, L. D., Orme, D., Osann, K., & Lott, I. T. (2001). Neurological changes and emotional functioning in adults with Down syndrome. *Journal of Intellectual Disability Research, 45*(Pt 5), 450–456.

Ng, M., Fleming, T., Robinson, M., Thomson, B., Graetz, N., Margono, C., . . . & Gakidou, E. (2014). Global, regional, and national prevalence of overweight and obesity in children and adults during 1980–2013: A systematic analysis for the Global Burden of Disease Study 2013. *Lancet, 384*(9945), 766–781.

Olley, J. G., & Cox, A. W. (2008). Assessment of adaptive behavior in adult forensic cases: The use of the Adaptive Behavior Assessment System-II. In T. Oakland & P. Harrison (Eds.), *Adaptive behavior assessment system-II: Clinical use and interpretation* (pp. 381–398). New York, NY: Elsevier.

Ranjan, S., Nasser, J. A., & Fisher, K. (2017). Prevalence and potential factors associated with overweight and obesity status in adults with intellectual developmental disorders. *Journal of Applied Research in Intellectual Disabilities.*

Rumsey, J. M., Rapoport, J. L., & Sceery, W. R. (1985). Autistic children as adults: Psychiatric, social, and behavioral outcomes. *Journal of the American Academy of Child Psychiatry, 24*(4), 465–473.

Saulnier, C. A., & Klin, A. (2007). Brief report: Social and communication abilities and disabilities in higher functioning individuals with autism and Asperger syndrome. *Journal of Autism and Developmental Disorders, 37*(4), 788–793.

Shattuck, P. T., Wagner, M., Narendorf, S., Sterzing, P., & Hensley, M. (2011). Post-high school service use among young adults with an autism spectrum disorder. *Archives of Pediatrics & Adolescent Medicine, 165*(2), 141–146.

Smith, K. R. M., & Matson, J. L. (2010). Psychopathology: Differences among adults with intellectually disabled, comorbid autism spectrum disorders and epilepsy. *Research in Developmental Disabilities, 31*(3), 743–749.

Smith, L. E., Hong, J., Greenberg, J. S., & Mailick, M. R. (2016). Change in the behavioral phenotype of adolescents and adults with FXS: Role of the family environment. *Journal of Autism and Developmental Disorders, 46*(5), 1824–1833.

Soenen, S., Van Berckelaer-Onnes, I., & Scholte, E. (2009). Patterns of intellectual, adaptive and behavioral functioning in individuals with mild mental retardation. *Research in Developmental Disabilities, 30*(3), 433–444.

Sparrow, S. S., Cicchetti, D. V., & Balla, D. A. (2005). *Vineland adaptive behavior scales* (2nd ed.). Circle Pines, MN: American Guidance Service.

Sparrow, S. S., Cicchetti, D. V., & Saulnier, C. A. (2016). *Vineland adaptive behavior scales* (3rd ed.). Bloomington, MN: NCS Pearson.

Stevens, K. B., & Price, J. R. (2006). Adaptive behavior, mental retardation, and the death penalty. *Journal of Forensic Psychology Practice, 6*(3), 1–29.

Su, C. Y., Lin, Y. H., Wu, Y. Y., & Chen, C. C. (2008). The role of cognition and adaptive behavior in employment of people with mental retardation. *Research in Developmental Disabilities, 29*(1), 83–95.

van Schrojenstein Lantman-de Valk, H. M., van den Akker, M., Maaskant, M. A., Haveman, M. J., Urlings, H. F., Kessels, A. G., & Crebolder, H. F. (1997). Prevalence and incidence of health problems in people with intellectual disability. *Journal of Intellectual Disability Research, 41*(Pt 1), 42–51.

Voelker, S. L., Shore, D. L., Brown-More, C., Hill, L. C., Miller, L. T., & Perry, J. (1990). Validity of self-report of adaptive behavior skills by adults with mental retardation. *Mental Retardation, 28*(5), 305–309.

Whitehouse, A. J. O., Watt, H. J., Line, E. A., & Bishop, D. V. M. (2009). Adult psychosocial outcomes of children with specific language impairment, pragmatic language impairment and autism. *International Journal of Language & Communication Disorders, 44*(4), 511–528.

Widaman, K. F., & Siperstein, G. N. (2009). Assessing adaptive behavior of criminal defendants in capital cases: A reconsideration. *American Journal of Forensic Psychology, 27*(2), 15–32.

Woodman, A. C., Mailick, M. R., Anderson, K. A., & Esbensen, A. J. (2014). Residential transitions among adults with intellectual disability across 20 years. *American Journal on Intellectual and Developmental Disabilities, 119*(6), 496–515.

Woolf, S., Woolf, C. M., & Oakland, T. (2010). Adaptive behavior among adults with intellectual disabilities and its relationship to community independence. *Intellectual and Developmental Disabilities, 48*(3), 209–215.

CHAPTER EIGHT

Baker, B. L., & Brightman, A. J. (1997). *Steps to independence: Teaching everyday skills to children with special needs* (3rd ed.). Baltimore, MD: Brookes.

Baker, B. L., & Brightman, A. J. (2004). *Steps to independence* (4th ed.). Baltimore, MD: Brookes.

Barron, A. M., & Foot, H. (1991). Peer tutoring and tutor training. *Educational Research, 33,* 174–185.

Bellini, S., & Akulian, J. (2007). A meta-analysis of video-modeling and self-modeling for children with ASDs. *Exceptional Child, 73,* 261–284.

Bruininks, R. H., Morreau, L. E., Gilman, C. J., & Anderson, J. L. (1991). *Adaptive living skills curriculum.* Boston, MA: Houghton Mifflin Harcourt.

Campbell, J. M., Ferguson, J. E., Herzinger, C. V., Jackson, J. N., & Marino, C. A. (2004). Combined descriptive and explanatory information improves peers' perceptions of autism. *Research in Developmental Disabilities, 25*(4), 321–339.

Cicero, F. (2012). *Toilet training success: A guide for teaching individuals with developmental disabilities.* New York, NY: DRL Books.

Dawson, G., Rogers, S., Munson, J., Smith, M., Winter, J., Greenson, J., . . . & Varley, J. (2010). Randomized, controlled trial of an intervention for toddlers with autism: The Early Start Denver model. *Pediatrics, 125*(1), e17–e23.

Durand, M. (2014). *Sleep better! A guide to improving sleep for children with special needs* (rev. ed.). Baltimore, MD: Brookes.

Dykens, E. M., Hodapp, R. M., & Finucane, B. M. (2000). *Genetics and mental retardation syndromes: A new look at behavior and interventions.* Baltimore, MD: Brookes.

Estes, A., Munson, J., Rogers, S. J., Greenson, J., Winter, J., & Dawson, G. (2015). Long-term outcomes of early intervention in 6-year-old children with autism spectrum disorder. *Journal of the American Academy of Child and Adolescent Psychiatry, 54*(7), 580–587.

Fein, D., Barton, M., Eigsti, I. M., Kelley, E., Naigles, L., Schultz, R. T., Stevens, M., Helt, M., Orinstein, A., Rosenthal, M., Troyb, E., & Tyson, K. (2013). Optimal outcome in individuals with a history of autism. *Journal of Child Psychology and Psychiatry, 54*(2),195–205.

Garfinkle, A., & Schwartz, I. (2002). Peer imitation: Increasing social interactions in children with autism and other developmental disabilities in inclusive preschool classrooms. *Topics in Early Childhood Special Education, 22*(1), 26–38.

Gruber, B., Reeser, R., & Reid, D. H. (1979). Providing a less restrictive environment for profoundly retarded persons by teaching independent walking skills. *Journal of Applied Behavior Analysis, 12*(2), 285–297.

Haring, T. G., & Kennedy, C. H. (1988). Units of analysis in task-analytic research. *Journal of Applied Behavior Analysis, 21*(2), 207–215.

Haring, T. G., Kennedy, C. H., Adams, M. J., & Pitts-Conway, V. (1987). Teaching generalization of purchasing skills across community settings to autistic youth using videotape modeling. *Journal of Applied Behavior Analysis, 20*, 89–96.

Hodgdon, L. A. (1999). *Solving behavior problems in autism: Improving communication with visual strategies.* Troy, MI: Quirk Roberts Publishing.

Kamps, D., Royer, J., Dugan, E., Kravits, T., Gonzalez-Lopez, A., Garcia, J., . . . & Kane, L. G. (2002). Peer training to facilitate social interactions for elementary students with autism and their peers. *Exceptional Children, 68*(2), 173–187.

Kasari, C., Freeman, S., & Paparella, T. (2006). Joint attention and symbolic play in young children with autism: A randomized controlled intervention study. *Journal of Child Psychology and Psychiatry and Allied Disciplines, 47*(6), 611–620.

Koegel, L. (1995). Communication and language intervention. In R. Koegel & L. Koegel (Eds.), *Teaching children with autism.* Baltimore, MD: Brookes.

Koegel, L., Koegel, R., Yoshen, Y., & McNerney, E. (1999). Pivotal response intervention. II. Preliminary long-term outcome data. *Journal of the Association for Persons with Severe Handicaps, 24*, 186–198.

Lovaas, O. I. (1981). *The "me" book.* Baltimore, MD: University Park Press.

Lowe, M. L., & Cuvo, A. J. (1976). Teaching coin summation to the mentally retarded. *Journal of Applied Behavior Analysis, 9*(4), 483–489.

Magiati, I., Charman, T., & Howlin, P. (2007). A two-year prospective follow-up study of community-based early intensive behavioural intervention and specialist nursery provision for children with autism spectrum disorders. *Journal of Child Psychology and Psychiatry, and Allied Disciplines, 48*(8), 803–812.

Matson, J. L., Mahan, S., & LoVullo, S. V. (2009). Parent training: A review of methods for children with developmental disabilities. *Research in Developmental Disabilities, 30*(5), 961–968.

McCarney, S. B., McCain, B. R., & Bauer, A. M. (2006a). *Adaptive behavior intervention manual: 13–18 years* (S. N. House, Ed.). Columbia, MO: Hawthorne Educational Services.

McCarney, S. B., McCain, B. R., & Bauer, A. M. (2006b). *Adaptive behavior intervention manual: 4–12 years; Goals, objectives and intervention strategies for adaptive behavior.* Columbia, MO: Hawthorne Educational Services.

McEachin, J. J., Smith, T., & Lovaas, O. I. (1993). Long-term outcome for children with autism who received early intensive behavioral treatment. *American Journal on Mental Retardation, 97*, 359–372.

McGee, G. G., Morrier, M. J., & Daly, T. (1999). An incidental teaching approach to early intervention for toddlers with autism. *Journal of the Association for Persons with Severe Handicaps, 24*(3), 133–146.

Miller, M. A., Cuvo, A. J., & Borakove, L. S. (1977). Teaching naming of coin values—comprehension before production versus production alone. *Journal of Applied Behavior Analysis, 10*(4), 735–736.

Morgan, L., Hooker, J. L., Sparapani, N., Rinehardt, V., Schatschneider, C., & Wetherby, A. (in preparation). Cluster randomized trial of the classroom SCERTS intervention for students with autism spectrum disorder.

National Research Council. (2001). *Educating children with autism.* Washington, DC: National Academies Press.

O'Brien, F., Bugle, C., & Azrin, N. H. (1972). Training and maintaining a retarded child's proper eating. *Journal of Applied Behavior Analysis, 5*, 67–72.

Page, T. J., Iwata, B. A., & Neef, N. A. (1976). Teaching pedestrian skills to retarded persons: Generalization from the classroom to the natural environment. *Journal of Applied Behavior Analysis, 9*(4), 433–444.

Pierce, K., & Schreibman, L. (1997a). Multiple peer use of pivotal response training to increase social behaviors of classmates with autism: Results from trained and untrained peers. *Journal of Applied Behavior Analysis, 30*(1), 157–160.

Pierce, K., & Schreibman, L. (1997b). Using peer trainers to promote social behavior in autism: Are they effective at enhancing multiple social modalities? *Focus on Autism and Other Developmental Disabilities, 12*(4), 207–218.

Prizant, B. M., Wetherby, A. M., Rubin, E., Laurent, A. C., & Rydell, J. P. (2006). *The SCERTS model* (Vols. I and II). Baltimore, MD: Brookes.

Scahill, L., Bearss, K., Lecavalier, L., Smith, T., Swiezy, N., Aman, M. G., . . . & Johnson, C. (2016). Effect of parent training on adaptive behavior in children with autism spectrum disorder and disruptive behavior: Results of a randomized trial. *Journal of the American Academy of Child and Adolescent Psychiatry, 55*(7), 601–608.

Scahill, L., McDougle, C. J., Aman, M. G., Johnson, C., Handen, B., Bearss, K., . . . & Research Units on Pediatric Psychopharmacology Autism Network. (2012). Effects of risperidone and parent training on adaptive functioning in children with pervasive developmental disorders and serious behavioral problems. *Journal of the American Academy of Child and Adolescent Psychiatry, 51*(2), 136–146.

Sparapani, N., Morgan, L., Reinhardt, V. P., Schatschneider, C., & Wetherby, A. M. (2016). Evaluation of classroom active engagement in elementary students with autism spectrum disorder. *Journal of Autism and Developmental Disorders, 46*(3), 782–796.

Stahmer, A. C., Akshoomoff, N., & Cunningham, A. B. (2011). Inclusion for toddlers with autism spectrum disorders: The first ten years of a community program. *Autism, 15*(5), 625–641.

Sutera, S., Pandey, J., Esser, E. L., Rosenthal, M. A., Wilson, L. B., Barton, M., Green, J., Hodgson, S., Robins, D. L., Dumont-Mathieu, T., & Fein, D. (2007). Predictors of optimal outcome in toddlers diagnosed with autism spectrum disorders. *Journal of Autism Developmental Disorders, 37*(1), 98–107.

Wetherby, A. M., Guthrie, W., Woods, J., Schatschneider, C., Holland, R. D., Morgan, L., & Lord, C. (2014). Parent-implemented social intervention for toddlers with autism: An RCT. *Pediatrics, 134*(6), 1084–1093.

Wilson, P. G., Reid, D. H., Phillips, J. F., & Burgio, L. D. (1984). Normalization of institutional mealtimes for profoundly retarded persons: Effects and noneffects of teaching family-style dining. *Journal of Applied Behavior Analysis, 17*, 189–201.

Woods, J. J., & Wetherby, A. M. (2003). Early identification of and intervention for infants and toddlers who are at risk for autism spectrum disorder. *Language, Speech, and Hearing Services in Schools, 34*(3), 180–193.

ABOUT THE AUTHORS

Saulnier, C. A., & Ventola, P. (2012). *Essentials of autism spectrum disorders evaluation and assessment*. Hoboken, NJ: Wiley.

Sparrow, S. S., Cicchetti, D. V., & Saulnier, C. A. (2016). *Vineland Adaptive Behavior Scales* (3rd ed.). Bloomington, MN: NCS Pearson.

About the Authors

Celine A. Saulnier, PhD, is an associate professor in the Division of Autism and Related Disorders, Department of Pediatrics, at Emory University School of Medicine. She obtained her doctorate in clinical psychology from the University of Connecticut under the mentorship of Dr. Deborah Fein. She then completed a postdoctoral fellowship at the Yale Child Study Center before joining Yale's faculty. At Yale, Dr. Saulnier was the clinical director and the training director for the autism program. Celine's research focuses on adaptive behavior profiles in autism as well as on early detection and diagnosis of autism in infants and toddlers. She is coauthor of the *Essentials of Autism Spectrum Disorders Evaluation and Assessment* (Saulnier & Ventola, 2012) and an author of *Vineland Adaptive Behavior Scales,* Third Edition (Sparrow, Cicchetti, & Saulnier, 2016).

    Cheryl Klaiman, PhD, is an associate professor in the Division of Autism and Related Disorders, Department of Pediatrics, at Emory University School of Medicine. She obtained her doctorate in school and applied child psychology at McGill University under the mentorship of Dr. Jacob Burack. She then completed her pre- and post-doctoral fellowship at the Yale Child Study Center under the mentorship of Drs. Ami Klin, Sara Sparrow, and Robert Schultz before joining Yale's faculty. At Yale, she worked with Dr. Robert Schultz to study novel treatment programs for autism as well as to better understand clinical profiles of individuals with Williams syndrome, Prader-Willi syndrome, and autism. She then moved to California where she was the director of the autism and related disorders unit at Children's Health Council and research faculty at Stanford University, where she studied longitudinal adaptive behavior profiles in individuals with fragile X syndrome. Her current research focuses on early detection of autism symptomatology and developmental delays across a range of neurodevelopmental disabilities.

Index

A

AAIDD (*American Association on Intellectual and Developmental Disabilities*), 12, 13, 35–36, 38, 45, 59

ABA (*Applied behavior analysis*), 130–134, 136

ABAS (*Adaptive Behavior Assessment System*), 6, 7, 26, 46–47, 54, 79
adult form, 47
parent form, 47
teacher form, 47

ABAS-II (Adaptive Behavior Assessment System, Second Edition), 47–49, 54, 72, 79, 84, 96, 103, 117, 118
adult form, 48
conceptual skills, 48
infant-preschool forms, 48
practical skills, 48
psychometrics, 49
social skills, 48

ABAS-3 (Adaptive Behavior Assessment System, Third Edition), 49, 55, 79
adult form, 49
intervention planner, 49
parent form, 49
parent/primary caregiver form, 49
psychometrics, 49
teacher/daycare provider form, 49
teacher form, 49

ABES-3 (*Adaptive Behavior Evaluation Scale, Third Edition*), 51–52, 55
psychometrics, 52

ABS (*Adaptive Behavior Scale*), 36, 54

ABS-PSV (*Adaptive Behavior Scale, Public School Version*), 36, 54
psychometrics, 36

ABS-S:2 (*American Association of Mental Retardation Adaptive Behavior Scale–School: 2*), 37–38, 54

ABS-School Edition (*Adaptive Behavior Scale, School Edition*), 37, 54

Adaptive behavior:
AAMR adaptive behavior constructs, 7
age, correlations with, 82–83
assessment tools, 6
birth of, 1–2
clinical psychology use, 18
declines with age, 69, 70, 99, 100
definition of, 1

Doll's definition, 34
domains, 37, 41, 47, 48, 58
DSM-5 definition of, 57–58
in IEP development, 18
intelligence and, 60
intervention targets, 126–127
and mental illness, 62
in minorities, 29, 89
principles of, 9–13
school psychology use, 18
three-factor structure of, 5
treatment goals, 124

Adaptive Behavior Assessment System see ABAS (*Adaptive Behavior Assessment System*)

Adaptive Behavior Assessment System, Second Edition see ABAS-II (Adaptive Behavior Assessment System, Second Edition)

Adaptive Behavior Assessment System, Third Edition see ABAS-3 (Adaptive Behavior Assessment System, Third Edition)

Adaptive Behavior Evaluation Scale, Third Edition see ABES-3 (*Adaptive Behavior Evaluation Scale, Third Edition*)

Adaptive Behavior Intervention manual, 52, 126

Adaptive Behavior Scale see ABS (*Adaptive Behavior Scale*)

Adaptive Behavior Scale, Public School Version see ABS-PSV (*Adaptive Behavior Scale, Public School Version*)

Adaptive Behavior Scale, School Edition see ABS, School Edition (*Adaptive Behavior Scale, School Edition*)

Adaptive Living Skills Curriculum, 137

American Association on Intellectual and Developmental Disabilities *see* AAIDD (*American Association on Intellectual and Developmental Disabilities*)

American Association on Mental Deficiency, 36

American Association on Mental Deficiency Adaptive Behavior Scale, 6, 26

American Association of Mental Retardation Adaptive Behavior Scale–School: 2 see ABS-S:2 (*American Association of Mental Retardation Adaptive Behavior Scale–School: 2*)